Praise for *If All the Seas Were Ink*

"*If All the Seas Were Ink* is such a moving memoir. I was taken by the perfect balance Ilana Kurshan achieved between revealing her own story while describing her daily study of the Talmud. Her portrait of everyday life in Jerusalem enriches her recounting of connecting to centuries of intellectual curiosity and conversing with bygone generations. How wonderful to explore this great volume with such a sensitive and thoughtful guide."

—SUSAN ISAACS, author of *Long Time No See*

"In this deeply personal and often hilarious story, Kurshan shows us how the Talmud's thousands of strange and demanding pages, read at one page a day for seven years, become a conversation about how best to live one's life in an imperfect world. Kurshan awakens us to our imperfect world's hidden magnificence— and to the power of literature to inspire human resilience. A stunning, gorgeous memoir."

—DARA HORN, author of *The World to Come*

"*If All the Seas Were Ink* is a book about passion of many varieties—romantic passion, religious passion, aesthetic passion, but above all else, passion for knowledge. The word scholarship is too tame to do justice to Kurshan's wild passion for the written word, whether the word is found on a page of Talmud or in a sonnet of Wordsworth. The blend of her loves makes for a rich and fascinating life, which makes for a rich and fascinating book."

—REBECCA NEWBERGER GOLDSTEIN, author of *Plato at the Googleplex: Why Philosophy Won't Go Away*

"With this memoir, Ilana Kurshan enters the exclusive club of daf yomi learners, a club that was, for generations, restricted to men.

With sincerity, humor, and insight, she invites readers into her experience of studying Talmud as a young woman in Jerusalem. Hers is a stunningly original voice in the world of Torah and the world of literature. Go run and read this book."

—RUTH CALDERON, author of *A Bride for One Night*

"Kurshan's beautiful prose weaves the trials and tribulations of her personal seven-year journey together with the Talmud texts she's learning. I applaud, and am awed, by this moving and remarkable memoir."

—MAGGIE ANTON, author of *Rashi's Daughters*

"An intimate and eloquent portrait of a young woman's passionate loves and fears . . . Kurshan writes as a woman of (as she puts it) 'Dickensonian sensibilities:' clinging to her privacy while exposing her vulnerability, seeking the resonances between her mind, soul and body, and revealing an acutely sensitive intelligence, a wry self-awareness, and an active sense of the absurd . . . Highly recommended."

—AVIVAH ZORNBERG, author of *The Murmuring Deep*

"When a woman as incredibly well-read as Ilana Kurshan commits herself to studying the Talmud daily for seven-and-a-half years, the results are mind-expanding, both for her and for readers of *If All the Seas Were Ink*. An utterly original book about the Talmud, long time students of Jewish texts will be reminded of precious Talmudic passages they had forgotten, and newcomers will gain a sense of how much wisdom there is in this ancient, but very vibrant, text."

—RABBI JOSEPH TELUSHKIN, author of *Jewish Literacy, Rebbe,* and *A Code of Jewish Ethics*

If All the Seas Were Ink

If All the Seas Were Ink

A Memoir

Ilana Kurshan

St. Martin's Press   New York

Grateful acknowledgment to Hadassah, Nashim, the World Jewish Digest, and
Lilith magazine—independent, Jewish & frankly feminist—where excerpts from
this book originally appeared in variant form.

www.stmartins.com

Design by Meryl Sussman Levavi

Cataloging-in-Publication Data is available from the Library of Congress.

ISBN 9781250121264 (hardcover)

ISBN 9781250121271 (e-book)

Our books may be purchased in bulk for promotional, educational, or
business use. Please contact your local bookseller or the Macmillan
Corporate and Premium Sales Department at 1-800-221-7945, extension
5442, or by e-mail at MacmillanSpecialMarkets@macmillan.com.

First Edition: September 2017

10 9 8 7 6 5 4 3 2

To my parents
Who taught me
It is a tree of life

And to Daniel
Who taught me
Be happy, hold fast.

CONTENTS

꙳

Said Rabbah: Even though our ancestors have left us a scroll of the Torah, it is our duty to write one for ourselves.

—BABYLONIAN TALMUD, SANHEDRIN 21B

It's a funny thing that people are always quite ready to admit it if they've no real talent for drawing or music, whereas everyone imagines that they themselves are capable of true love, which is a talent like any other, only far more rare.

—NANCY MITFORD

AUTHOR'S NOTE

The names of several of the people in this book have been changed. While this is a true story, I have tried to protect the privacy of the people I have written about, who appear here more as characters than as real people. Anything I say about these individuals is far more revealing of myself than of them.

If All the Seas Were Ink

INTRODUCTION

One Day Wiser

The house was quiet and the world was calm.
The reader became the book . . .

—WALLACE STEVENS

IT IS EARLY IN THE MORNING—THE HOUSE IS QUIET AND the world is calm, and I steal out of bed and tiptoe to the bathroom. I wash my hands and reach for my toothbrush, but in the predawn light it is hard to distinguish my turquoise toothbrush from my husband's white one, so I hold them up to the faint rays of sunlight struggling to make their way through the window. I put on my slippers and open the door as quietly as possible—my twins sleep in the bedroom across the hall, and if one of them stirs, my gain will be canceled out by my loss. The rabbis of the Talmud say that every night is divided into three watches—in the first watch, the donkeys bray; in the second watch, the dogs bark; and in the third watch, the mother nurses her child and whispers to her husband. But my husband and children are blessedly still asleep; no dog whets its tongue, and I don't even hear the first honks of morning traffic from the highway down the hill as I open the volume of Talmud waiting for me on the couch. This quiet is part of the meaning, part of the mind, my access to the perfection of the page. King David, too, used to study while it was still dark, roused by the dancing of the wind on the strings of his Aeolian harp at exactly midnight. But David, like all kings, had the luxury of sleeping three hours past dawn, whereas I must soon begin my day. I know that I have to learn quickly, that the Talmudic page is like a ruined Temple and that Elijah will hurry me along if I linger. I lean over the page, want to lean, want most to be the scholar to whom this book is true. And just when the reader is becoming the book—just when I think I can hear the Holy One Blessed Be He wailing like a dove, moaning the destruction of the Temple and the banishment of His children from His table—I realize that the moaning is in fact my daughter, and she is hungry and crying, and it is time for another watch to begin.

⁊

My commitment to studying Talmud began nearly a decade ago, on another early morning, when my friend Andrea and I were running hills—the only kind of running one can do in Jerusalem. The air was cool and crisp, but we were already sweating in the knee-length shorts we wore in deference to the city's unwritten modesty code. As we huffed and puffed up the steep hill to the Knesset, I turned to Andrea and joked, "We will ascend Jerusalem at the height of our joy"—a paraphrase of a biblical verse recited at traditional Jewish weddings. I thought briefly about how I'd recited those words at my own wedding one year earlier, a moment I winced to recollect. But my quotation made Andrea think of the text and not its marital context, or so it seemed, because she turned back to look at me, a few paces behind, and casually remarked, "Did I tell you? I've started learning a page of Talmud a day."

My jaw dropped. "What did you say?" I pushed myself to keep up because I wanted to hear more. The Andrea I knew enjoyed hanging out in bars, reading paperback thrillers, and staying in shape. It was hard to imagine why she'd be interested in the Talmud, a vast compendium of Jewish law and narrative dating back to the first few centuries of the Common Era. The Talmud is famous for its nonlinear argumentation, sprawling digressions, and complex analysis of the finer points of Jewish religious law. A far cry from the latest Stephen King. What business did Andrea have with the Talmud?

"It's called *daf yomi*," she told me, and I recognized the phrase, Hebrew for "daily page," though it's more accurately translated as "daily folio," since every page of Talmud consists of two sides, back and front, with no square inch lying fallow—each page brims with printed Hebrew letters, leaving only the narrowest margins. Just recently there had been a widely publicized daf yomi celebration in Madison Square Garden, with thousands of Jews gathering to mark the completion of their study of the Talmud. They were mostly men in black suits and white shirts, with corkscrew curls hanging down over their ears. "Anyone can do it," Andrea added, as if reading my thoughts. "You go through a page of Talmud a day, and you finish in seven and a half years. How cool is that? In seven and a half years you've read what is arguably the most important book of Jewish law."

"But why?" I asked her. "Why do you care so much about Jewish law? I mean, you don't keep Shabbat, you've dated non-Jewish guys—why do you want all these rabbis peering over your shoulder?"

"Because they're not just talking about legal stuff. They're arguing with their wives, insulting their students, one-upping their colleagues—and when talking about law, they're not telling you what to do. They're figuring it all out, invoking not just the Bible but also folk tales, fables, and cultural myths. On yesterday's page I read about the three entrances to hell—one of which was in Jerusalem." Andrea smiled at me from beneath the brim of her baseball cap.

"I guess," I said, wondering where exactly that gateway to hell was located as we wove through the streets of the ancient city. "But what do you hope to get out of it? All that Talmud, I mean."

"I don't know," Andrea said and shrugged, rivulets of sweat

trickling down her shoulders. "I think it's partially the thrill of the challenge. You know, like running a marathon. It's fun to set impossible goals and then slowly make them more possible." I thought of the story of the great second-century sage Rabbi Akiva chipping away at a mountain stone by stone, gradually uprooting it and casting it into the Jordan River (Avot de Rabbi Natan, version A, chapter 6). It is a metaphor for how this sage, who began learning relatively late in life, came to master the whole Torah. But that was Rabbi Akiva.

We finished running by 7:00 a.m. and parted ways, but I couldn't stop thinking about what Andrea had told me. What would it be like to take on a seven-and-a-half-year project? It was almost impossible to imagine my life in seven and a half years. Would I still be living in Israel? Would I still feel saddled by the pain and shame I carried around with me? Would I finally manage to "move on," as everyone kept assuring me I would? "Time does not bring relief / you all have lied," wrote Edna St. Vincent Millay in a sonnet I often quoted to myself. Time did not bring relief but seemed to stretch inexorably, and I couldn't bear the thought that in seven and a half years I might still be grieving.

At the time I could barely get through the days, let alone commit to getting through the entire Babylonian Talmud, a text divided into six orders (or sections), 37 tractates (or volumes), and some twenty-seven hundred pages. But then I thought about how moving on is about putting one foot in front of the other, or turning page after page. If every day I turned a page, then eventually a new chapter would have to begin.

One chapter would lead to another, and then another, and before long I'd have completed an entire tractate. What a healthy relationship to time, viewing it not as a mark of age but as an opportunity to grow in wisdom. If I learned a page a day, then instead of resigning myself to being one day older, I could aspire to be one day wiser. Eventually I learned that this is in fact the Jewish view of time: the rabbis teach in tractate Avot (5:23) that five is the age for studying Torah, ten is the age for studying Mishnah, and fifteen is the age for studying Talmud.

At that point I was nearly twice the age stipulated in Avot, but as we learn elsewhere in that text, "If not now, when?" (1:14). Perhaps it was time to step on the treadmill and let the pull of the daf yomi schedule carry me along. At least I might stop feeling so stuck and ashamed of how the past year had unfolded. The previous summer Paul and I had married and immediately boarded a plane for Israel. I left my job and my community in New York to follow him—all too willingly—to a place I did not know. In the romanticized version of the Exodus story related by the prophet Jeremiah, the Israelites follow God through the wilderness, and God later tells them, "I remember the devotion of your youth, how as a bride you loved me and followed me through the wilderness, through a land not sown" (Jeremiah 2:2).[1] I loved Paul and followed him to a land barren of family and friends, a land where I'd have to try to put down new roots. But by spring, the season of growth and rebirth, any love we'd known had been uprooted, like a patch of grass ripped out of the soil. Paul and I soon cut off all connection, and I was on my own. Days would go by when I spoke only to the lady who checked coats at the library or the man at the corner store who sold me my milk and bread.

Even Andrea, one of my few friends, soon became too busy to jog with me. But the Talmud teaches that "[o]ne who is walking on his way and has no companion should occupy himself with Torah study" (Eruvin 54a). And so I did, in incremental steps. When I began learning daf yomi, I did not even own a volume of Talmud, nor did I buy one right away. Heading out to the bookstore seemed too presumptuous, as if in buying Yoma—the volume that the daf yomi community was up to at the time—I were committing to the full seven and a half years. After so recently marrying and divorcing, I was reluctant to commit to anything. And so instead I found a podcast with a daily fifty-minute class on the daf, and I started listening on my morning runs.

Sometimes it was difficult to keep track of the line of argumentation without the Talmud page in front of me, but I followed the directional cues of the text as I wound my way through the city. The names of the streets in Jerusalem are organized thematically with each neighborhood depicting a particular historical period, set of characters, or field of scholarship. The leafy hills of Rehavia are named for medieval biblical commentators; the narrow alleys of Baka are named for the twelve tribes; and the quaint side streets of the German Colony are named for nineteenth-century European rabbis. I did not follow a predetermined course when I jogged; instead, I followed the text wherever it led me. I took a left on Rabbi Akiva and then a right on Hillel and noted how, in a moment of concession, Rabbi Hisda turned into Rabbi Meir at a quiet intersection.

Eventually one morning I ended my run at a religious bookstore, where I was conspicuously both the only woman and the only runner. (At least my sporty bandana looked like a modest head covering.) Acting quickly, I pulled out some bills from my pocket and left with my own copy of tractate Yoma. Yoma is Aramaic for "the day," and this volume of Talmud deals with Yom Kippur, the holiest day on the Jewish calendar. But I studied it on unremarkable summer evenings, as the sweltering days cooled off into clear, bright nights. I sat in bed next to an open screenless window with the Talmud perched on my bent knees, reading its marginal notes and adding my own, the moonlight casting a glow on my page.

In the classic printing of the Talmud, which dates back to nineteenth-century Vilna, the Talmudic text appears in the center of the page and is surrounded by commentaries in the margins. I learned not from this classic printing but from an edition published by Rabbi Adin Steinsaltz, whose modern Hebrew commentary explicates and elucidates the text. Hebrew is the language of the oldest sections of the Talmud (which also includes Aramaic, the lingua franca of the rabbis who wrote it), and it is the language of the Jewish people living in the modern State of Israel, where I was making my home. But the Talmud is also a book of the diaspora, and Jews studied it for two thousand years wherever in the world they found themselves. Even when Jews did not have a homeland, and even when hardly any Jews spoke Hebrew, they continued to study Talmud. I had immigrated from the diaspora, and by studying Talmud in Hebrew in Israel, I was in my own way bringing the text back home.

However, one need not know Hebrew to study Talmud, a text that is available in multiple English translations. One need not even be Jewish, or at all religious. Indeed, sometimes the rabbis are so bold and heretical that their statements may be best appreciated by those who are not themselves devout. "Were it not written, it would be impossible to say it," they sometimes warn, and then go on to twist a verse written in the Bible into a startling theological conclusion. Unlike later works that followed from it, the Talmud is not a law code intended to tell Jews how to behave but a record of rabbinic legal conversations in which many of the questions are left open and unresolved. It is a text for those who are living the questions rather than those who have found the answers.

Still, that is not to say that I didn't try to figure it all out for myself. My copy of Yoma—and of all subsequent volumes, which I continued for a long time to purchase one by one—became filled with penciled notations that rained down the margins: question marks where I was confused, exclamation points where I was taken by surprise, boxed summaries of the major topics under discussion, and underlined references to other texts that came to mind while I was learning. Various passages of Talmud resonated with works of literature I'd studied previously—as an undergraduate at Harvard, as a graduate student at Cambridge, and as a book editor and literary agent in New York and Jerusalem. I'd spent my whole life reading books, but here was a book I could imagine spending my whole life reading.

A teacher once told me that nothing is as exciting as the next page of Talmud, and this rang true for me. The Talmud is a highly discursive text, proceeding primarily by association rather than by any rational scheme. Often there is no way of knowing how the stream of rabbinic consciousness will flow from one page to the next: the text meanders from a discussion about marking time to the dating of legal documents to a map of the night sky on the eve of the flood—all in the space of the opening pages of tractate Rosh Hashanah. The Talmud surprised me at nearly every turn, and while there were topics I found less interesting than others, there was something that caught my eye on almost every page—a folk remedy employed to heal an ailing sage, a rude insult leveled at one rabbi by another, a sudden interjection from a rabbi's angry wife. Often I was less focused on what the rabbis were discussing than on how they transitioned subtly from one subject to another, such that a discussion of sex with a virgin suddenly morphs into a discussion of how to avoid hearing something untoward by sticking one's fingers in one's ears—as if to suggest that all acts of penetration are one and the same. I found myself carried along for the ride, caught up in the flow of the argumentation and tossed around like a rough wave when the back-and-forth between the rabbis became particularly stormy.

I began to feel increasingly at home in the world of the Talmudic rabbis, who spent their time gathered in study groups to learn and debate the Mishnah. Contemporary scholars disagree about the social role the rabbis occupied. Were they a class of intellectual elites or just isolated members of society? At least some had day jobs, like Rabbi Yohanan the sandler and Rabbi Yitzhak the smith. The more prominent sages, like Rav and Rabbi Yohanan, were the heads of large Talmudic academies with numerous disciples. As I got to know the individual rabbis through my encounters with the text, many became as familiar to me as old friends: Ben Azzai, who loved studying Torah so much that he couldn't bear to sacrifice precious learning time to raise a family; Rabbi Eliezer, who left his family's huge farming estate against his father's will to go learn Torah in Jerusalem; and Rabbi Yehoshua, who developed his love of Torah in the womb because his mother used to pass by the study house when she was pregnant with him. I'd been working in book publishing for years, but driven by my interest in the Talmudic sages, I began moonlighting as a translator of rabbinic biographies. I learned about the individual rabbis, as well as about their wives and daughters and the women in their communities who sought their guidance.

As a woman, I grew excited about the possibilities open to me when encountering this text that for fifteen hundred years has been regarded primarily as the province of only the male half of the population. In the past few decades, more women have begun studying Talmud, both in the yeshiva, an institution for the religious study of Jewish texts, and in the academy—but this is only a recent phenomenon, and there are still very few women with enough years of learning under their belt to rival their male counterparts. I was raised with a strong feminist sensibility. My father served for decades as the rabbi of an egalitarian synagogue in which men and women participate equally in the service, and my mother worked as a top executive in the Jewish nonprofit sector. My parents always taught me that women had the same intellectual capacities as men. The Talmud, though, teaches otherwise.

The sages of the Talmud explicitly state that women are not obligated in the commandment to study Torah (Kidushin 29b), and Rabbi Eliezer declares that "anyone who teaches his daughter Torah teaches her frivolity" (Sotah 20a). But the Talmud includes a dissenting opinion, attributed to Ben Azzai, who insists that a man is obligated to teach his daughter Torah so that, were she to be rightfully accused of adultery, she would understand that though her merits might delay her punishment, it would inevitably come. As this example reflects, most of the women in the Talmud are sexual objects who are seduced or raped or subjected

to virginity tests. Those few women who are depicted as learned—
Yalta, Beruriah, Rav Hisda's daughter—have surprisingly violent
streaks, perhaps a testament to their force of personality. But they
are rare exceptions in a text whose heroes are almost all men, not
to mention men who considered themselves experts in women's
psychology and anatomy.

As a modern woman reader of Talmud, I was fascinated by
the rabbis' assumptions about women's attitudes toward marriage
and children, and I wondered whether they still resonate with
women today. After my divorce, I thought about whether it is still
true, as the rabbis insist, that *tav l'meitav tan du m'l'meitav
armelu*—that a woman would prefer to be married than to be
alone, even if, as the rabbis go on to assert, her husband is "the size
of an ant." Does this principle hold in an age when, at least in
many parts of the world, women can own property, live independently, and have children out of wedlock without undue social
sanction?

It soon became clear to me that by the Talmud's standards,
I am a man rather than a woman—if "man" is defined as an independent, self-sufficient adult, whereas "woman" is a dependent
generally living in either her father's or her husband's home. In
some ways this was a relief because I could regard the Talmud's
gender stereotypes as historical curiosities rather than infuriating
provocations. The Talmud did not offend me because I was de-
fying its classifications through my very engagement with the
text. So many of the classical interpretations of the Talmud reflect gendered assumptions, and these texts have the potential to
take on radically new meaning when regarded through feminine
eyes. Though plowed through by generations of scholars before
me, the Talmud was fertile ground for gleaning new insights and
fresh perspectives.

I kept a journal about what I learned, where I learned it, and
what moved me most deeply. Learning daf yomi is like zooming
through a safari on a motorbike; there is so much to take in, but

you are moving along at an impossibly rapid clip. By writing, I was better able to remember some of my favorite passages. And so I set for myself the challenge of writing a limerick or sonnet corresponding to each page I learned. These poems served as mnemonics that enabled me to summon, even years later, those passages I'd particularly enjoyed, such as the following from the end of tractate Rosh Hashanah (35a):

> Rav Yehuda did not like to pray
> He preferred to learn Torah and say:
> "You may call my soul dirty
> But one day in thirty
> Is better than three times a day."

The rabbis of the Talmud, too, often relied on mnemonic devices, which were essential given the text's oral transmission. Though in some ways I was rewriting the Talmud by rendering it in verse, in another sense I was doing just what the sages of the Talmud had done—I was trying to make my learning so much a part of me that I, like Rabbi Eliezer, might someday be able to refer to "my two arms, like two wrapped Torah scrolls" (Sanhedrin 68a)—as if I, too, could inscribe Torah on my heart.

On the cover of my journal I wrote "Dyo ilu yamey," a quotation from the Aramaic poem *Akdamut,* composed in the eleventh century and traditionally recited on Shavuot, the holiday celebrating the giving of the Torah at Sinai. The author of the poem, Rabbi Meir bar Yitzhak, plays off a trope that appears in variant forms throughout rabbinic literature: "God's eternal glory could not be described even if the heavens were parchment, and the forests quills; if all the seas were ink, as well as every gathered water; even if the earth's inhabitants were scribes and recorders of initials." My journal was an attempt to set my quill to parchment, to try and capture some of what I learned each day—always fearing that, as Rabbi Eliezer declared on his deathbed, "I skimmed only as much knowledge as a dog laps from the sea" (Sanhe-drin 68a).

Looking back now, I see that these journal entries unfolded as a record not just of my learning but also of my life, drawing from deep wells of sadness and fear and, with time, from over-flowing fountains of joy. I began learning as a divorced woman living alone in Jerusalem, with no idea of what the future might hold. It took me a while—quite a few tractates—before I found my stride. (And yes, like T. S. Eliot's J. Alfred Prufrock, who mea-sured out his life in coffee spoons, I have come to measure out mine in tractates, referring to periods in my life by what I was up to in the Talmud.) Eventually I began to make a home for myself in Jerusalem, even though I was thousands of miles away from my family and closest friends. One day I saw a sign for a morning daf yomi class in a synagogue down the street, and I decided to join. I was the only woman, but the rabbi greeted me with a welcoming smile and I soon became one of the guys—the rest of whom were retired old men. After class the men went to pray in the syna-gogue sanctuary and I slipped my Talmud into my bag and headed to the local pool, where I swam laps while reviewing in my mind the page I'd just learned.

Daf yomi, though initially a solitary pursuit, soon brought community into my life. Perhaps this should not have been surpris-ing. Tens of thousands of Jews around the world learn daf yomi, and they are all literally on the same page. This is because daf yomi is not just about learning a page of Talmud a day. It's about learn-ing a specific page, the same page that everyone else is learning, following a schedule that was fixed in 1923 when Rabbi Meir Shapiro of the Lublin Yeshiva first conceived of the program. Rabbi Shapiro described his vision of daf yomi as a way of unify-ing the Jewish world:

What a great thing! A Jew travels by boat and takes gemara *Berachot* [the first volume of the Talmud] under his arm. He travels for 15 days from Eretz Yisrael [the land of Israel] to America, and each day he learns the *daf*. When he arrives in America, he enters a *beit midrash* [study house] in New York and finds Jews learning the very same *daf* that he studied on that day, and he gladly joins them. Another Jew leaves the States and travels to Brazil or Japan, and he first goes to the *beit midrash*, where he finds everyone learning the same *daf* that he himself learned that day. Could there be greater unity of hearts than this?[2]

For Rabbi Shapiro, the whole world was a vast Talmud classroom with students connected by a worldwide web of conversational threads. Invoking a similar image, the rabbis of the Talmud described the class as a vineyard, with students seated in rows like an orderly arrangement of vines. I experienced daf yomi as a way of inhabiting a virtual classroom, sitting in a seemingly empty row and learning by myself while at the same time sensing the ghostly presences of those in the front rows who had studied those same passages in previous generations. And there were other presences, too, because my row was not in fact empty; it was populated by fellow daf yomi learners sitting just a few seats over—on the other side of Jerusalem, in Bnei Brak, and farther down the row in Europe, America, Australia, and wherever in the world there were people of the book.

Those connections only deepened. A year after I started daf yomi, I began dating again—just when I got up to the order known as Nashim (Women), a large section of the Talmud encompassing seven tractates that deal with issues of marriage and personal status. Over the course of Seder Nashim (the Order of Women) I fell in and out of love several times. Four years after my divorce I met the man I would go on to marry—who also began studying daf yomi—at a class on the weekly Torah portion, the section of the Torah that would be read in synagogue on the upcoming Shabbat. And so Torah became a companion, but it also brought my companion into my life. Daniel and I married just a few months after we met, and by our third anniversary we had three children, a son and twin daughters. When I finished my first daf yomi cycle at age thirty-five, our son was two and a half, our girls were approaching their first birthday, and I was stealing those predawn hours to learn before they woke up.

Throughout it all, daf yomi has remained a constant in my life. I have never missed a day of learning, though that learning has taken different forms over the years. When I was single I learned over dinner, careful not to drip tomato sauce upon discussions about the sprinkling of blood on the Temple altar. Once I got married to Daniel we learned together, one of us reading the daf aloud while the other washed dishes or folded laundry. After our children were born, I came to the end of my learning not at the bottom of the page but whenever the baby woke up; the pages from these months are filled with sudden slashes that mark the points where I was interrupted. Then I picked up later, in bed, falling asleep with the rabbis still arguing in my head about just how late a person can recite the bedtime Shema prayer.

And so I followed the text, but the text also followed me through the various twists and turns my life took. During particularly tough periods, on days when it was hard to remember why I bothered to get up in the morning, my daily Talmud study was an anchor, if not a life raft. Even if I accomplished nothing else that day, I managed to get through the daf. And on the most wondrous days of my life—when I gave birth to my children— daf yomi reminded me that I am, first and foremost, a reader and a lover of texts. I read Talmud aloud to each of my infants while they nursed at my breast, and they imbibed words of Torah with their mother's milk.

The Talmudic rabbis famously teach that "one is not obligated to complete a task, nor is one free to desist from it" (Avot 2:16). And so I kept learning regardless of where I found myself. Over the past seven and a half years, I've learned Talmud in libraries, cafes, airplanes, supermarket lines, and hospital waiting rooms. Whenever possible, I tried to learn with a pencil in hand so I could jot down my thoughts. Those pencil jottings formed the basis for this book, an effort to trace the path of my learning and living these past seven and a half years—from those initial jogs with Andrea, when I thought I'd never be happy again, to this morning, when I managed to fit in half a page before I heard my daughter's cries. Seven and a half years ago I felt only despair for what lay ahead; looking back, I feel blessed by the lessons I have been privileged to learn—from the text, from the world beyond the text, and from the ever-widening intersection of text and life in which I write these words.

A NOTE ON
THE TALMUD

~⦿~

THE TALMUD IS THE MAIN TEXT OF RABBINIC LITERA-
ture, covering the vast array of Jewish law and lore. It is in fact not
one literary corpus, but two. There is the **Jerusalem Talmud**,
compiled in the Galilee of the land of Israel, and the **Babylonian
Talmud**, compiled in Persian-dominated **Babylonia** (now Iraq).
It is the Babylonian Talmud that has been more widely studied in
traditional Jewish circles and that is the subject of daf yomi study,
and of this book.

Written over the course of several centuries, the Talmud began with the **Mishnah**, a collection of legal statements from rabbis living in the land of Israel during the first two centuries of the
Common Era. The Mishnah was compiled after the **Temple**, the
centralized site of ancient Jewish worship and sacrifice located in
Jerusalem, was destroyed by the Roman Empire in 70 C.E. Subsequent generations of scholars in the Galilee and in Babylonia in-
terpreted and commented on the Mishnah, incorporating their
own legal opinions as well as personal anecdotes and longer narrative accounts. They also quoted biblical verses to provide a basis

for rulings in the Mishnah and to substantiate their own legal opinions. All of these rabbinic conversations formed the core of the Talmud, which was revised and redacted over the next four hundred years.

The order of the Talmud follows the order of the Mishnah, with each section of Talmud commenting on a particular **mishnah**—the lowercase "m" is used to distinguish the smaller subsections from the entire capital "M" corpus. Together the Talmud and Mishnah comprise the **Oral Torah**, so called because it was transmitted orally for generations and not written down in its entirety until many years after its completion. Although the rabbis committed the Oral Torah to writing more than twelve hundred years ago, it is still referred to as the Oral Torah, and it is often studied aloud in partnership between two individuals. It stands in contrast to the **Written Torah**, the first five books of the Bible, also known as the Five Books of Moses. In the Talmud the term **Torah** is used to refer both to the Written and the Oral Torah, and so **Torah study** may refer to the study of Talmud as well.

The Babylonian Talmud is divided into thirty-seven volumes, known as **tractates**, each of which deals with different aspects of Jewish law, from vows to marriage to sacrificial worship. The tractates are grouped into six broader sections known as **orders**, with the tractates in each order arranged from longest to shortest by the number of chapters. Nearly all the tractates consist of both *halachah*—legal material—and *aggadah*—homiletical, ethical, and narrative passages. Weaving together halachah and aggadah, the Talmud is one of the most intensely edited books in all of world literature, its legal passages juxtaposing the rulings of different sages and its stories reworked into tight literary units in which no detail is extraneous and little is transparent.

Students of Talmud rely on commentators both ancient and modern to explain and interpret the text. The most famous and widely studied rabbinic commentator is the eleventh-century

French rabbi known by the acronym **Rashi** (Rabbi Solomon ben Isaac), whose running commentary covers almost the entire Talmud. But the project of explaining the Talmud is ongoing, and every new book about the Talmud is a commentary on the text.

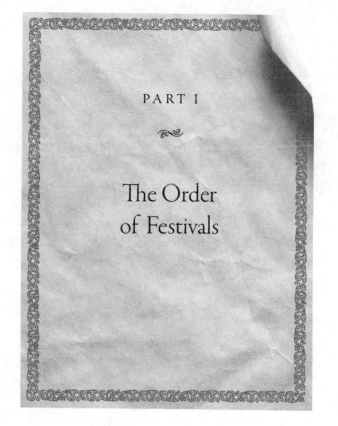

PART I

The Order
of Festivals

YOMA

❧

Alone in Jerusalem

WHEN I BEGAN STUDYING TRACTATE YOMA, I HUNG A xeroxed map of the Temple inside the front door of my studio apartment—right in the spot where hotels generally feature a floor map with the nearest fire exits marked. Most of the tractate is essentially a guided tour of the Temple, following in the footsteps of the high priest as he enacts the various rituals of Yom Kippur. With each page of Yoma I tracked my path on the map as I wound through the Temple's chambers and vestibules. I witnessed as the high priest slaughtered goats, sprinkled blood on the altar, and donned gold-and-white vestments with a breastplate and tinkling bells.

My apartment was tiny and square, with a kitchen counter and mini-fridge against one wall, a bathroom in the opposite corner, and a desk along the adjacent wall beneath my only window, where I hung my laundry out to dry over a narrow ledge that my cultured European landlady generously referred to as a "Romeo and Yooliet balcony." The floor was made of square tiles decorated in a green-and-brown floral pattern. There was no couch or armchair or other place to sit, but I so rarely had visitors that it didn't seem to matter. My bed was lofted above the kitchen area up a steep and rickety ladder leading toward a high ceiling, and it wasn't a proper bed but just a mattress that I'd purchased second-hand and transported home precariously on the roof of a cab. I had no proper bookshelves, so I stacked my books in the closet. Another stack of books served as a nightstand on which I rested my glasses if I remembered to take them off. Most nights I fell asleep reading with the lights on, my novel collapsed over my face like a tent with my nose marking my place.

The heroine in one of Margaret Drabble's novels revels in the "spinsterish delight" of crawling alone into bed with a book, and I could relate—not just at the beginning of the night but also at 3:00 a.m., when I woke up pleased to have those stolen mid-night moments to my conscious self; and in the early morning hours, when I arose before my alarm clock and read by the light streaming through my open window. I had books I would read only in bed; they lived under the blankets and waited patiently while I read more respectable volumes during daylight hours. Writing in bed, too, was a newfound pleasure. There were entries in my journal that I was able to write only under cover of darkness, as if I could not expose these negatives to the harsh light of day. And there were, if I was honest, many negatives. But I was rarely honest.

For a while I could not own up to the reality of my situation because I did not even know who I was. Each morning I walked mechanically to the library to continue working on the book about the Temple's destruction I'd begun ghostwriting during the year my marriage fell apart. I was grateful that the material was not my own because I was incapable of original thought. I felt cut off from the ideas that had once animated me and from the emotions that had once transported me. One night Andrea came over to regale me with stories of her latest crush. "He works at the coffee shop where I've been writing my articles," she gushed.

"I mean, just to make some money on the side. He's really a writer. He's given me a draft of his novel to read, and it's a love story! How much should I read into that?" I didn't know what to tell her. Romantic love seemed like a thing of the past, a place where I had once lived and whose hills and valleys I could map out with complete accuracy, yet a place to which I was sure I would never return. I resolved that if I was destined to spend the rest of my life alone, then at least I should not feel lonely. While I remained warm toward the few friends I had, I treated myself with cool indifference. I imagined that if the temperatures within plummeted low enough, then any hopes I dared to harbor would scamper to the corners and die in the cold.

Every so often, though, those feelings rose to the surface, and I had to confront what I knew to be true: That I have always been a hopeless romantic, and that my sense of romance is deeply bound up in my passion for literature. That I memorized "The Lady of Shalott," Tennyson's long ballad about unrequited love, when I was a teenager. That in college, I used to stroll along the Charles River at sunset reciting Byron's "So We'll Go No More A-Roving"—not to a man, but to whichever girlfriends were willing to put up with my romantic melodrama. That I dated several men in college and beyond, but I was still imagining myself as Anne of Green Gables, and none could measure up to Gilbert Blythe. That ultimately curling up with a good book always surpassed the inevitable awkwardness of real courtship, with its silly questions of what to wear and when it was OK to write back and how to interpret that passing glance. That all this seemed to change when I met Paul, who wanted to curl up with me and my books and play Paolo to my Francesca. And that when our marriage collapsed, the entire edifice of literary romanticism that I had constructed for myself seemed to collapse beneath me, and I was convinced that my love life—that imaginative world informed by Byron, Barrett-Browning, and the Brontës—was over forever.

But I spoke of this to no one, even when Andrea suddenly grew self-conscious after all her enraptured gushing and said to me soberly, "And what about you? How are you?" The Talmud in Yoma (75a) cites a debate between two rabbis about what a person should do when distressed, based on a verse from Proverbs: "If there is distress in a man's mind, let him quash it" (12:25). The Hebrew word for "quash it," *yashhena*, sounds like *yashena*, "distract," but also like *yisihena*, "tell." According to Rabbi Ami, the distressed individual should distract himself with other things. According to Rabbi Assi, he should tell of his woes to others so that he feels less burdened by them. I followed Rabbi Ami, choosing distraction over confession. Were I to attempt to narrate our failed marriage, I would surely just blame myself: I was not mature enough, I had not sufficiently taken into account the needs of others, I had not worked hard enough at it. I may have been a self-avowed romantic, but I'd failed at the most important romantic relationship. *How had this happened, how?* I wondered, echoing the repeated "how" of Lamentations—the book of the Bible known in Hebrew as Eichah (how), in which the prophet Jeremiah elegizes the Temple. I fingered the drawstring on the window shade above my desk as I read about the crimson thread in the Temple that miraculously turned white at the moment on Yom Kippur when the people's sins were forgiven.

Living alone, I identified with the high priest who was sequestered for seven days prior to Yom Kippur in a special chamber of the Temple to prevent him from contracting impurity. During this period other priests appointed a "backup wife" for him in case his wife were to die, since he was required to atone for his household and could not do so unless he had one. This may sound terribly unromantic, and indeed the Talmud is often regarded as a highly unromantic text, particularly when it comes to the transactional nature of marriage. But this is only because, for the rabbis, the object of longing was rarely wives, or even other women. Rather, when the rabbis wax most poetic, they are fre-

quently speaking about the Temple, which was destroyed generations before the Talmud's inception.

In learning Yoma, I became swept up in the romance of
Temple lore. I dreamed of the seven-branched golden candelabra,
the sink where the priests rinsed their hands, and the *muchni*, the
clanking mechanical pulley system that lowered the sink into a
pit of water beneath the Temple floor. I shared in the rabbis' nostalgia for the Temple's glory days—particularly the First Temple
era, when the priests were not yet corrupt (or so the rabbis claim)
and the ark of the covenant still stood in the Holy of Holies. By
the time of the Second Temple, the Talmud teaches, the Holy of
Holies was empty and the ark had disappeared, leading to mystery and intrigue surrounding its whereabouts.

There is a Talmudic story about a priest engaged in Temple
service who once noticed that one of the paving stones in the
floor was slightly higher than the rest (Yoma 54a). He went out to
report on his discovery to his fellow priests, but "he had not yet
finished speaking when suddenly he died." (This kind of instan-
taneous zapping is a common trope in rabbinic stories.) The Talmud concludes that this must have been the place where the ark
of the covenant was buried. Surely anyone who came so close to
discovering the hidden ark would not live to tell the tale. This
passage continues with a story about two priests who were busy
picking worms out of the wood that was set aside for burning on
the altar. One of them dropped his axe—presumably on the spot
where the ark was buried—and immediately a fire broke out and
consumed him.

The more dramatic the Talmud's stories, the more they took
on a life of their own. One evening while washing the floor of my
apartment, I noticed that one of the tiles was loose. I had already
covered the floor with soapy water and was soaking it all up with
a rag affixed to a *sponga* pole—the traditional way to clean the
floors in Israel—when I came to that loose tile and trembled. I
approached it with trepidation, half expecting fire to come forth

and consume me if I put down my bucket of soapy water in the wrong place.

The rabbinic discussion of the Temple is fiery and passionate, at times bordering on the erotic. The rabbis relate that even though Jericho is a full ten-parsa distance from Jerusalem, the women of Jericho did not need to put on perfume because the scent of the incense wafting from Jerusalem was so powerful. Even the goats of Jericho would sneeze when their nostrils were tickled by the fragrance. In Jerusalem the scent was so concentrated that it was not just ordinary women but also brides who could forgo any fragrance. The incense, made of cinnamon, saffron, cassia, myrrh, and other spices whose names are as seductive as their scents, intoxicated the sages of the Talmud. As one elder reports, "Once I went to Shiloh [the site of the portable sanctuary where Jews worshipped prior to the First Temple], and I breathed in the scent of the incense from between its walls" (Yoma 39b). As I imagined the spices wafting from the Temple's clefts, I could almost hear the breathless panting.

Of course, there is no nostalgia for what remains; nostalgia is the longing for what once was. No one who is happily wed grows nostalgic about marriage, as Byron quipped in *Don Juan*: "Think you, if Laura had been Petrarch's *wife* / He would have written sonnets all his life?" And one does not speak nostalgically of a Temple that is still standing and operational. Not surprisingly, the opening chapter of tractate Yoma includes a lengthy discussion of the reasons for the Temple's destruction. When it comes to the First Temple, these reasons are all related to the Jewish people's sins against God: the Temple was destroyed because of the sins of idolatry, or adultery, or murder. In explaining the sin of idolatry, Rabbi Yohanan quotes a verse from Isaiah (28:20): "For the bed shall be too short for a man to stretch himself out on it." He explains that this verse refers to a couch too narrow for both God and an idol to lie on (Yoma 9b). The imagery invoked is the intimate space of a bedroom, a reminder that the Temple was the space of the most intimate connection between God and Israel. As Rav K'tina states, "At the time when Israel would go to the Temple on the festivals, they would roll back the ark curtain to reveal the cherubs, who were hugging each other, and they would say: Look at how beloved you are of God, like the love between a man and a woman" (Yoma 54a). This same passage compares the poles that protruded through the ark curtain to a woman's breasts poking through the fabric of her dress. God has no place to sleep because there is an idol in His bed, and on account of that idol, His most intimate chamber is destroyed.

One evening as I sat learning daf yomi on my Romeo and Juliet balcony, I was suddenly transported to fair Verona, where I laid my scene. I imagined Juliet leaning her cheek against her gloved hand as Romeo gazes up at her under cover of darkness. Juliet sighs ("Ay me!"), and Romeo hangs on to her every sound and gesture ("She speaks! O, speak again, bright angel"), wooing her from below in language reminiscent of the Song of Songs, which Shakespeare seems occasionally to invoke ("Stony limits cannot hold love out"). I imagined the balcony as the site of many subsequent late-night trysts, as it is the one place where the lovers can speak freely to one another without risking the wrath of the Montague and Capulet clans. Surely Juliet longs, each day, for night to come, so she can go out on her balcony to speak to Romeo.

And then I imagined that one day, Juliet comes home to find that her parents have boarded up her balcony. Her window is covered with wooden planks fixed crudely to the wall, and pieces of the railing, hacked at with axes and spades, lie strewn on the street below. "Her gates have sunk into the ground, he has smashed her bars to bits" (Lamentations 2:9). Juliet is utterly distraught: how will she see Romeo that evening? How will she communicate with her lover? "See, O Lord, the distress I am in! My heart is in anguish" (Lamentations 1:20). It is not only her balcony she has lost, but the whole elaborate system of semaphores and scheduling that she and her lover have constructed to ensure that they see each other regularly. Juliet wails. "Bitterly she weeps in the night, her cheeks wet with tears. There is none to comfort her of all her friends" (Lamentations 1:2).

The rabbis, in mourning the Temple, were not just mourning a physical edifice but an entire system of connecting with God—one that involved daily sacrifice, fragrant incense, elaborate vestments, and golden trumpets. I, too, felt that I was mourning not just my marriage but all my romantic dreams—dreams that involved late-night roving and star-crossed love. I'm not sure if, after the destruction of the First Temple, the Jews dared hope that there might someday be a second. I only know that in my own life I harbored no such expectations.

I was convinced I'd never re-marry, but one night my imagination got the better of me and I pictured myself again a bride. It was late Friday afternoon during that magical, mystical time the rabbis refer to as "between the suns," on the cusp of the day that is waning and the night about to fall. (I suppose the English equivalent is twilight, meaning "two lights.") Uneasy about the prospect of a long evening alone, I put on a long white flowing dress and walked outside to head toward synagogue. But then I changed my mind and instead set my steps toward the walls of the Old City, entered the stone gate, and walked down the narrow cobblestone paths to the Kotel, the last remaining wall of the Temple, singing the prayers to welcome Shabbat along the way. I've never felt any special connection to the Kotel, but I was eager to visit the site of all the rituals I'd been reading about for weeks in tractate Yoma. And there was something thrilling about the notion that the Temple Mount—the object of thousands of years of Jewish longing and the place toward which Jews the world over direct their prayers—was just a half-hour walk from my apartment. "Arise and shake off the dust of the earth / Wear glorious garments reflecting your worth," I sang, feeling my soul increasingly uplifted with each successive stanza of the mystical prayer Lecha Dodi, "Come My Beloved," in which the Sabbath is greeted like a bride.

When I reached the Kotel I had already finished chanting Maariv, the evening service, and so I whispered a few words of silent petition and turned back toward home. I learned in Yoma that the high priest was supposed to enter the Holy of Holies and offer only a short prayer, lest the people waiting anxiously outside grow worried that he had somehow behaved incorrectly and would never emerge from that holiest of places (Yoma 52b). My prayers, too, lasted only seconds, and I didn't even bother to elbow my way through the crowds of devout worshippers between me and the wall. I did not need to touch the cold stones because I could feel the weight of their history when I pressed my fingers against the Talmudic page. By the time I got home, the sky was pitch black, and I was hungry and exhausted, ready to learn daf yomi over dinner and collapse into bed.

Since I usually ate my Shabbat meals alone, I rarely bothered to prepare anything elaborate. Often on Friday afternoons I would cook while listening to recordings of daf yomi classes on my laptop. One week I was preparing a salmon while listening to daf yomi, which suddenly turned to the subject of fish (Yoma 75a). The rabbi teaching the class quoted a biblical verse cited on that day's page of Talmud: "We remember the fish that we ate in Egypt for free" (Numbers 11:5). I was intrigued, but I had to keep cooking or I would not be ready in time for Shabbat. I unwrapped the salmon and rinsed the soft pink flesh in the sink, trying to make out the voice on the computer that was narrating the Talmud's discussion.

I turned off the tap and listened closely. On Yom Kippur we are commanded to engage in self-affliction. The manna we ate in the desert was a form of affliction as well, since the children of Israel received only enough to eat every day and had to endure the uncertainty of whether there would be new manna tomorrow. Instead of the manna, the Israelites really wanted fish, which is the reason that they complained to Moses: "We remember the fish that we ate in Egypt for free."

But did the Israelites really eat free fish in Egypt? Weren't they slaves? The leading third-century Babylonian sages, Rav and Shmuel, try to make heads and tails of the verse. While listening to their debate, I sliced the salmon fillet in two halves, dubbing them Rav and Shmuel. I sprinkled some oregano and lemon juice on Rav and put him in my toaster oven, which was the only oven that fit in my pokey apartment. Shmuel would have to wait on the counter for a while.

The Talmud goes on to quote the sages' conflicting opinions. Rav says, "Fish means fish," insisting on a literal reading of the biblical text. Shmuel says, "Fish means illicit sexual relations," invoking the pervasive Talmudic analogy between food and sex. I closed the toaster door, but they kept at it. Rav says, "It says 'the fish that we ate'—this must be a literal reference to food." Shmuel says, "It says 'for free'—did we really get free food? It must mean the illicit sexual relations that the Israelites were free to engage in before they received the Torah." Rav tries to defend himself, flapping his half-tail vigorously: "When the Israelites were in Egypt, they used to dip their jugs into the Nile. God would cause a miracle to happen: fish would get swept into the jugs as well, and they would have food to eat." Shmuel insists that eating is a euphemism for something else. He quotes a verse from Proverbs: "Such is the way of the adulteress. She eats, wipes her mouth, and says, 'I have done no wrong'" (30:20).

Shmuel, what a dirty mind you have, I scolded the piece of fish lying limply on the counter. I covered him up with a piece of foil and hoped that my neighbors could not hear. Rav, modestly browning in the oven, has his comeback prepared. "The daughters of Israel were not adulteresses! They were not loose women! After all, as it says in the Song of Songs: 'A locked garden is my beloved bride'" (4:12).

Shmuel is not so sure. "But it says that when the Israelites were in the desert, they were crying for their families! What do you think that means, 'for their families' (Numbers 11:10)? They were bemoaning the fact that now that they had the Torah, they could not just sleep around with any woman they wanted."

"Ding!" went the toaster. Rav was ready to come out. I unwrapped Shmuel and rested him gently on the oven tray.

"Ha v'ha havay," says the Talmud, affirming that both are correct and making peace between the pieces. The Israelites were crying both because they missed the fish and because they missed the illicit sexual relations they enjoyed in Egypt.

"Ha v'ha havay," I sighed placatingly, placing the two pieces of fish side by side in a glass dish. Resolved, I picked up the phone to call a friend. "Do you want to come over for dinner tonight? I just made fish."

☎

I did not always cook for Shabbat. Through my editing work I had met Hedva and Ari, a warm and friendly young couple with three small children who often invited me to join them for Shabbat meals. Hedva was just a few years older but seemed light years ahead of me. She was a preschool teacher with a soft, calming smile, and she was beautiful in a put-together sort of way, her hair neatly combed, her clothes flattering but not fancy. Ari, an academic whose dissertation I'd edited, was smart and kind and gracious, and I idealized the couple's seemingly perfect marriage, their starched white tablecloth, their beaming children, and the delicious golden challah loaves that Hedva baked every week. The Talmud in Yoma (38a) speaks of the priestly bakers of the Garmu family who refused to share their bread recipes with anyone else. I was sure Hedva would share her recipe with me if I asked, but there was no way I would bother baking challah when I lived alone. I could easily get by with a couple of mass-produced rolls from the corner store, which were enough to satisfy the requirement to make a blessing over two loaves of bread on Shabbat. I thought of a line from Yoma: "One cannot compare a person who has bread in his basket to a person who does not have bread in his basket" (74b). The phrase recurs several times throughout the Talmud, and refers not just to food but also to sex. One cannot compare the haves and the have-nots. Hedva and Ari made delicious challah, but whenever I said goodbye to them on their doorstep and walked back home on Friday nights, I was left thinking not about what they had but about what I had not.

In those early days after my divorce, I jogged every morning. I would wake up convinced that if it weren't for the compulsion to hit the pavement, I would never summon the willpower to get down from my loft bed. If I were going to run, it had to be before the 7:00 a.m. traffic clogged the streets, which meant I had to get out of bed right away. And so I did, each morning. In winter I dressed in leggings with a warm protective headband covering my ears; I did not mind the cold because it, along with the adrenaline rush, jolted me out of my morning despondency. By the time I got back from my run through the hills and valleys of Jerusalem, I was too sweaty to do anything but shower. Then I naturally got dressed, at which point I figured I might as well start the day. And so by running I staved off despair.

I had been a runner since I was a teenager, when I was a proud member of my high school track and field team. I used to train in the summers with my friend Kitty, who shared my love of poetry. Each week we would choose another poem to memorize while running around the track. I kept a photocopy of the poem folded up in the pocket of my gym shorts, and the two of us took turns testing each other, consulting the text only when necessary. We started with Milton's sonnets, which were easy to memorize because their iambic meter matched the pounding of our feet against the pavement: "When *I* Con*si*der *How* My *Light* Is *Spent.*" As we built up our endurance, we moved on to longer works like Tennyson's "The Lady of Shalott," which I returned to when I was embowered in my Jerusalem studio with its lofted bed, romanticizing my solitude.

Like most of my classmates, Kitty wasn't Jewish, and each time a Jewish holiday came around I had to explain why I was missing another day of school. One summer day she asked me why I wouldn't be able to join her for a run, and I told her it was Tisha b'Av, the fast day commemorating the Temple's destruction. At the time, our local synagogue was undergoing renovations to build a new youth wing. My father was the rabbi and we lived on the synagogue property, as Kitty knew from her occasional visits to our home. Nonetheless, perhaps I should have anticipated her confusion. "I'm sorry I can't join you today. I have to fast. Why? The Temple was destroyed." Kitty paused, puzzled by my explanation. "The Temple was destroyed?" she questioned, raising her eyebrows. "I thought they were just renovating."

፝፝ℰℭ

I felt like my world, too, was destroyed when I broke my foot that Yoma summer. Ever oblivious to my body, I'm not sure exactly how it happened, but one morning I returned from my run, tried to get into the shower, and realized I could no longer walk on my left foot. Tears were streaming down my cheeks as I reluctantly hobbled into a cab to head to the emergency clinic. I was crying not out of pain—I can bear tremendous amounts of pain as long as it's merely physical—but out of fear that if my foot were broken, I might have to stay off it. One of my greatest pleasures was walking the streets of Jerusalem. Since I'd first moved to Israel with Paul two years earlier, my feet had traced a continuous path throughout the streets of the city. I rarely took buses or cabs, preferring to take in the city at my own pace, attuned to its daily rhythms and its subtle changes in light. Only occasionally would I lift my feet from the surface of the ground—not because I regard the land of Israel as holy, but because I am a lover of texts, and my reading and learning have always been intimately connected to walking. Whenever possible, I read novels set in Jerusalem, and then visited the places described—the YMCA stadium (sadly demolished a few years later) where David Grossman's Rhino used to watch soccer games in *Someone to Run With*; the old Arab house where Batya Gur's Zahava was brutally bludgeoned in *Murder on Bethlehem Road*; the park in San Simon where the tour guide in Meir Shalev's *A Pigeon and a Boy* describes the War of Independence battle that took place there.

For a while, though, I was going to have to rest. The X-ray results were unequivocal, as were the doctor's instructions: "Minimal walking, and no running for six weeks." That night as I lay in bed with my leg propped up on a stack of books—I owned only one pillow, and needed it for my head—I came across a story in Yoma about two priests who raced each other up a ramp to the Temple altar. Whoever got there first would get to do *trumat hadeshen*, the first sacrificial ritual performed in the Temple each morning, which involved clearing off the ashes from the previous day's sacrifices (22a). When the two were neck and neck, one pushed his fellow aside, causing him to fall and break his foot. I wondered whether the injured priest was struck, as I was, by the words we recite every Shabbat morning: "God guards all [my] bones; not one of them breaks" (Psalms 34:21). The ideal, of course, is for "all my bones to say, 'O Lord, who is like You?'" (Psalms 35:10), as we recite elsewhere in the liturgy. But my bones were not cooperating.

The next day was the first day of Elul, the final month of the Jewish calendar, a month that is devoted to repentance in preparation for Yom Kippur. Jewish tradition teaches that throughout

Elul our lives hang in the balance—will we put our best foot forward or stumble over the obstacles in our path? Will we be inscribed for life or death? The liturgy of the Al Chet, the long confessional prayer recited many times on Yom Kippur, links most of the sins to the parts of the human body: "For the sin of wanton eyes, for the sin of being stiff-necked, for the sin of the evil tongue." And then, of course, there is the line that involves feet: "For the sin of running with our legs toward iniquity." At least I wasn't able to do that in my present state.

In my more upbeat moments, I hoped that staying off my feet might offer me an excuse to turn my gaze inward. The Yom Kippur liturgy states that "God searches all the inner chambers of the stomach and checks the kidneys and the heart." God gives the ultimate internal exam, and we are supposed to follow His example. I had been running for so long—away from my loneliness, away from my shame, away from my sadness. But now, huddled over Yoma with my broken foot, it was all catching up with me.

Looking back now I realize that in mapping out the Temple I was, almost in spite of myself, mapping out my heart. Elsewhere in the Talmud Rabbi Akiva teaches that the Hebrew word for man, *ish,* and the Hebrew word for woman, *isha,* differ only in the letter *hey,* which is the symbolic representation of God's name (Sotah 17a). The other two letters common to both words are *aleph* and *shin,* which spell *aish,* fire. If a man and woman's union has merit, the divine Hey will reside between them; if not, a fire will break forth and consume them, perhaps emerging from the uneven floorboards.

It's a moment I so rarely let myself recollect, but the last night that Paul and I broke bread together, we sat down for Shabbat dinner at our small wooden table that faced a bare wall in our rental apartment. The Shabbat candles were flickering behind us, but suddenly I realized that something else was flickering too— no, not flickering, but burning. Burning! The yard behind our apartment was swept up in flames that leapt higher and higher outside our ground-floor windows. I gasped, momentarily paralyzed by shock. And then what happened? Seeing the flames, Paul reached for the phone to call for emergency help. I lunged for his hand to pull him along with me but then let go and bolted out the door myself. I ran and ran, perhaps sensing that if I didn't flee then, I never would. And then for a long time I kept running.

When the Temple was destroyed, the rabbis began compiling their teachings to form the Mishnah, which led to the Talmud, and ultimately text study occupied much of the central religious role that had formerly been the province of Temple ritual. My marriage, like the Temple, had ended in conflagration. But for a while at least, studying Yoma was my sanctuary.

SUKKAH / BEITZAH

❧

Temporary Homes

I WAS WALKING WITH MY SISTER IN MANHATTAN DURING one of my visits back from Israel in the aftermath of my divorce. "Can you imagine where you'll be in ten years?" she asked me as we crossed at 96th Street. The traffic was at a standstill, and ten years seemed like an eternity. I always forget, until the light turns green again, how fast the cars whizz by. I looked at my sister, wishing I could answer for her instead. Her future seemed so much more certain: she was in a stable marriage, pregnant with her first child, and enrolled in medical school. I, though two years her senior, was between apartments, still taking it day by day, and I had no idea how to respond.

I was, at the time, a bit like the children of Israel in the wilderness, who wandered for forty years following their liberation from Egypt. During this itinerant period they complained about the food, complained about their leader, and built temporary huts known as *sukkot*, or booths, the plural form of *sukkah*, from which the tractate takes its name. In the middle of my study of tractate Sukkah, I moved from one temporary apartment to another, unable to commit to anything long term. Indeed, in the span of my first two years of daf yomi learning, I lived in four different apartments, wandering through the wilderness even though I'd already arrived in the promised land.

Sukkot is also the name of an autumn holiday in which Jews commemorate the period of the Israelites' wandering through the wilderness by leaving the comfort of their homes to dwell for a week in small huts that they build in their backyards or on their apartment porches. Much of tractate Sukkah deals with the construction of these huts—what materials they may be made of, how tall they must be, how many walls they must have. I studied these laws diligently, but I never built a sukkah of my own— perhaps because the idea of a temporary home seemed superfluous at a time when my regular home seemed so short term.

During that period, the main source of stability in my life was not my home but my work. Shortly after the divorce I landed a job at a small literary agency in Jerusalem, where I sold foreign rights to Israeli publishers. My job involved reading book catalogues in search of titles that would be suitable for the Israeli market, speaking with Israeli editors about their acquisitions interests, answering e-mails from colleagues abroad who were pitching their new titles, and conducting auctions among Israeli publishers competing for rights to publish the same book. Beyond the nature of the work, which I enjoyed, the need to report to an office on a regular basis provided a basic framework for my days, and I never lacked for what to read.

The best part of the job was definitely the books. Twice a week our assistant came back from the post office dragging a metal granny cart overflowing with packages, each filled with the latest offerings hot off the presses of the major American publishers. I read through the glossy book catalogues like a kid in a candy store and ordered not just what I thought we could sell, but anything I wanted to read—literary novels, the collected works of my favorite contemporary poets, the latest academic books on Talmud and Jewish studies. Opening the mail was like getting birthday presents every day, and I told myself that with all those books, I could never possibly be lonely.

My obsession with books was hardly new. In my high school job as an aptly named "page" in the local public library, I was once nearly fired when my boss found me in the basement where I was supposed to be sorting through recent book donations. Instead, though, I was crouched among piles of books with my notebook and pen, copying out a favorite passage from a tattered paperback copy of A. S. Byatt's *Possession*—which opens with a scholar poring over marginalia in a library basement. At Harvard, too, I worked as a circulation clerk at the Widener Library and spent most of my remaining hours deep in the stacks, munching cold pancakes purloined from the dining hall breakfast and scouring Victorian novels for references to contemporaneous scientific ideas, or making forays to the Judaica department six flights up. I spent the year after graduation studying British romantic poetry at Cambridge and then worked for three years in the editorial department of Random House, reading poetry aloud to myself as I walked the streets of Manhattan to and from work. When Paul and I married, I left that job to follow him to Israel, where at first I worked as an editor and ghostwriter before starting at the literary agency. If I had to append an epigraph to my CV, it would probably be from Ecclesiastes, which is chanted on Sukkot each year: "The making of books is endless" (12:12).

In addition to the books, other highlights of my job at the literary agency included my annual trips to the international book fairs in Frankfurt and London. I attended my first Frankfurt fair in October 2006, which coincided with tractate Sukkah in the daf yomi cycle. The Frankfurt International Book Fair is the world's oldest and largest, dating back over five hundred years to shortly after Johannes Gutenberg's invention of moveable type. Originally attended by local booksellers and readers— Hilary Mantel writes in *Wolf Hall* that Oliver Cromwell stopped by—the fair has become the single most important international publishing event. It is held on the sprawling grounds of the Messe, a trade fair in downtown Frankfurt that includes several multistory exhibition halls connected by escalators, moving walkways, and a tram service. But on that first visit I was most struck not by the scale of the fair but by the setup of the exhibition halls. A different floor is devoted to each country, and the floors are arranged in numbered rows and lettered aisles, such that every exhibitor is located by its coordinates: S972 for Random House, P973 for Norton, H17 for HarperCollins. Along these rows and aisles, each publisher or agency sets up a booth to exhibit its recent and forthcoming books. And so the Frankfurt Book Fair, which appropriately falls out right around Sukkot every year, is in fact a festival of booths.

I spent my first Frankfurt Fair lugging around a briefcase with foreign rights guides, book catalogues, and my copy of tractate Sukkah, which I tried to learn discreetly between meetings. But it is hard to do anything discreetly at the fair, where it is all about suits and trappings, and nothing passes show. Editors and publishers dress to the nines in fancy business suits, elegant high-heeled shoes, and expensive silk blouses. One of the reasons I love living in Israel is because of the informality of the dress code: I can get by dressing for work in jeans and sweaters. But in Frankfurt I had to wear black dress pants, an elegant frilly sweater, and uncomfortable leather shoes that I would not be caught dead wearing on any other occasion. My colleague, with whom I shared a hotel room, often tried to convince me to put on makeup, though I could not bring myself to go that far. Makeup has always seemed to me like a colossal waste of time and money. But looking around the fair, I realized that I might be the only woman who was not in lipstick, and I was surely the only woman carrying around a volume of Talmud.

As I made my way from booth to booth for meetings scheduled every half hour, I couldn't help but examine each one to see if it would qualify as kosher—that is, fit for religious purposes.

And so instead of thinking about world rights and preemptive bids, I was counting walls, hollowing out imaginary holes in the ceiling above, and estimating dimensions using the rabbinic measurements of *amot* and *t'fachim*, the length of a forearm and the width of a fist. Contrary to what I might have expected, there were indeed several kosher sukkot at the Frankfurt festival of booths. If you hold by *dofen akumah*, the notion that a right angle may be considered as constituting part of a single wall, then the HarperCollins booth, with its small skylight, would be kosher. On the other hand, the Hanser booth, with its two walls completely open, was certainly not. The Random House booth took up a full row in the American hall and was lined by framed and backlit full-color book jackets of forthcoming Spring 2007 titles; this was definitely what the rabbis would call *noi*, elaborate decoration. Penguin Putnam's booth had a giant black-and-white penguin painted on one of its walls, but the rabbis explicitly say that an animal cannot serve as a sukkah wall. And so I continued to take note of each booth as I wandered through the wilderness of the Frankfurt Buchmesse.

One night I was obligated to attend a fancy reception for the German publisher Suhrkamp in a private room at a five-star hotel. All around me, women with elaborate hairdos and men with manicured mustaches leaned in to kiss one another on both cheeks. I tried to blend in with the beige curtains, hoping that I could hide in the corner by the tray of Swiss chocolates. Choking in a cloud of cigarette smoke, I dreamed of the clouds of God's glory that accompanied the Israelites throughout their desert wanderings. I looked forward to eating a home-cooked meal in my friend's sukkah when I got back. In Frankfurt, kosher food was hard to come by—it was basically sausages or starve. Fortunately, I had brought four boxes of granola bars with me, which I nibbled on between meetings, but I had not eaten a proper sit-down meal since arriving in Germany. To invoke the Talmud's term for the type of snacking that is permissible when not eating in a sukkah, it was all "temporary eating," *achilat aray*, or, as I came to refer to it, "achilat awry."

When I returned to Jerusalem, my friend Yael's parents invited me to join them in their rooftop sukkah for the first night of the holiday. It was a lovely evening. The sukkah swayed in the breeze and I shivered in the white sweater I wore over a light floral dress; by day it was still summer, but the nights had grown chilly. Yael sat opposite her parents, who were flanked by two older couples, neither of whom I had previously met. Yael's mother turned to me. "I hear you've been learning daf yomi," she said. "Perhaps you'd like to share some words of Torah with all of us?" At that point I had been learning for only a few months; I was hardly a Torah scholar. Nor had I embarked on my study plan with the intention of teaching others. But I realized for the first time that night that a commitment to studying Torah bore with it a responsibility to share that learning. And so I pulled out my volume of Talmud, which I was accustomed to carrying with me at all times, and read about a debate between Rabbi Akiva and Rabban Gamliel, glancing occasionally over at Yael, who was the only one who knew why the text spoke to me so powerfully.

The sages discuss the case of a person who builds a sukkah on a boat, presumably while taking a long overseas voyage during the holiday. Rabbi Akiva argues that such a sukkah is kosher, but Rabban Gamliel disagrees. The Talmud then goes on to relate the following punchy anecdote:

> There is a story about Rabban Gamliel and Rabbi Akiva who were once sailing aboard a ship. Rabbi Akiva stood up and built his sukkah on the ship. The next day, a wind blew and overturned it. Rabban Gamliel said to him, "Akiva, where's your sukkah?" (Sukkah 23a)

Rabban Gamliel disagrees with Rabbi Akiva's decision to build a sukkah aboard a ship, presumably on the grounds that such a sukkah is inherently unstable. When Akiva's sukkah indeed collapses, Rabban Gamliel essentially says "I told you so," knocking the wind out of Akiva's sails.

As the subsequent Talmudic debate demonstrates, the disagreement between these two sages hinges on their differing understandings of how stable a sukkah must be. According to Rabbi Akiva, a sukkah is kosher so long as it can withstand regular, predictable weather. But Rabban Gamliel maintains that a sukkah must be stable enough to withstand more than it is likely to confront—even those raging gales that blow only rarely. Otherwise, as Rabban Gamliel might have put it, all is just "futility and pursuit of wind," to quote again from a refrain in the book of Ecclesiastes.

The dispute between Rabban Gamliel and Rabbi Akiva is one I played out in my head all the time. "OK," I'd tell myself, "you're managing your life right now, but what if you suddenly lost your job? What if your very few friends were to leave the country? What if you had to move again?" I thought of the empty cardboard boxes collapsed in my closet. Each time I'd moved, I'd packed up my possessions. I had started saving them between moves, which seemed to make sense given how frequently I kept packing up and relocating. Suddenly the routine I had constructed for myself seemed to be as flimsy as those cardboard boxes. Yes, I was in a place where I could withstand the little breezes that destabilized me every so often—a lost bus pass, a missed appointment—but what if another gale were to blow? Where would my sukkah be then?

Ultimately, I sided with Rabbi Akiva. It is OK, I decided, to be in a place in life where I can withstand only those winds that are blowing right here and right now. Perhaps there are stronger winds that would knock me over—certainly they had knocked me over in the past, and were they to blow again, I had no doubt that I'd be flat on my back, flailing helplessly. And yet, as Matthew Arnold wrote in "Dover Beach," the world has no certitude, but "the sea is calm tonight." The winds were not blowing at this very moment, and in my friend's parents' sukkah, where I was eating a homemade meal with good people, the colorful paper chains hanging from the ceiling were dancing in the breeze, and my volume of Talmud lay open before me. Of all the biblical holidays, it is Sukkot—when we leave the security of our homes and subject ourselves to the elements—that is referred to in the Bible as "the time of our rejoicing." Joy, then, is about the ability to celebrate what we have right now, to see our half-full cup as running over. As we are exhorted each year on Sukkot by Ecclesiastes, "I commend rejoicing in life, because there is nothing better for a person under the sun than to eat and drink and rejoice" (8:15). And so I took another sip of wine, relished the sweet honeyed challah, and rejoiced in the moment.

જી

I had a crisis in my home just when I moved on from Sukkah to Beitzah, the tractate that deals with festival observance, specifically those restrictions imposed on ordinary human activity so as to enhance the sanctity of the day. The Hebrew word *beitzah* means "egg," and the name of the tractate comes from its opening mishnah, which has to do with whether it is permissible to eat an egg that is laid by a chicken on a festival. As the rabbis explain, everything must be designated for festival use in advance of the day, which is impossible if something is not yet born. The first few pages of the tractate continue this avian theme, exploring such questions as the sexual habits of various fowl, the permissibility of moving a ladder from one dovecote to another, and the collection of eggs from a bird's nest. Given this preoccupation with all things bird related, perhaps I should have been less surprised when I came home a few days after starting tractate Beitzah to discover two pigeons roosting in my apartment.

At the time I was accustomed to leaving my apartment before

dawn and returning long after dusk. Since I lived alone, there was no reason to hang around in the morning or to rush home for dinner. I would leave home hastily, eager to start the day. One morning I forgot to close my kitchen window. When I walked in the door that evening, ready to collapse on the couch and learn the next page of Beitzah, I was startled to discover the two pigeons. One was perched atop my Shabbat water heater, its beak tucked underneath its neck contentedly. The other sat on my bookcase between my prayer book and my dictionary, as if it were prepared not just to teach itself the traditional prayers, but also to learn what they meant.

I do not react well to unexpected guests, and so for the first few minutes I simply shrieked at the top of my lungs, hoping that I would frighten away the intruders. But these birds were the pictures of equanimity, and even when I began flailing my arms wildly in their direction, they merely cocked their heads at me curiously as if we were playing a game of charades and it was their turn to guess. I was loud enough to attract the attention of my neighbor Amir, who rapped on my door to find out what was going on. Amir was a single Israeli guy in his late thirties who was always inviting large groups of people over for raucous Shabbat meals that he encouraged me to join. I rarely did, preferring to eat alone with a book. But this time, for a change, the racket was coming from my side of the wall. When Amir walked in I was still so discombobulated that I did not know what to say. But when words fail me, poetry usually comes to the rescue: "Unmerciful disaster," I croaked as I pointed to the intruders in my chamber.

If Amir had read Poe, it was certainly not in English. Ignoring what I'd said, he instead tried to calm me down. When this didn't work, he told me that he was running out to find some equipment. "Sit down," he encouraged me, and somehow I did. I gazed up at the birds, neither of which had budged. Seeing as they didn't seem to be going anywhere, I picked up a volume of forgotten lore and decided to make my best attempt at resuming my regularly scheduled evening activity:

> Beit Shammai say: One may not move a ladder from one dovecote to another, but he can tilt it from window to window. Beit Hillel permit this. (Beitzah 9a)

I wondered if Amir was going to return with a ladder, since the birds could easily fly out of reach. But then I had an idea. I have always thought that the only aspect of owning a pet that I would actually enjoy would be naming the creature. *Tell me what thy lordly name is on the Night's Plutonian shore. . . .* In tribute to tractate Beitzah, where the Mishnah records many disputes between the houses of Hillel and Shammai, I named my intruders after these first-century sages who founded opposing schools of thought. "But this is my house," I insisted, as I watched Hillel flit to my Shabbat hot plate as if preparing to engage me in conversation about its halachic status.

> One who traps pigeons that live in dovecotes and pigeons that live in attics is liable. (Beitzah 24a)

Just then Amir burst in with a broomstick, a wig, a towel, a laundry basin, and a can of anti-roach spray—a curious approach to the problem, aimed both at making me laugh and at banishing the offending creatures. He sent me out to the hallway and then summoned me back a few minutes later to show me that the birds were now perched on the windowsill outside, looking in. I thought of Hillel the sage, who learned Torah by peering down through a skylight when he could not afford to pay the entrance fee to the study hall, and wondered if these feathered scholars were hoping to listen in on my daf yomi study. *And the Raven, never flitting, still is sitting, still is sitting.* It was with some degree

of triumph that I shut the casement window tight and collapsed
into bed.

ॐ

It was not just my apartments that seemed temporary, but also
my residence in Israel. Although I had a full-time salaried job,
most of my friends were American students who came to Israel
for the academic year and then returned home in the summer.
When September rolled around I would scroll through the list of
contacts in my cell phone and delete half the names and numbers,
a revolving door of Davids, Talyas, and Rachels. I wondered if
this was how grade school teachers felt when they said goodbye to
their students each June and greeted the new crop in September.
Still, my job had gone a long way toward making me feel less
stuck, as had the steady pace of turning the next page of daf yomi.

Friends both in Israel and America often asked me, "Are you
in Israel *for good*?" and I didn't know what to answer. I had come
to Israel in love with a man, but the place had a romance of its
own, and it exerted a hold on me. Once I had begun creating a life
on the other side of the world, it was hard to imagine picking up
and leaving it all behind. My family was supportive of my decision to stay, so long as I came back to visit once a year. But even on
those annual visits back to New York, it was unclear to me—and
to my parents—whether I should head back to Israel with fuller
suitcases and transport more and more of my possessions east
across the Atlantic. Where would I ultimately make my home? I
had not committed to staying in Israel for the long term. How
could I, as a single woman in a rental apartment? Besides, what
does it mean to be in a place for good? Do people ask that question about other parts of the world?

Eventually I began to think of "for good" as the English translation of *l'tovah,* for goodness, as in the blessing that we recite on
the Shabbat before each new Jewish month: "May all our heart's
wishes be fulfilled *for good*." And so I would respond that yes, I

hoped that everything I did in life was toward a positive end. More than that, though, I could not say. Israel was the place where I had a job, and that job kept me rooted for the time being. Like the children of Israel in the wilderness, I would often pick up and relocate, but each of my temporary homes afforded me stability and shelter. And so even though I couldn't answer my sister's question about what the future held in store, I—unlike the children of Israel—was not complaining.

ROSH HASHANAH

༄

The Book of Life

ROSH HASHANAH IS COMMONLY TRANSLATED AS THE
Jewish new year, an occasion for dipping apples in honey and
spending long hours in synagogue praying to God for a year of
blessing. But in tractate Rosh Hashanah there is not one Jewish
new year, but four: one for festivals and the dating of legal documents, one for tithing cattle, one for agriculture, and one for trees.
These various ways of marking time do not present a conflict until
Rabbi Eliezer and Rabbi Yehoshua break out in a fierce debate
about when the world was created (10b): on the first of Tishrei
(Rosh Hashanah as we know it) or the first of Nisan (the month
of Passover, when the Jews were freed from Egyptian bondage).
Each rabbi marshals an elaborate body of evidence in support
of his contention, and the resolution of their debate ultimately
hinges—rather surprisingly—on the astrological map of the sky
on the night of Noah's flood, which the Torah tells us took place
"in the second month on the seventeenth day of the month"
(Genesis 7:11).

My cosmological sensibilities are different, but I relate to the notion that there are various ways of marking time. Since high school I have kept track of my schedule using daily planners—notebooks with space to record daily appointments, commitments, and deadlines. When I lived in New York I bought my planners at the corner drugstore and had to annotate them before I could use them. Each year I'd copy over from my Jewish calendar all the dates of the Jewish holidays, the Shabbat candle-lighting times, and the names of the weekly Torah portions, superimposing Jewish time on secular time.

When I came to Israel, I brought my American planner with me, but it wasn't until Rosh Hashanah rolled around that I realized how backward that was. The new year was starting now. Why did my planner not end until December 31? And so I bought a new planner that started with Rosh Hashanah. In Israel, I discovered, the holiday season refers not to the break between Christmas and New Year's but to the festive month of Tishrei, in which there are rarely more than three consecutive work days in any given week. I learned to follow not just the holiday cycle but the fruits that come in and out of season: the pomegranates that redden and ripen in time for Rosh Hashanah, the citrus that turns from green to yellow as the autumn days grow shorter, the apples and persimmons that dominate the open-air market in winter, and the moist tender apricots available for one month right around Shavuot. When shopping for produce I feel connected to the cycle of the seasons and the growing patterns of the land, whose fruit is sweet to my palate.

The question of how to mark time and the seasons is central to tractate Rosh Hashanah, much of which deals with the laws governing the sighting of the new moon and the fixing of the calendar. On the Jewish calendar, every month has either twenty-nine or thirty days, depending on when the new moon appears. In ancient times the start of a new month was based on the testimony of witnesses who would come to the central court in

Jerusalem to report on their sighting of the new moon in the sky. Sometimes these stories were quite colorful (and hence suspect): "I was climbing a hill in Maale Adumim when I saw the moon prancing between two rocks, its head resembling a calf, its ears resembling a goat, its horns resembling a deer, and its tail resting between its thighs" (Rosh Hashanah 22b). For witnesses who lacked such descriptive power, the patriarch Rabban Gamliel would hold up a chart with various diagrams of the moon so that the witnesses might choose which image most closely resembled what they had seen in the sky. The patriarch and the court in the land of Israel had exclusive control over the establishment of the calendar, which became a hallmark of rabbinic authority as well as a means of asserting the land of Israel's centrality.

In Israel it is not just the years but also the weeks that follow a different pattern: the Israeli weekend falls out on Friday and Saturday, while Sundays are regular working days. Many of my American friends living here lament that the loss of Sundays is the most difficult part of moving to Israel, but I don't see it that way. I have never liked Sundays. In college a friend and I coined the term "Sunday doldrums" to refer to that sinking feeling of having so much to do and seemingly infinite time in which to do it—with the consequence that nothing gets done at all. This disorder was clinically labeled by the early twentieth-century neurologist Sándor Ferenczi as "Sunday neurosis," consisting of "headaches or stomach disturbances that were wont to appear on this day without any particular cause, and often utterly spoilt the young people's one free day of the week."[3] This was my affliction as a college student. I set my alarm for 7:00 a.m. every Sunday and forced myself to be up and out by 7:30, determined to take advantage of every minute. But twelve hours later, when the sun set and I was thoroughly exhausted, I felt like I'd gotten nothing done.

Sundays in America seemed to slip away into the late, empty

hours of the night, never quite living up to their promise. But Fridays in Israel have an energizing, even frenetic arc, with each hour drawing closer to Shabbat. I wake up on Friday and I know exactly how many hours I have until sunset to accomplish everything on my to-do list. So I throw in a load of laundry, dash to the bakery to pick up fresh challah, come home to roast vegetables for a salad, hang out the laundry to dry, finish editing a paper I promised to return to someone that week, dash off a few e-mails, fold the laundry, and then wash the floor before the sun begins to make its descent. Even the most mundane tasks become infused with an aura of sanctity because they are performed "lichvod Shabbat"—in honor of Shabbat. It is the loss of this sanctity that the great twentieth-century theologian Rabbi Joseph Soloveitchik lamented when he described Shabbat in America:

> It is not for Shabbat that my heart aches; it is for the forgotten "erev Shabbat" [eve of the Sabbath]. There are Shabbat-observing Jews in America, but there are no "erev Shabbat" Jews who go out to greet Shabbat with beating hearts and pulsating souls.[4]

Here in Jerusalem, where the restaurants close and the traffic disappears from the streets and time seems to slow down as Shabbat begins, erev Shabbat has its own unique character. The moment the sun sets, I put away my Friday to-do list. I have checked off everything that absolutely must get done, and the rest can no longer plague me once I light the candles and slip into the slow, peaceful rhythm of the day of rest. Only after Havdalah, the ceremony that concludes Shabbat, do I take out my planner once again to see what awaits me in the coming week.

God, too, keeps a planner of sorts, mapping out not His days but ours in advance of Rosh Hashanah. The Talmud (Rosh Hashanah 16b) relates that on the Day of Judgment God inscribes the names and fates of all the Jewish people in three different books. The first is reserved for those who are completely righteous; God records their names in this book of life and signs it on Rosh Hashanah. The next book is reserved for those who are thoroughly wicked; God records their names in this book of death and it, too, is signed on Rosh Hashanah. The third book contains the names of all the rest of us, those in the middle; God enters our names in pencil, so to speak, on Rosh Hashanah, but then waits until Yom Kippur before sealing our fates for life or death. It is during this period that God plans out our years, deciding who will live and who will die, who will make it into the book of life and who will not.

My own book of life, though, is not just my planner. In my planner I record the external realities—where I need to be when, and with whom. But then there is my journal, a record of what happens beneath the surface, in the deep and rocky emotional terrain of my heart, a landscape that sometimes feels so alien and barren that it may as well be on the moon—orbiting the earth, and keeping pace with sublunary reality, but a different thing entirely. Like the moon, my journal entries are merely a product of my own reflections, waxing and waning depending on how much light I shed on to the page.

I began chronicling my days in second grade when my parents gave me a Rainbow Brite journal, each page of which was a different bold color. When I flipped back to read what I'd written, I could make out my pencil etchings only on the yellow and orange days; the red and blue days were illegible. Still, I tended to write more on "blue" days than on "yellow" days—on days when I was sad or worried, rather than on days when I was happy and carefree. After all, if I was carefree, then why bother reflecting? My journal writing was never a celebration but more of a wallowing or, at best, a series of determined resolutions fiercely pounded onto the page.

The Hasidic sage Rabbi Levi Yitzchak of Berditchev would go to bed each night and examine his thoughts and deeds for that day. If he found fault with them, he would say to himself, "Levi Yitzchak will not do this again." Then he would chide himself, "Levi Yitzchak said exactly the same thing yesterday." And then he would reply, "Yesterday Levi Yitzchak did not speak the truth, but he does speak the truth today."[5] I can relate. I tell myself that by writing and reflecting on my life, I will become a better person. So many of my faults and bad habits seem to be a product of merely failing to live deliberately, with a heightened consciousness of what I am doing and why. Surely there are only so many times that I can scribble, "I will not eat chocolate after 10:00 p.m." before I finally start listening to myself. So writing becomes a sort of *shofar*, the ram's horn blown throughout the holiday season to call on us to mend our ways.

The shofar is sounded at the conclusion of daily morning services in the month leading up to Rosh Hashanah. In Jerusalem there may be as many as three or four synagogues on a given block, and when I jogged around the city at dawn, I heard one after another. Hearing the shofar on Rosh Hashanah is a religious commandment, and the rabbis in tractate Rosh Hashanah (27b) discuss whether a person who happens to be walking past a synagogue on the holiday and overhears the shofar blast has fulfilled his ritual obligation. They conclude that a person has fulfilled this obligation only if he "directed his heart," that is, if he listened to the sound of the shofar with deliberate intentionality—an indication that what is most important is not the sound of the shofar but how that sound resonates within us.

The shofar is supposed to remind us to repent, a notion reflected in the rabbinic discussion of the case of a broken shofar. The Mishnah in Rosh Hashanah (27a) considers the case of a shofar that is cracked and is then put back together. Is such a shofar kosher for use on the holiday? What if one adds on extra materials—such as glue—to put the shards back together? Is the glued shofar kosher? The rabbinic discussion is reminiscent of the ancient Greek paradox known as the Ship of Theseus, which deals with the question of whether an object that has had all its component parts replaced remains fundamentally the same object. Consider a ship that is comprised of wooden planks. One plank decays, and is replaced by a new plank. Then another plank decays, and it too is replaced. This process continues until none of the original planks remain. Is the vessel still the same ship?

Like the paradox of the ship, the Talmud deals with the question of when things change and when they stay the same. When is a shofar still a kosher shofar, and when is it changed into something else? Given that we are who we are, how much can we reasonably be expected to transform ourselves? In "Archaic Torso of Apollo," Rilke describes standing before the statue of a Greek god and finding himself utterly in its thrall. The statue—although it is missing a head and eyes—seems to look back at him with dazzling intensity. The poem climactically concludes with the terrifying charge, "You must change your life."

This is also the charge of Rosh Hashanah. Each year we recite in the Rosh Hashanah liturgy, "Repentance, prayer, and righteousness avert the evil decree." And so I strive for transformation not just while scribbling in my journal but also while standing before God in prayer—on Rosh Hashanah, and throughout the year.

∾

"Know Before Whom You Stand," read the gold letters above the ark in the synagogue in which I grew up. But around the time I learned tractate Rosh Hashanah, my "standing before God" took place not in a proper synagogue, but in a *minyan*, a small prayer community that I organized along with a group of friends. New prayer communities are always popping up in Jerusalem, a city in which finding the ideal synagogue is a quest that can rival Orwell's search for the perfect pub. Our minyan, Kedem, was fully egalitarian, with men and women participating equally in all parts of the service. We followed the traditional liturgy and read the full Torah portion every Shabbat morning. In a country divided into religious and secular camps—and in which gender egalitarianism is generally assumed to belong solely to the latter—Kedem was for a long time an anomaly on the Israeli synagogue scene. But having grown up in an egalitarian synagogue, I felt uncomfortable praying in a segregated space where women and men played different roles. At Kedem our constituents were mostly Americans living abroad, particularly students, so the minyan had a very transient feel, with many members departing at the end of the summer. When September rolled around, we scrambled to find volunteers to blow the shofar and lead the many high holiday services, as well as to help with setting up the physical space—we met in the music room of an elementary school, stacking the prayer books atop the grand piano.

On Chanukah, when we borrowed an extra Torah scroll from another synagogue but had no room for it in our makeshift ark, I volunteered to house it in my studio apartment. I laid the scroll on my desk and covered it with a prayer shawl, but I was all too conscious of its presence. I did not feel comfortable walking out of the bathroom in a towel because I did not want to uncover my nakedness when there was so much holiness in the room. Nor did I feel I could gossip on the phone with friends, lest the verse prohibiting tale-bearing rise off the page to rebuke me. Rather, I conducted myself with the utmost propriety for the thirty-six hours I was roommates with the Torah scroll—and then breathed a sigh of relief when it was time to give it back.

The Talmud teaches that "a person should always first arrange his prayers, and then pray" (Rosh Hashanah 35a), and the Hebrew word for prayer book, *siddur*, also means "arrangement." By serving as a coordinator of the minyan, I took this dictum very seriously. Most weeks I spent many hours preparing for and organizing services for the upcoming Shabbat, and so my whole week felt oriented toward that day, which is indeed what the rabbis mandate: in tractate Rosh Hashanah (31a), Rabbi Akiva teaches that there is a special psalm for each day of the week. The psalms for the first six days are about the creation of the world, and the psalm for Shabbat is about the world to come. In our daily prayers, we precede the psalm for each day by counting that day with reference to Shabbat: today is the first day of the Sabbath, today is the second day of the Sabbath, and so on. This counting resonated deeply with me as each week I took stock of how many days I had left to organize services for the coming Shabbat.

During services, I spent most of my time making sure there were enough chairs, reminding people when to open the ark, and redirecting visitors who accidentally wandered into our minyan in search of one of the many other synagogues located on the same street. Leading the minyan was ironically both a reason to come to synagogue and an excuse not to pray. With all my administrative responsibilities, who had time to concentrate on speaking to God? At the end of tractate Rosh Hashanah (35a), we learn that Rabban Gamliel would excuse field laborers from the responsibility to pray regularly, since they were busy in the fields and could not afford to leave their crops unattended. I was also too busy to pray, and I wondered whether making it possible for others to pray was also an acceptable form of worship.

Since I rarely had focused time in synagogue, I carried my siddur with me wherever I went. In moments when I felt totally lost—when I could not bring myself to show up for any of my appointments, or even bear to write about how I was feeling—I spoke to God through the siddur. I didn't always use it, but I wanted to know it was there if I needed it. I also never left the house without my planner and my journal—to stay organized, and to ensure that I had a place to record my thoughts. Suffice to say I did not travel lightly. My planner, my journal, my siddur— they are, each in their own way, my books of life.

TAANIT

꩜

Two by Two

ON ROSH HASHANAH WE COMMIT TO CHANGING OUR lives, and then we spend the rest of the year trying to make good on that promise. For months I'd persuaded myself to bask in my solitude as if it were summer sunlight, not realizing how parched it left me until, unexpectedly, the soil of my soul began thirsting again. I was ready for a change. Appropriately, it was around this time that I started learning tractate Taanit, which deals largely with fasting in times of drought. I looked up to the heavens like the thirsty rabbis, and suddenly Omri fell into my life.

I met Omri just before I studied the mishnah at the end of Taanit about courtship rituals in the land of Israel, which took place, surprisingly, on the most serious and somber fast day of the Jewish calendar: "Never were there any more joyous festivals in Israel than the fifteenth of Av and the Day of Atonement, for on them, the maidens of Jerusalem would go forth dressed in white garments—borrowed ones, so as not to cause shame to those who had none of their own. . . . The maidens went out and danced in the vineyards, saying, 'Young men, look and observe well whom you are about to choose. Regard not beauty alone, but rather look for a virtuous family, for 'Grace is false and beauty is vain'" (26b).

I was not wearing a white dress when I first met Omri, nor was I out dancing in the vineyards, but there was something enchanted about our first few dates. He was on reserve duty in the Israeli army and I was busy preparing for the Jerusalem book fair, a biennial international event in which a group of editors and agents from around the world come to Jerusalem for a week to learn about book publishing and Israeli literary culture. I spent the week at a hotel with the other participants, and so when Omri came back on leave, I told him to meet me in my hotel room, as if I were accustomed to such assignations. He came after dark and crept out before dawn to return to his base, and I pretended we were having a clandestine tryst under wartime curfew.

At the time I found it difficult to think of myself as attractive, let alone beautiful. "Grace is false and beauty is vain," I said to myself as I put on the same clothes I'd worn the day before— why bother with a new shirt when the current one wasn't yet smelly? I dressed in long denim skirts with large pockets and elbow-length sleeves that worked for both winter and summer, obviating the need for separate wardrobes. I had no patience for sartorial distractions, insisting with Jane Austen that "[d]ress is at all times a frivolous distinction, and excessive solicitude about it often destroys its own aim."[6] Instead I prided myself in my dedication to learning, a passion Omri and I shared.

When I prepared for dates with Omri, I didn't try on clothes, but I tried out various Talmudic passages I might share with him. On one of our early dates we walked through the Cardo—the main thoroughfare in Roman Jerusalem of Hadrian's time—and discussed the Talmud's story about the encounter between the Caesar's daughter and the reportedly ugly Rabbi Yehoshua ben Hanania (Taanit 7a). The Caesar's daughter inquires about the implications of an ugly man being such a great scholar of Torah. "How can such beautiful wisdom be contained in so ugly a vessel?" Rabbi Yehoshua responds with a challenge: "Does your father the Caesar keep wine in gold vessels?" "Of course not," the Caesar's daughter responds. "But he is the Caesar. Shouldn't he use the finest vessels?" So the Caesar's daughter promptly transfers all her father's wine to gold vessels, and of course the wine spoils. It is not the vessel that matters, but what is contained inside, as the rabbis teach in a mishnah (Avot 4:20). Or so I thought at first, but Omri saw it differently.

"The Caesar's wine spoils when it's placed in gold vessels," he pointed out.

"Yes, but it is the wine that matters and not the container," I responded, thinking of the mishnah in Avot.

"Is it?" Omri questioned. "Had the wine been placed in clay vessels, it would have been just fine. The fact that the vessels were gold made a difference. The vessel matters. Besides, wine is a liquid."

"So?" I asked. Omri had clearly given this more thought than I had.

"A liquid takes the shape of its container. The wine assumed the shape of the gold vessel."

Omri transformed the way I understood this Talmudic story. I'm no longer as dismissive of the vessel, or of what is on the outside. Who I am is related to what I learn because I give shape to my learning, just as the vessel gives shape to the wine poured inside it. Moreover, just as a gold vessel spoils the wine it contains, there is some sort of chemical reaction that takes place between me and the Torah I learn. I am transformed by the Torah I study, and the Torah I study is transformed by my insights.

My study dates with Omri opened my eyes to a new kind of relationship in which the Torah we studied not only took our shape but also filled the space between us, like the optical illusion of the vase that is also two faces. Although Omri and I learned much Torah together, we were not learning the same Torah. It is impossible for any two people to learn the exact same Torah, because the moment someone internalizes what he or she has learned, that learning begins to assume his or her shape. In this sense, the vessel and the contents are inherently interrelated.

Of course the vessel—the outside—is not just who I am but how I look. Yeats insisted that "to be born a woman is to know—although they do not talk of it at school—that we must labor to be beautiful." I first encountered those lines in a high school poetry class, where I resolved that I cared too much about what they actually did talk about in school to be bothered with what they did not. In college I refused to wear my hair down even though, on the rare occasions when my hair band snapped and I had no choice but to let my hair free, I was always met with compliments. It was not just that I was suspicious of beauty. I was well aware of the power of beauty to turn heads, but I wanted to know that I would have that power in reserve should I ever need it. If I wore my hair down every day, I thought, then no one would comment. So long as I looked ordinary 99 percent of the time, people would notice the moment I made any effort whatsoever, and so I'd have an easy way to make myself pretty when necessary. It was like, say, having a superpower that I saved only for those critical moments when I was being pursued by the archvillain and had to suddenly fly or become invisible.

With Omri I did not feel I needed any superpowers, at least not at first, when our relationship seemed to be soaring. After a few months of dating I tried to persuade him to take up daf yomi so we could learn together, but I soon realized that this was a mistake. Omri was a thorough student who could not bear to leave any stone unturned, and so I would forever be trying to turn the page while he would stay my hand. He needed to understand every turn of phrase and every logical leap in the Talmudic text, whereas daf yomi demands a certain degree of superficiality or it is impossible to keep pace. I was as exasperated with his slowness as he was with my speed, and in the end we gave up.

Tractate Taanit discusses the ideal study partnership and teaches that a person cannot learn Torah alone. "Rabbi Hama said in the name of Rabbi Hanina: Why is it written, 'Iron and iron together' (Proverbs 27:17)? Just as iron sharpens iron, two scholars sharpen each other's teachings. Rabbi bar bar Hana said: Why is Torah analogized to fire? As it is written, 'Are all my words not like fire? spoke the Lord' (Jeremiah 23:29). To teach that just as fire cannot ignite on its own, so too do words of Torah not endure in the single individual" (Taanit 7a). Learning Torah, like falling in love, is supposed to set us on fire. I believed that I would know I had met the right man when we had the right "learning chemistry" as well as the right "romantic chemistry." But the heart and the head are not always in the same place, and Omri and I stayed together even after we began learning alone.

On some level I was so committed to the relationship because Omri protected me from loneliness. I thought of Honi the Circle Drawer, whose name comes from a story in Taanit (23a) in which he draws a circle and refuses to move from it until God brings rain during a season of drought. In another tale on the same page of Taanit, Honi plants a carob tree even though he knows he will not be able to eat from it. As he explains to a passerby, he is planting the carob tree for his descendants, just as his ancestors planted for him. Honi then proceeds to fall into a deep sleep lasting seventy years. When he wakes, no one recognizes him anymore or accords him respect. He sinks into depression and prays to God that he might die. The story concludes with Honi's death and another rabbi's declaration that a person cannot live in social isolation: "Either companionship or death." Omri was a companion during what would otherwise have been a very lonely stretch of life.

It is Omri I have to thank for much of my knowledge of Jerusalem. He loved to explore the city and used to take me on late-night rambles around its lesser-known neighborhoods and alleyways. Like me, he walked everywhere, rain or shine. But he always carried an umbrella with him, whereas I couldn't be bothered. It seems that there are two types of people—the raincoat wearers and the umbrella carriers—and I am the former. Raincoat wearers cover themselves up as best as possible, hoping that they will be sufficiently protected by their waterproof outer layer. Umbrella carriers are more proactive; they lift a protective covering over their heads and carve out a corner of the world where the rain will not fall. I thought of the story of Rabbi Hanina ben Dosa, who once set out on his way when it started to rain. "Master of the Universe," he cried out, "the whole world is at peace but Hanina is distressed?" The rain ceased. When he got home, he cried out, "Master of the Universe, the whole world is distressed and Hanina is at peace?" And then the rain came (Taanit 24b). Unlike Hanina, I don't feel the need to carve out my own corner of dryness. I'm happy to let the rain fall on me and on the trees and flowers that need it, covering myself with a raincoat and accepting, come what may, the inevitable inconvenience.

The inconvenience of rain is exacerbated by the fact that in Israel, where the daily news report includes mention of the water levels in the Sea of Galilee, one is never allowed to complain about precipitation. "Rain is a blessing," as Omri often rebuked me when I complained. Or, as the rabbis declare in Taanit (7b), "A rainy day is as great as the day that the heavens and earth were created." I tried to celebrate the romance of the rain, particularly when I watched it pour down my windows at work while I was safe and dry inside, bundled in the warm afghan I kept folded in my desk drawer. I told myself that in an era of global warming, I ought to feel grateful that the seasons still change, the rainbow comes and goes, and all this glory has not passed away from the earth. Each time it rained, no matter where I was and how little protective gear I had with me, I tried to respond like the sage Nahum Ish Gamzu in tractate Taanit (21a), who would greet every calamity that befell him with the faith that "this, too, is for the best."

Growing up in the American Northeast, I, like so many others, took rain for granted. There was always an abundance of water, and the question was not whether it would rain enough to fill the sea, but whether the sun would come out tomorrow. But Israel has distinct wet and dry seasons. It may rain any day from October to March, but then it is completely dry in the spring and summer months. Often the start of the rainy season comes unexpectedly: the sky is no more overcast than usual; the forecast is the same as the day before and the day before that; no one thinks to carry an umbrella. And then suddenly, unexpectedly, the skies heave. Within moments, the streets are flooded and the sidewalks are dotted with muddy brown puddles. Bus drivers try to remember where the switch for the windshield wipers is located on the dashboard, pedestrians duck under the awning of the local grocery for cover, and students rummage through their backpacks for a plastic bag to put over their books. Everyone remembers where they were at the moment the rainy season began—it is an event worthy even of its own name, biblical in origin: the *yoreh*.

The rabbis in Taanit link the name yoreh to the teaching of Torah, which comes from the same root word. They assert that a day of rain is as great as the day that Torah is given (7a). Torah was given from a heavenly God to human beings on earth, just as rain falls from the heavens to nourish the soil. The rabbis invoke the image of a groom meeting a bride to describe how rain falls to meet the earth (Taanit 6b), and they analogize the giving of the Torah to a wedding ceremony between God and Israel (Taanit 26b). When I learned Taanit, the yoreh coincided with the Shabbat on which we read the Torah portion about Noah, and the floodgates of the heavens suddenly and dramatically opened while we were in synagogue chanting the story of the ark and the flood. I was still testing the waters with Omri, uncertain if our relationship was strong enough to weather the storms. Still, when the heavens opened, I was grateful that I had someone to go inside with, two by two.

⁊

It was nearly two years later that Omri and I finally broke up, which is a long time in daf yomi terms. We were together for the rest of Seder Moed (the Order of Festivals) and the entirety of Seder Nashim (the Order of Women). By the start of Seder Nezikin, which deals with the laws of damages, I knew it was time to end things. One evening we were shopping in the *shuk*, the open-air market, for fruit and vegetables. It was late, and we were tired and irritable, and it probably wasn't a good time to make a date of our shopping excursion. I went over to a vendor selling apples and started filling a plastic bag. In the Song of Songs, apples symbolize the awakening of young love: "Under the apple tree I roused you" (8:5). But that was not how Omri saw it. "What are you doing," he rebuked me. "You have to check each one carefully to make sure it's not bruised." He poured back my bag of apples into the pile, much to the vendor's dismay, and began examining each apple painstakingly before adding it to the bag. At some point, I was convinced that I had made a thorough enough examination of Omri, and although he was not perfect—we all have our bruises and scars—I felt that we could make a life together. Omri, even two years later, was still deliberating whether to add me to his bag. And so, not without heavy hearts, we parted ways. The next time the rain fell, I was on my own. But like Nahum Ish Gamzu, I told myself that this, too, was for the best.

MEGILLAH

❧

Who Knows?

Tʀᴀᴄᴛᴀᴛᴇ ᴍᴇɢɪʟʟᴀʜ ɪs ᴀʙᴏᴜᴛ ᴛʜᴇ ᴘᴜʀɪᴍ ʜᴏʟɪᴅᴀʏ and the Scroll of Esther, which may have had special significance to the sages because it describes a postrevelatory world in which there is nonetheless faith in God's manifest presence. In the Scroll of Esther, known commonly as the *megillah*, the deliverance of the Jews from the evil villain Haman seems to come about entirely by human hands; there is famously no mention of God in the scroll. But the rabbis of the Talmud connect the name of Esther—the story's celebrated heroine—to the Hebrew word for "hiddenness," and they identify the world of the megillah as one of *hester panim*, a world where God pulls all the strings though no one can see His face.

This sense of God's hiddenness is one that I have long struggled with, particularly during my short-lived marriage. Each morning Paul woke up and prayed to God with supreme powers of concentration, moving his lips fervently in the absolute conviction that he was engaging an interlocutor whose existence was beyond doubt. His God did not seem to be the God of the megillah—the God of hester panim—but rather the God who revealed himself in visions to Abraham, Isaac, and Jacob; who spoke to Moses through a burning bush; and who stopped the sun in the sky for Joshua, performing miracles in broad daylight.

I would stand beside Paul with my prayer book open and despair. Most days, when I prayed, nothing happened for me. I uttered the words mechanically, out of a sense of obligation, but I rarely felt that my prayers drew me closer to God. Unlike Paul, I knew God—and I continue to know God—primarily in shadows cast by other people. I would see someone reach out to a stranger, or watch a friend marshal reserves of hidden strength, and I would imagine that I was seeing the light of God reflected off human presences. Paul saw God the way some people can look straight up at the sun, and he felt that anyone who could not see the radiance was surely blind. I sought out God the way a traveler through the forest might seek out the moon through the trees; sometimes it was hidden, other days it was just a faint crescent, still other days it was a full orb with mountains and valleys of variegated hues. But it was still just a play of shadows, as all moonlight is.

These different ways of knowing God are discussed by the major twentieth-century American scholar Rav Yizhak Hutner in his writing about Purim and Pesach in the *Pahad Yitzhak* (Purim, 34). Rav Hutner explains that on Pesach— Passover—we come to know God through the overt and explicit miracles that He performs with His outstretched arm in Egypt, as again and again we are reminded that "this is the finger of God." Rav Hutner invokes the metaphor of a person stumbling around in the darkness, trying to recognize a face before him. Pesach, says Rav Hutner, is like the person who shines a flashlight in order to identify the shape before him. He holds up the light, and immediately he is able to apprehend the image.

But Purim, Rav Hutner explains, is like the person who has no flashlight and must therefore use other, less obvious, clues. This night traveler needs to rely on a sort of sixth sense to intuit the identity of the presence before him. In the same way, we sense God's presence in the Purim story only indirectly. The miracle of Purim is not one of divine intervention—there are no catastrophic plagues or dramatic sea-splittings. Paradoxically, God can be found in the Purim story only in the halo created by the concealment of His glory, like the glow of a total eclipse. It is in the absence of God that we intuit His presence. This requires not just faith but also imagination, a notion that calls to mind a passage from *A Midsummer Night's Dream*:

> And as imagination bodies forth
> The forms of things unknown, the poet's pen
> Turns them to shapes and gives to airy nothing
> A local habitation and a name.
> Such tricks hath strong imagination,
> That if it would but apprehend some joy,
> It comprehends some bringer of that joy;
> Or in the night, imagining some fear,
> How easy is a bush supposed a bear!

To know God in Purim mode is to give shape to the shadows. But to know God in Pesach mode is to live in a world of absolute black and white, where everything has its reason and everything is clearly part of a larger providential plan. One night Paul and I were sitting at the dinner table when we heard the siren wail of an ambulance passing by, and he began moving his lips in silent, devout prayer. "What are you saying?" I inquired. "I am asking God to make sure that the person in that ambulance will be OK," he told me, as if he had a direct line to the divine.

Sometimes when I had trouble praying, I read fiction instead. When I was struck by a brilliant turn of phrase or moved by a beautiful passage, I experienced sensations that I hoped prayer would arouse, but which it rarely did. The notion of finding spiritual inspiration in a literary text was not foreign to the rabbis of the Talmud, who based the order of the blessings in the Amidah—the "standing prayer," the central prayer in Jewish liturgy—on a series of biblical verses. The rabbis in tractate Megillah (17b) ask why certain prayers are included in the Amidah— Why mention the patriarchs? Why mention God's strength?—and in each case, the answer is based on the Bible. If literary narrative is the source for prayer, I reasoned, then perhaps sometimes it's all right to read instead of praying.

But this was not a notion that Paul could accept. One evening he asked me if I was ready to recite the evening prayer, and I said, "I'd so much rather finish this chapter of *Don Quixote*. I'm skipping Maariv." He became visibly agitated. "What's wrong?" I asked. "I just can't relate to a person who thinks it is more important to read *Don Quixote* than to pray to God," he said. If only I'd had the courage to tell him what I know now—that God, for me, was more likely to be found in the pages of *Don Quixote*, where the intricate narrative craft reminds me that the world is about so much more than what we sense at any given moment. My God is the God of *hester panim*, but He is no less real. Perhaps it is fitting that it was on Purim that I intuitively sensed that our marriage was ending, and it was the day before Pesach that Paul told me in no uncertain terms—as I stood in the kitchen cleaning out the refrigerator for the holiday, holding up a half-rotten apple—that he no longer wanted to be married to me. For him, I imagine that was the end of it. Whereas I, for a while, continued to sense his presence in the shadows.

Getting over Paul was a process of trying to willfully forget even as I was flooded by memory. This conflict between memory and forgetting is a key theme of the Shabbat before Purim, which is known as Shabbat Zachor—the Shabbat of remembering. Tractate Megillah (29a) explains that each Shabbat in the month of Adar is characterized by special additional readings from the Torah. On Shabbat Zachor, the second of these four weeks, we read Moses's account of a brazen attack on Israel just after the exodus from Egypt, committed by the infamous nation Amalek, from whom Haman is descended: "Remember what Amalek did to you on your journey, after you left Egypt—how, undeterred by fear of God, he surprised you on the march, when you were famished and weary. . . . Therefore, when the Lord your God grants you safety from all your enemies . . . you shall blot out the memory of Amalek from under heaven. Do not forget!" (Deuteronomy 25:17–19).

This commandment seems to contain two contradictory injunctions. On the one hand, the Torah commands us to "remember" and "do not forget." On the other hand, the Torah charges us to "blot out the memory of Amalek," which suggests that we should forget Amalek entirely, leaving not even a mental trace. Were we to fulfill the second injunction successfully, the first would make no sense: how can we remember what has already been blotted out? I found my answer not in the Talmud, but in a poem by Edna St. Vincent Millay, who describes how she is afraid to go to so many places lest she find herself overcome by memories of her lover. In an effort to forget him, she seeks out a place where he is blotted out from under heaven. But it is his very absence that brings back a torrent of memories:

> I say, "There is no memory of him here!"
> And so stand stricken, so remembering him.[7]

On Purim, the act of remembering is critical. The Talmud teaches that if Purim falls on Shabbat, then the Zachor portion must be read the week before, "so as not to precede doing with remembering" (30a). That is, we are not supposed to "do" the Purim celebration and blot out Haman's name until we first remember Amalek. On Purim day, when we sound noisemakers upon hearing the name of Haman read in the megillah, we should not be so loud that we drown out the name of the villain completely. As a result of these rabbinic injunctions, Amalek and Haman continue to lurk in the shadows of Jewish experience, never fully erased from collective memory. I think back to those first painful months after Paul and I parted ways, when it seemed as if I would never be happy again. But then, with felicitous inevitability, I was proven wrong—happiness caught up with me after all.

⁊

"When the month of Adar enters, we increase in happiness," the Talmud teaches in a nod to tractate Megillah at the end of Taanit (29a). Since Adar contains the holiday that celebrates the miraculous deliverance of the Jewish people, we are supposed to be happy from the moment the month begins. When I first moved to Israel I was surprised to discover how seriously this injunction is taken. In the month before Purim, storefronts throughout the city are converted into costume bazaars (kings, queens, pirates, cowboys, fairies, and butterflies) and the vendors in the shuk who sold dried fruit for Tu Bishvat now stock mini chocolate bars and gummy candy for inclusion in *mishloach manot*, the packages of food distributed to neighbors and friends on the holiday. Even the phrase "When the month of Adar enters, we increase in happiness" becomes a jingle that is played in shops all over the city, as ubiquitous as "Jingle Bells" during American Decembers. Somehow, when the month containing the holiday of Purim arrives, we are supposed to become automatically happy, as if on demand. But is that really possible?

In the academic and literary world, this question has spurred a field of research known as positive psychology. A wave of books published in recent years have raised such issues as whether we can know what makes us happy (*Stumbling on Happiness* by Daniel Gilbert), the implications of positive psychology in the political sphere (*The Politics of Happiness* by Derek Bok), and whether women's happiness differs from that of men (*Bluebird* by Ariel Gore). These books posit that happiness is something that can be attained, albeit with a bit of hard work, if we better understand our own mental processes. In response, a countergenre has emerged from those who question whether the pursuit of happiness is really such a good thing after all (*Bright-Sided* by Barbara Ehrenreich and *Against Happiness* by Eric Wilson).

Several of these books argue that a key to happiness is to cultivate gratitude. The Israeli happiness guru Tal Ben-Shahar writes of the importance of recording five occasions for gratitude each night before falling asleep. I have not made this a daily ritual, but I try to make it at least an annual one. Purim each year reminds me of Purims past, and, when I unfurl the scroll of my life, there is always some reason to rejoice. When I learned tractate Megillah in daf yomi I felt grateful, at least on some level, that I was no longer with a man who had not wanted to be married to me. I felt grateful that I had started dating again. And I felt grateful, too, that I remained in an evolving relationship with God, even if it seemed like we were forever engaged in a game of hide-and-seek, with God lurking in the shadows. I'm not sure if I was happy, but the possibility of happiness began to seem less elusive.

☙

Each year, the happiness at the end of the Purim story is supposed to come as a surprise. The rabbis teach in tractate Megillah (17a) that one of the laws governing the reading of the Scroll of Esther is that the megillah may not be read backward. The story unfolds in linear progression, moving from "sorrow to joy and from mourning to festivity," as we learn only in the penultimate chapter (Esther 9:22). Of course, since we read the megillah every Purim, we already know how it will end—with the triumphant hanging of Haman, whose plot to exterminate the Jews was foiled by the beautiful Queen Esther. Even so, we are commanded each year to read the megillah in order, without jumping backward to read into what already happened, and without jumping forward to imagine what is yet to come. In my own life, though, I am forever doing both.

When I first learned tractate Megillah I would never have guessed that six years later, on the eve of Purim, I'd be nine months pregnant with twins. It was a leap year on the Jewish calendar, which meant there was an extra month of Adar, such that my due date coincided with Purim. The Hebrew term for leap year is *shana me'uberet*, literally a pregnant year. I lay there propped up in bed with my volume of Talmud, as pregnant as the year. In my favorite verse in the megillah, Mordechai instructs his niece Esther to go before the Persian king Ahasuerus and entreat him to save the Jews of his kingdom. Esther has already been crowned queen of Persia, but Ahasuerus is unaware that she is a Jew. Mordechai tells her that she must risk her life by appearing before the king even though she has not been summoned, "because who knows if it was for this moment that you attained a royal position?" (Esther 4:14). Perhaps Esther is destined to save her people.

"Who knows?" Mordechai tells Esther, throwing into question the whole enterprise of looking backward and forward in time. Mordechai implies that none of us can know whether any particular moment of our lives is the reason that we were created. Was my first marriage part of a larger providential plan to bring me to Israel, where I might meet the man with whom I'd share my life? Or was the purpose of remarrying so that I might someday have children who would have unique destinies of their own? Who knows? The point of Mordechai's question is not that every moment has larger—perhaps even cosmic—significance, but that we can never know for sure which moment does.

The megillah relates that Esther enjoined the people to come together in fervent prayer that all should proceed smoothly when she risks her life to approach King Ahasuerus. In the first chapter of tractate Megillah the sages interpret the unusual verb that describes Esther's reaction to hearing of the king's decree to destroy and massacre all the Jews: "What is *va-tithalhal*? Rav says: She became a menstruant. Rabbi Yirmiya says: She lost control of her bowels" (15a). The classical rabbinic commentator Rashi explains that the cavities of her body dissolved. All these interpreters are playing with the etymological similarity between *va-tithalhal* and *halal*, the Hebrew word for "cavity" or "hole" and the hallmark of the feminine; the Hebrew word *nekeva*, female, literally means "hole."

The highly sexualized Esther of the Talmud does indeed seem to fit this epithet: she sleeps with both Mordechai and Ahasuerus, getting up from the lap of one and sitting down in the lap of the other (Megillah 13b). But for all that she is sexualized, the Talmud's Esther is also exonerated: the sages relate that Esther derived no pleasure from sleeping with Ahasuerus, because she was like "the ground of the earth" (Sanhedrin 74b)—she lay under him unmoving as he went about his business. However, when she heard that Ahasuerus planned to destroy her people, she realized she could not be passive any longer, and the cavities of her body dissolved. I wonder if Esther felt like she was in labor, bearing inside her womb the destiny of the Jewish people.

During those weeks before Purim I was very pregnant indeed. Unable to see past my belly to my feet, I could not know what the next few days and weeks held in store. Would I give birth on Purim, as my due date predicted? Would the births be smooth and the babies healthy? What would it be like to be a mother of twins? I could no more have told you at that moment than I could have foretold, back when I first learned tractate Megillah, that one day I would remarry, create a new life for myself, and bring new life into the world. And so aware that I could not predict the future, I resolved that I would instead pray that one day, when I read the story of my life backward, this chapter would have a happy ending.

MOED KATAN

❧

Trapdoor Days

IF MEGILLAH IS THE HAPPINESS TRACTATE, THEN MOED Katan appears all the way at the other end of the emotional spectrum—certainly when it comes to the third and final chapter, which deals with the laws of mourning. I identified with the themes of this tractate, thankfully not as a mourner but rather as one who has been, at various points in my life, acquainted with the night.

I write of my bouts of depression tentatively, with head hung low. I am all too familiar with the tendency to romanticize dark feelings—to say that they are the sign of a creative, artistic soul, or that they reflect a capacity to feel more deeply. I acknowledge the validity of mental illness, but my own depressive tendencies have always struck me as the failure to develop adequate coping mechanisms. Perhaps I have been blessed with such a supportive family and social network that I have never had to learn to combat the demons on my own. The Talmud in Moed Katan (17a) states that anyone who feels that his evil inclination is getting the better of him should "dress in black, and wrap himself in black,

and go to a place where no one knows him." The sages are referring to someone who is tempted by sin and desperate for an out-
let, but the tendency to spiral down into the dark pit of depression
is a temptation too, and I can certainly identify with the impulse
to wear all black and avoid social contact. The problem is that
wherever you go, there you are. Even in that dark place where no
one knows me, I am still stuck with myself, and the aloneness often serves only to exacerbate the dark feelings.

That was how I felt the year my marriage fell apart, which
was also the year I tried, for the first time, to wear *tefillin*—a subject that comes up with surprising frequency in Moed Katan.
Tefillin are small leather boxes containing parchment inscribed
with verses from the Bible. They are essentially miniature Torah
scrolls worn on the forehead and arm so that the wearer may
embody Torah and remain cognizant of its teachings. The commandment to wear tefillin was taken very seriously by the sages
of the Talmud. We are told in Moed Katan (25a) that Rav Huna,
upon discovering that one of his tefillin straps had turned over,
fasted for forty days in penance. Although in modern times tefillin
are worn only during morning weekday prayers, in Talmudic
times—and in subsequent generations—they were worn all day
and had no special association with prayer. For instance, the Talmud (Moed Katan 26a) relates an anecdote about a man who
took off his tefillin to go to the bathroom at some point during
the day, only to return and find an ostrich pecking at them!

The origin of the commandment to wear tefillin appears in
the book of Exodus: "It shall be for you a sign upon your arm and
a reminder between your eyes, so that God's teaching will be in
your mouth, for God took you out of Egypt with a mighty arm"
(Exodus 13:9). Tefillin serve as a direct link between the intentions of the mind and the actions of the arm, both of which
should be guided by the Torah's values. In the Talmud, studying
Torah and wearing tefillin are intimately related. The sages state
explicitly that women are exempt from tefillin because they are

exempt from Torah study (Kidushin 34a). But in our modern egalitarian world where women like myself learn Torah alongside men, I was hard-pressed to find a compelling reason not to adopt tefillin as a regular practice. And so as I watched Paul put on tefillin every morning, I decided I would join him.

Upon wrapping tefillin around one's hand, it is traditional to recite a verse from Hosea (2:21–22) that is also associated with Jewish wedding ceremonies: "I will betroth you to Me forever, and I will betroth you to Me with righteousness, justice, kindness, and mercy. I will betroth you to Me with fidelity, and you shall know God." With each day that I wrapped tefillin around my arm, our marriage increasingly unraveled. Paul and I prayed side by side in the mornings, standing at our kitchen table overlooking the unkempt garden outside our ground-floor window. But we seemed to spend more time engaged in conversations with God than with each other. Much as toddlers parallel play, oblivious to one another's presence, we parallel prayed. This was particularly ironic since it was prayer that had originally brought us together: we'd met in a synagogue, where we'd tried to ignore each other's stolen glances and concentrate instead on speaking to God. On more hopeful days I thought of a line from a poem by Frank Bidart: "The love I have known is not the love of two people looking into each other's eyes, but of two people looking in the same direction." But I had no way of knowing if we were in fact directing our prayers toward the same desired end.

Paul and I had been married in the heat of summer, but already by winter a chill had set in. The growing awareness that we were no longer joined together in kindness and mercy drove me into a dark place in which I found it very difficult to pray. "The worst is not, so long as we can say this is the worst," I kept telling myself, quoting *King Lear*, but then things would get even worse. Perhaps the Jewish equivalent to this quote is "From the depths I have cried out to God" (Psalms 130:1), because there is something about hitting that lowest point that moves the soul to the uplifting experience of prayer, like a diver's feet buoyed up by contact with the ocean floor. But I still felt quite sunk, and it was not long before I found it impossible to wear tefillin anymore.

The rabbis draw a connection between tefillin and sadness in their discussion of mourning in Moed Katan (15a). They teach that a mourner is forbidden from wearing tefillin based on a passage in Ezekiel in which God tells the prophet that He is going to take his wife from him but that Ezekiel may not mourn her. Ezekiel, living in the early years of the sixth century BCE just before the destruction of the First Temple, serves as an object lesson for the Jewish people: God would soon destroy their Temple, but the people would not be allowed to mourn it because they were at fault in their failure to obey God. "Put on your splendor," God says to Ezekiel (24:17), and the rabbis interpret splendor as a reference to tefillin, which are regarded as a form of adornment. Ezekiel is supposed to wear his tefillin as a sign that he is not observing mourning practices for his wife, and thus the rabbis conclude that under ordinary circumstances, a mourner should not wear tefillin.

I was not aware of this law during the year I tried to wear tefillin, but I understood intuitively that tefillin and depression did not mix. I had many trapdoor days, as I came to refer to them—days when I just wanted to fall through the floor and escape my life. As is often the case with depression, the mornings were the worst. I'd wake up by Paul's side as if he were a total stranger. Some days I was too unhappy to shower and I just wore the clothes draped over my chair from the day before, with no frills or accessories. If I could not even be bothered to put on earrings, how could I adorn myself in the splendor that tefillin represent? Other mornings I showered but then couldn't put on tefillin until my hair had dried. So there were logistical complications in addition to emotional ones. Once it became clear that it was impossible for me to put on tefillin every day, I gave up on the practice altogether. It remains bound up in associations far removed from kindness and mercy, and I have been unable to return to it since.

༄

The notion of a trapdoor day came to me during the year after I graduated Harvard, when I was at the peak of my academic career. I graduated with highest honors and won a one-year fellowship to study in Cambridge. "From Cambridge to Cambridge, there is nothing like Cambridge," I initially quipped, just as Moses Maimonides famously stated that "from Moses to Moses, there was no one like Moses." But for me, Cambridge, England, was a far cry from Cambridge, Massachusetts. At Harvard I was part of a warm and vibrant Jewish community where I organized a Conservative minyan and spent my free time sitting in on large lecture classes about intellectual history, literature, neuroscience, religious thought, and anything that captured my interest. The world felt dazzlingly alive and I woke up each morning determined to use every moment to the fullest. But in Cambridge, England, where the weather was overcast and dreary and the sun set two hours before dinner, the world seemed to be closing in on me.

I came to Cambridge as the recipient of a John Harvard Fellowship, which entitled me to a generous stipend while I lived in what was reputedly the bedroom of the original John Harvard, who went on to donate his estate and library to a new school in the Massachusetts Bay Colony. John Harvard was a student at Emmanuel College, Cambridge, in the 1630s, and his room—or his "rooms," as they were known—seemed not to have changed much since the seventeenth century. The main sitting room was large and cavernous, with wood-paneled walls and a low ceiling. The mantel was decorated with badminton rackets, oars, and rugby balls, and atop the sealed fireplace hung the Harvard Veritas shield and the Emmanuel purple lion. I had to duck to enter the front door, which was made for a time when the average person was considerably shorter. A metal plaque on the lintel read

"Mind your head," though I often forgot. A story in Moed Katan (25a) tells of Rav Huna's deathbed, which the sages were unable to fit through the doorway of his house. How then could they remove his body for burial? One sage suggested raising it through a hole in the roof, but this was not acceptable because "the honor of a scholar demands that he pass only through the door." In the end, they had to beat down the door so as to remove Rav Huna. I regarded my low doorway somewhat morbidly. My fellowship was supposed to be a great honor, but there was no way my bed could possibly fit through the entry.

John Harvard's "rooms" included a bedroom with a sloped floor made of creaky, uneven boards that groaned whenever I put my feet down. There was also an immense wardrobe with the bar for hanging clothes protruding from the back to the front so that I could see only one item of clothing at a time. I referred to it as my "Lion, Witch, and the Wardrobe wardrobe" and had dreams about getting swallowed up inside it and emerging halfway around the world in the other Cambridge. Adjacent to the bedroom was a study that was formerly a "gyp room," or servants' quarters, with a large mahogany desk I found far too intimidating for the humble nature of my academic work. I generally preferred to perch on my bed with my laptop, my back leaning against the dark paneled walls.

But the Harvard rooms were most notable for what they lacked—namely, a bathroom. The closest toilets were one courtyard to the right, and the showers were one courtyard to the left. I slept with my shoes on at night because inevitably I had to wake up to use the loo, and I did not want to have to fumble for footwear in the dark. I am told that the long line of Harvard scholars who preceded me in those rooms—all men, as far as I know—used to pee out the window and aim for the duck pond for which the college is famous. Often it was the quacking of the ducks that woke me up at night, and I glared at them irritably on my way to the bathroom under cover of darkness.

No doubt the John Harvard Fellowship is a dream come true for most of those who receive it, and I would never want to sound ungrateful. The year was entirely unstructured, with nothing demanded of me except to receive any visitors graciously and to enjoy the opportunity for intellectual exploration. Officially I was enrolled in the English department pursuing a master's in early nineteenth-century literature. That is, I was studying Wordsworth on the same campus where Wordsworth received his formative education. What could be more thrilling? And yet, as I read a section of Wordsworth's autobiographical poem *The Prelude* while sitting on the grass beside the duck pond, I identified all too much with the poem's ponderous tone:

> I was detached
> Internally from academic cares,
> From every hope of prowess and reward,
> And wished to be a lodger in that house
> Of letters, and more: and should have been
> Even such, but for some personal concerns
> That hung about me in my own despite
> Perpetually.

I, too, wished to be a lodger in the house of letters, and should have been—but some personal concerns held me back.

At Cambridge I discovered that I cannot abide unstructured time. Most days I woke up in the morning with absolutely nowhere I had to be and nothing I had to do. There was much that I wanted to read—I was determined to make it through Coleridge's intellectual autobiography, among other classics of British Romanticism—but no one was checking up on me or reading alongside me, nor did I have the support of a daf yomi community. Had I been learning daf yomi that year, I suspect I would have had a less isolating experience and that I would have sought out connections with others who were on the same page. Instead my only scholarly relationships were secular. Once a week I met with a leading expert on Wordsworth and Coleridge who sat in a tall-backed rocking chair, swayed back and forth, and looked at me with piercing eyes. He waited for me to direct the conversation, and I struggled each week to think of a brilliant question to pose. Then, with the sun already set on a cold winter afternoon, I retreated back to my dark John Harvard rooms to read until I fell asleep.

My days at Cambridge were painfully lonely. The Talmud in Moed Katan (15a) teaches that a mourner is forbidden to engage in *sheilat shalom*, that is, to greet other people and inquire after their welfare, as part of a general avoidance of unnecessary speech. I thought about this concept of *sheilat shalom* on days when I saw no familiar faces, such that there was no opportunity to greet or be greeted. Socializing among students primarily took place in the local pubs with names like The Red Lion or The Queen's Arms. I don't enjoy drinking and I was uncomfortable socializing in pubs, nor did I want to come home with my black clothes— only black seemed cool enough—reeking of smoke.

A few weeks into the Michaelmas term I found a home in a Shakespeare reading group that met every Friday night to read an entire Shakespeare play aloud, in parts. Reading Shakespeare became my alternative to Shabbat dinner. It was also a way to dress in black and wrap myself in black—that is, to shed my own skin and assume another identity for a few hours. Thankfully the group met in an empty classroom and not in a pub, though there was plenty of wine to go around.

I was also at home in the library, where I spent long hours reading about Coleridge's opinions on mesmerism, phrenology, and other ideas we'd dismiss today as pseudoscientific—a continuation of my undergraduate work. I was interested in how poetry became a medium for Wordsworth and Coleridge to engage in dialogue about the reigning scientific ideas of their day, and how these ideas, though subsequently debunked, became enshrined in their work. One day I wandered into an old curiosity shop and bought myself a phrenology bust—a statue of a head with all the mental functions mapped on to the skull. According to the principles of phrenology, human character may be deduced from the bumps on the skull. Phrenology paved the way for our contemporary understanding of cerebral localization, the idea that particular brain functions correspond to specific regions in the brain. But the notion that character is reflected in the shape of the skull is no longer the province of science, but of boardwalk fortune telling.

Now that phrenology bust sits on the windowsill above my desk in Jerusalem, where it serves as a reminder of fallen myths. A few months into my fellowship I learned that John Harvard did not actually live in the John Harvard rooms, and in fact the building that contains them was not completed until at least a year after he graduated. The fellowship, too, was not all it was cracked up to be—at least not for me. The Harvard suite radiated an aura of privilege and prestige, but the dim rooms with their groaning floorboards were cold and haunting. As the John Harvard fellow at Cambridge I learned that the dream of hours of uninterrupted time to read and study will forever tempt but inevitably frustrate me. My year in England taught me that the fellowship of others is more important than any academic fellowship. Armed with that lesson, I have learned, for the most part, to stave off despair.

∽

I write this book as the mother of three children under the age of three, at a time in my life when quiet is hard to come by. In the evenings when they are blessedly asleep I sit in the main room of our Jerusalem apartment at the long desk my husband and I share, lining the window. I translate literary texts while Daniel, a professor of English literature, grades student papers. My side of the windowsill contains my phrenology bust, which winks at me as I type, encouraging me when I struggle to find the right words. His side contains a framed photograph of his father, looking up at him with kind, twinkling eyes.

Daniel placed that photograph there while mourning his father, who died following a long battle with cancer one year after we were married. Sometimes when guests come to visit, they look at the figure in the photograph, who bears clear resemblance to Daniel. "Wow, your father looks so much like you," they exclaim, and we try to find a way to switch to the past tense so that they understand. Often we simply appeal to our toddler son Matan, who refers to the figure in the photograph as *Saba alav hashalom*, which translates as "Grandfather who rests in peace." Matan does not understand death, but he knows that Saba alav hashalom never comes to visit.

The laws of mourning in Moed Katan reflect an understanding that the death of a parent is different from any other loss. For instance, if a person learns of the death of a relative more than thirty days after the fact, he does not observe *shiva* or *shloshim*, the seven-day period of intense mourning and the thirty-day period of less intense mourning practices; however, if it was a parent who died, then shiva and shloshim are still observed (20a). Likewise, a person is obligated to rend a garment upon hearing the news of a relative's death; that rent garment may be stitched back together properly after the period of mourning, unless the deceased was a parent (22b). When a parent dies, the rent in the fabric of life is never fully repaired.

For the eleven months after his father's death, Daniel said Kaddish, the traditional mourner's prayer, three times a day. This was a significant commitment: each day he woke up early enough to get to morning minyan, and he interrupted his afternoon of research or teaching to find a minyan for the afternoon and evening prayers. Throughout that year I often thought of Emily Dickinson's poem about stopping for death: "Because I could not stop for death / He kindly stopped for me." It is not easy to stop for death, as we learn in Moed Katan. The Talmud cites several stories about rabbis who made it difficult for the Angel of Death to claim their souls (28a). Rav Hisda, for instance, never stopped learning Torah, such that Death—which has no power over Torah—could not snatch him up. Desperate, the Angel of Death went and climbed atop the central pillar holding up Rav Hisda's house, causing the pillar to collapse. Startled by the noise, Rav Hisda looked up from his learning, and at that moment, the Angel of Death catapulted him into his carriage, and off they drove.

As this story underscores, death never comes at a convenient time, and almost always the soul wants more. How much Daniel and I would have loved for his father to have been able to meet our twins, who were born one year later. But as the Talmud teaches in Moed Katan, "One's length of days, one's children, and one's food depend not on one's merits, but on fortune" (28a). And so Daniel honored his father by stopping for death three times a day, interrupting whatever he was doing to find the nearest minyan and recite the Kaddish. During that entire year, I never once saw him put on tefillin, because he did so only at synagogue. In my eyes, though, his steadfast commitment to his father crowned him in a sort of halo, a form of radiant splendor.

These days, Daniel prays at our desk by the window. Though he bows in the direction of the Temple Mount, which is visible in the distance, usually his attention is at least partially focused on our kids, who eat breakfast at the adjacent table. Sometimes when he is in a rush in the morning he leaves his tefillin on the windowsill, somewhere between the phrenology bust and the photograph of his father. Taken together, the phrenology bust and tefillin and photograph remind me of seventeenth-century vanitas still-life paintings, with their arrangements of skull and hourglass and flowering plant. "Still life with sadness," I might call our triptych, a reminder that in spite of divorce and in spite of depression and even in spite of the agony of death, there is still life. At the desk beneath the windowsill containing our vanitas, I type out this story of our lives.

HAGIGAH

❧

Torah from the Heavens

I WILL NEVER FORGET WHERE I WAS WHEN I LEARNED tractate Hagigah, because the volume still bears a luggage identification sticker. The tractate deals with the laws relating to the commandment to make a pilgrimage to Jerusalem three times a year, on Passover, Shavuot, and Sukkot. Appropriately, I was preparing to board a plane to Israel at the time, due to land just a few hours before the start of Passover. My trip was not a pilgrimage but the return flight after the London Book Fair. The rest of my flight consisted largely of British Jews who were heading to Israel for the holiday. Standing in line before the El Al ticket counter, I was surrounded by flocks of Hasidic men in black and white who were squawking through their beards and flapping their dress bags in a frenzy of preflight excitement. I'd begun learning on the long Tube ride from the fairgrounds at Earl's Court out to the Heathrow terminal, and I was still clutching my volume of Talmud in my arm when I walked over to join them in the queue.

I was dragging a huge suitcase full of the catalogues and foreign rights guides I had amassed at the book fair, but my luggage was nothing compared with what I saw all around me. Families with four or five young children were accompanied by caravans of suitcases, duffel bags, hatboxes, baby strollers, and diaper bags; pacifiers were being dropped by drooling babies hanging over their mothers' arms; and their oblivious fathers hid behind large leather-bound tomes and moved their lips in a feverish undertone. The line inched forward slowly, but none of the penguins around me seemed bothered by the glacial pace. And so it seemed only natural to me that while I was waiting, I'd open my Talmud and plow onward through the unlearned pages of daf yomi that had accumulated during my busy trip abroad.

I was up to the second chapter of tractate Hagigah, which contains the largest concentration of mystical material in the Talmud. Presumably this material is included in Hagigah because the Torah (Deuteronomy 16:16) commands that all Jews must appear before the face of God on the pilgrimage festivals that are the subject of this tractate, an encounter with the divine that inspires mystical musings. The opening mishnah enumerates those matters that should be studied very cautiously in small-group settings: the laws of forbidden sexual relations (which may be taught to no more than three students at a time), the details of the creation of the world (which may be taught only to a pair of students), and the prophet Ezekiel's vision of a chariot of fire (which must be taught only one-on-one). Without elaborating on any of these matters, the Mishnah goes on to caution, "Anyone who looks into four matters is deserving of never having been born: What is above, what is below, what is in front, and what is behind" (11b).

Absorbed in my learning, I was somewhat oblivious to what was going on in front of and behind me. Perhaps I ought to have noticed the flurry among the Hasidic men, who peered out over the tops of their books and glanced in my direction. Perhaps I should have listened to them whispering in Yiddish and noticed the nervous glances exchanged beneath raised eyebrows. But my head was buried in those matters that are wondrous and concealed and hidden, as Ben Sira, a sage from Jerusalem in the early second century BCE, would have it: "In that which is wondrous to you, do not expound. And in that which is concealed from you, do not investigate. Examine that which is permitted to you; you have no business with hidden matters." Ben Sira's text was excluded from the canonized Hebrew Bible, but his statements are occasionally quoted in the Talmud, as on the page of Hagigah I had open before me (13a). I imagined that all the Hasidic men around me were quoting from Ben Sira too, insisting that I had no business studying Talmud.

In the circles in which I travel—among liberal American Jews and religious Zionist Israelis—it is widely accepted that women may study the same Talmudic texts as men, and indeed there are several institutions of higher learning devoted to such purposes. In ultra-Orthodox circles, however, women's learning is generally restricted to Bible and religious ethical literature. I am not sure of the justification for this practice—are women told that Talmud study is beyond them? That it is unnecessary for them? One bewigged woman, standing behind me in line, leaned over and said to me in Yiddish-accented Hebrew, "It is Talmud? And you can understand something in it? A little bit?" Perhaps that was my opportunity to expound on the wondrous, but I merely nodded, without lifting my head from the book.

My learning was soon interrupted again by a tall uniformed Israeli man with a dark ponytail who wanted to know if I had packed my bags myself. I closed tractate Hagigah so that I could focus on his security questions: "Why are you going to Israel? You have family in Israel? No family? You live in Israel? Why do you live in Israel if you have no family? You are from America? Why don't you live there?" I tried to answer the security agent, but these were not questions with simple answers.

Why was I living in Israel, so far from my family and friends? I had come because of Paul, sure, but what was keeping me? Certainly it was not my apartment, since in those days I moved so frequently. Nor was it Omri or any of the men I'd dated, since none of these relationships seemed particularly promising. It was still just a couple of years after my divorce, and I was unprepared to make long-term commitments. Even Israel seemed at times like a temporary home, a place where I was living for the time being.

The agent had still more questions. How did I know Hebrew? Where had I learned it? I explained that I grew up in a family of Hebraists—my American parents spoke Hebrew to me as an infant—and that I went to an American Jewish day school with a rigorous Hebrew program. Since arriving in Israel, I told him, I'd tried to read a Hebrew novel every few months. Perhaps I should have added that I was also learning Aramaic through my Talmud study, since the Talmud is written in both languages. The Mishnah, the oldest part of the Talmud, was written in Hebrew in the land of Israel, and much of it deals directly with the land. I might have told him that for me, learning Jewish texts in English in the diaspora would always feel like a pale shadow of the real thing—which was why studying Talmud in Israel had taken on so much significance. But was I really expected to share all this? I was sure that no biblical pilgrim had ever been subjected to such rigorous interrogation.

The Mishnah warns against delving into "what is in front of you and what is behind you," which were the very questions the agent was getting at. What was behind me? How had I gotten to a place in life where I was living alone, halfway around the world from the people who knew me best? And what was ahead of me? Where was my life going, and what was I doing to ensure that it was heading in the direction I wanted? Even when I was by myself, scribbling away in my journal, I was loathe to ponder these matters too closely. The daily planner I carried in my backpack lasted until September of that year, and after then, I had no plan. What lay ahead?

"Gate C6," the clerk told me as if in answer to my question, stamping my boarding pass. I made my way to the gate and resumed learning. The Talmud functions as an elaboration on the text of the Mishnah, and so it is not surprising—though it is somewhat ironic—that the Talmud proceeds to expound at great length on each of the restricted subjects enumerated in the Mishnah. The rabbis brazenly ask about the details of the creation of the world: Was the heaven or the earth created first? How tall was the first man? How many layers did God create in the heavens? The rabbis describe each layer of heaven in surprisingly poetic terms: There is the layer known as Vilon, "where morning enters and evening exits, and creation is renewed." There is Shchakim, "where the millstones grind out manna for the righteous." And Ma'on, "where the ministering angels sing songs by night and are silent by day" (12b). Just when I got up to the final layer, a voice on the loudspeaker announced that my El Al flight was boarding, and soon we too would take off into the heavens.

My seat on the plane was right behind the wing, below which I could nearly make out the wheels on the runway. I thought of the mystical chariot of Ezekiel, which rose to heaven with wheels and wings. According to the Mishnah's hierarchy, this is the most esoteric subject of all; it is dangerous to learn about Ezekiel's chariot even one-on-one. The Talmud in Hagigah (13a) tells the story of a young child who sat reading about the chariot in his teacher's house when suddenly he was consumed by flames. Then there was Rabbi Elazar ben Arach, who expounded on the chariot before his teacher when at once a fire came down from the heavens and surrounded all the trees in the forest, which then burst into song (14b). Suddenly I felt light-headed. Was there a dip in cabin pressure? I looked out through the window to the endless expanse of sky and the outstretched wings of the plane with its wheels now tucked beneath. The page of Talmud danced before my eyes, and thinking of Yeats's Irish airman, I relished the lonely impulse of delight that I so often felt when studying Torah.

A few hours later, when I got up from my seat and made my way down the aisle toward the bathroom, I passed rows of men slumped over their own volumes of Talmud in exhaustion. "All who learn Torah at night—the Holy One Blessed Be He affixes to him a thread of loving-kindness by day" (Hagigah 12b). I returned to my seat and resumed learning as the plane flew through the night. One black-hatted man who was still awake and learning continued to peer at me suspiciously, but when I caught his eye I could only think about how we were both—at least literally—on the same page.

The same Talmudic sage who speaks in praise of learning Torah at night goes on to relate that night is not meant to be taken literally. He explains, "All who learn Torah in this world—which resembles night—the Holy One Blessed Be He affixes to him a thread of loving-kindness in the next world, which resembles day" (12b). As the plane began its descent, I considered how little in my life seemed clear and illuminated and how much took place under cover of darkness.

Finally grounded, I went through passport control and came to the arrivals section, where parents waited for their children with open arms, husbands awaited their wives with eager smiles, and important dignitaries were greeted by uniformed men carrying handwritten signs bearing their names in block letters. No one was waiting for me on this side of the ocean; I'd be traveling back from the airport in a public van to my studio apartment. Still, after a week at the London Book Fair, I felt like I was coming home. In their discussion of the laws of the pilgrimage festivals, the rabbis in tractate Hagigah focus on the biblical injunction that no one visit the Temple empty-handed (Exodus 23:15). Hence the mandate to bring sacrificial offerings on each of the pilgrimage festivals. When I disembarked the plane, as when I'd boarded, I was carrying my well-worn volume of Hagigah tucked under my arm. And so I was not making my pilgrimage back to the holy land empty-handed; for the time being, daf yomi was my offering.

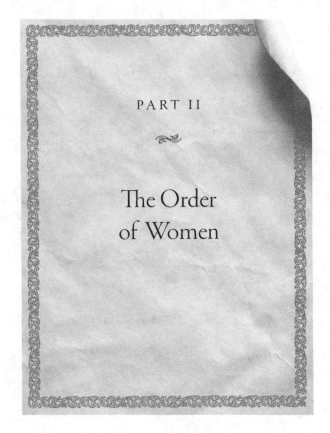

PART II

The Order
of Women

YEVAMOT

❧

Lentils in My Pot

I WAS UNMARRIED THROUGHOUT THE ENTIRE YEAR AND a half in which I learned the tractates in Seder Nashim, which deal with the relationships between husbands and wives. As I pored over Talmudic pages about who is permitted to marry whom, and how betrothal takes place, and what happens if a wife is suspected of being unfaithful, I thought of Rabbi Akiva's commentary about the plague of frogs in Egypt. "There was just one frog," said Akiva, interpreting the biblical verse that literally reads, "The frog came up and covered the land of Egypt" (Exodus 8:2). Akiva explained that this one frog in turn gave rise to enough frogs to cover the entire land. His colleague responded by invoking the classic distinction between halachah (law) and aggadah (legend). Akiva's expertise was the former, and so Rabbi Elazar ben Azarya chided, "Akiva, what are you doing studying aggadah? Desist from these words, and go study the laws of skin blemishes and impure tents" (Sanhedrin 67b). As a single woman living alone, I suppose I had as much business studying Seder Nashim as Rabbi Akiva had studying aggadah. But I could not help but daydream about that one and only Frog who would overlook my blemishes and come to my tent in the guise of a handsome prince.

Yevamot, the first tractate in Seder Nashim, literally means "sisters-in-law." The tractate deals with the biblical law of levirate marriage whereby a man is obligated to marry his deceased brother's widow so long as she is childless. This is the case even if the man already has a wife, since men in Talmudic times were permitted to marry more than one woman. The rival co-wives of polygamous men are known as *tzarot*, a word that also means "troubles." And so when I began learning this tractate during the summer of 2007, I jokingly referred to this period as my summer of tzarot. If nothing else, there was the trouble of how to understand the complicated family relationships discussed in this tractate, such as the case of a man whose brother is married to his mother-in-law, or the case of two men who accidentally switch wives under the wedding canopy, and other confusing liaisons.

And then there was the trouble of being single. Officially I was still dating Omri, but our relationship was faltering, and by that point I was pretty sure it wasn't meant to be. I probably ought to have broken up with him sooner than I did, but I was still more scared of being alone than of being with the wrong person—and that says a lot, given that I'd been married to the wrong person just two years earlier. That summer, in addition to learning Yevamot, I reread D. H. Lawrence's *Lady Chatterley's Lover* when a used copy appeared in the rack outside my local bookstore. Lawrence writes about the difficulty of finding a suitable mate: "The world is supposed to be full of possibilities, but they narrow down to pretty few, in most personal experiences. There's lots of good fish in the sea—maybe! But the vast masses seem to be mackerel or herring, and if you're not mackerel or herring yourself, you are likely to find very few good fish in the sea."[8] The lack of eligible single men in Jerusalem was a frequently voiced lament among my female friends, who always seemed to far outstrip their male counterparts. Lawrence says this explicitly, quoting a verse from Jeremiah (5:1): "'Go ye into the streets and by-ways of Jerusalem, and see if you can find *a man*.' It had been impossible to find a man in the Jerusalem of the prophet—though there were thousands of male humans. But *a man*! *C'est une autre chose!*"[9] Jeremiah, who prophesied the destruction of the Temple in the early sixth century BCE, was looking for any upright and godly person on the streets of Jerusalem. My own requirements, of course, were a bit more specific.

If I found no one in Jerusalem, I resolved, I would head to Harpania, a meeting place for singles who had no luck in their hometowns (Yevamot 17a). Rabbi Zeyra says that the name Harpania comes from the two Hebrew words *har* (mountain) and *poneh* (turn). Harpania is the mountain that people turn to if they come from such bad genealogical lines that no one wants to marry them: "Whoever cannot identify his family and his tribe turns there to find a mate." It is clear from the Talmud that the Jews of Talmudic Babylonia were very preoccupied with their family trees. They prided themselves in tracing their ancestry all the way back to the Babylonian exile in the days of King Yechonia (600 BCE). And they were interested in marrying only those of "pure lineage," those who could construct family trees back for generations. Certain parts of Babylonia were regarded as genealogically "purer" than others, and apparently Harpania was the worst; as the Talmudic sage Rava proclaims, "Harpania is deeper than hell." And so anyone who could not find someone to marry was encouraged to try his luck there.

Jerusalem was probably not quite as bad as Harpania, but even so, the dating scene did not look good for women. Once I accompanied a friend to a singles event—the only such event I ever attended—and was distressed to see that the women outnumbered the men by nearly two to one. And the gap was not just in quantity but in quality as well. Most of the women were dressed in stockings and modest but flattering fitted skirts, their stray gray hairs dyed, and any wrinkles or skin blemishes covered by painstakingly applied makeup. The men—their pants baggy, their hair disheveled—looked like they had just rolled out of bed. I thought of items on sale in a supermarket: The women were the perishables, stamped with expiration dates that were rapidly approaching. The men were the canned goods; they didn't look all that appealing, but they could remain on the shelves indefinitely until someone finally decided to pick them off. Everyone sat in a circle nibbling on stale cookies and drinking apple juice from a carton in plastic cups, playing silly icebreaker games led by a pretty woman in a bright purple dress, her hair wrapped in a colorful turban. Whenever it was my turn, she flashed me a smile that seemed kind but patronizing, as if I were a little child with a long way to go—even though I imagined that we were about the same age. She acted like she was a preschool teacher and the rest of us were her toddling charges. Since when had being single become so infantilizing?

Living in Jerusalem, I was surrounded by the assumption that everyone wanted to be married, and that those who weren't were incomplete and longing for things to be otherwise. Unlike in New York City or Cambridge, there was no respect for the high-powered businesswoman or the tenured professor; so long as she was single, she must be unhappy. I didn't mind being unmarried, but the thought of other people's pity made me cringe.

The Talmud, too, looks pitifully upon any woman who does not have a man with whom to share her life and, more specifically, her bed. Five times throughout the Babylonian Talmud, the sage Reish Lakish quotes a popular folk saying: *Tav l'meitav tan du m'l'meitav armelu*, meaning "It is better for a woman to sit as two than to sit alone by herself." The rabbis' discussion of this statement unleashes a flurry of colorful comments about how much a woman is willing to put up with just so that she can have a husband (Yevamot 118b):

Abayey said: Even if her husband is the size of an ant, she
is proud to place her chair among the free women.

Rav Papa said: Even if her husband is a carder, she hangs
him on the doorposts of her house and dwells in
matrimony.

Rav Ashi said: Even if her husband is a stalk, she does not
lack for lentils in her pot.

It seems the Talmud cannot imagine a woman who could be
both happy and single. Even so, Abayey, Rav Papa, and Rav Ashi
are not granted the last word. The passage concludes with the following assertion: "And all these women commit adultery and at-
tribute their offspring to their husbands." That is, all these women
who so desperately wish to be married are really just interested in
having a convenient excuse when they find themselves pregnant
as a result of their adulterous affairs. Why do they need husbands?
So that they can point to a legitimate father for their bastard
children!

This closing line, astonishing in its flippancy and subversive-
ness, casts the preceding statements in a new light: According
to the Talmudic sages, a woman needs a husband so that she can
"place her chair among the free women," that is, so that she
can count herself among those women who are free to have adulterous affairs! She doesn't care if her husband is a stalk, because
she's just using him as a cover so that she can gallivant off to her
extramarital affairs. For this reason it is better for a woman to be
married than to be alone.

To some extent Omri functioned as a similar cover for me.
He was not my husband, but as my long-term boyfriend he enabled me to place my chair among those who were free from the
torture of attending singles events and being "set up" by concerned, well-meaning strangers. "Are you looking to meet someone?" people often asked me, and immediately I would rush to

assure them that no, I had quite enough lentils in my pot, thank you very much.

Shortly after I studied this passage in Yevamot, a friend came for Shabbat dinner bearing the gift of a large glass jar full of hard candy. "When you finish all the sweets," she told me, "you can save the jar and use it as a vase for the next time Omri brings you flowers." I smiled, knowing that I would do no such thing. Instead, I washed out the jar, filled it with a kilo of lentils, and placed it in my cupboard alongside my beans, split peas, and other dried goods. I put a label on the jar with that line from Yevamot: "She does not lack for lentils in her pot." Most nights that summer I had lentil soup for dinner—alone.

֍

In the Talmud it is clear that men have the advantage when it comes to marriage, which is described as a one-way transaction in which a man acquires a woman and may be legally wed to several women at once. The Talmud speaks of the sanctity of marriage, but we hear other less conventional voices as well, such as the following account in Yevamot:

> When Rav would visit the city of Dardishir, he would an-
> nounce: "Who will be mine for a day?"
> And when Rav Nachman would visit the city of Shach-
> netziv, he would announce: "Who will be mine for a day?"
> (Yevamot 37b)

Rav and Rav Nachman, two prominent third-century Baby-lonian sages, apparently had a practice of marrying (or perhaps simply sleeping with) women for a single day. I understand what was in it for the sages, who presumably had to travel often and could not always take their wives with them. But I can't help but wonder what sort of women would be interested in these one-night stands. Perhaps they were so desperate for companionship that they would rather have a man for one night than be alone forever? Or perhaps they were enchanted by the notion of being associated with such a great rabbinic luminary? The Talmud contains not a hint of criticism of these practices, perhaps a testament to the surrounding culture's more relaxed attitude toward sexual ethics. But I find it hard to relate.

Personally I am drawn to those Talmudic stories—few and far between though they may be—of women who have free rein to choose among various men, rather than the opposite dynamic. This is the case with Rava's wife, who actively chooses her husband rather than waiting around like a wallflower to be plucked. She is introduced in the context of a discussion about marriage and fertility, in which the rabbis aver that "any woman who waits ten years after the death of her husband before remarrying will never give birth again" (Yevamot 34b). I first encountered this passage in the morning Talmud class I attended at a synagogue in Jerusalem, when mine was the only womb in the room. While I knew the Talmud wasn't talking about me personally, the discussion on the page before us was certainly more about me than about any of the men at the table. Suddenly I felt as conspicuous as Virginia Woolf traipsing across the all-male precincts of Oxbridge.

Rav Nahman goes on to qualify that "this was taught only with regard to one who did not intend to remarry; but if a woman intended to remarry, then she will indeed become pregnant." Rav Nahman, perhaps influenced by the Greek notion that female hysteria was caused by "wandering womb," suggests that a woman's psychology may affect her fertility. According to Rav Nahman, so long as a woman intends to have intercourse again, her reproductive organs will not wither. I was reassured, but the subject matter still seemed a little too close to home, and I hunched over my volume of Talmud with lowered eyes.

It is at this point in the passage that Rava's wife makes her appearance, though it seems like she was there all along, sitting in on an all-male study group just like me. Unlike me, however, she was not able to remain anonymous. Upon hearing the rabbis' assertions, Rava leans over to his wife and tells her that this is no hypothetical conversation: "The rabbis are murmuring about you." She, too, had been previously married and it seems she had waited a long time before remarrying and becoming Rava's wife. Rushing to her own defense, Rava's wife seizes upon Rav Nahman's corollary. She assures Rava that although she did not remarry for over a decade, her womb did not close up because she always intended to remarry. Or, as she tells Rava somewhat romantically, "My eye was on you all along."

I am impressed by the bravado of this woman who sits next to her husband while he is studying Torah with his colleagues and defends herself by professing her longstanding romantic interest. She clearly has a will of her own, even though she remains nameless. We learn more about her elsewhere in the Talmud, where she is known as the daughter of Rav Hisda. The Talmud relates the following anecdote from her youth:

> The daughter of Rav Hisda was sitting on her father's lap. They were seated before Rava and Rami bar Hama. Rav Hisda said to his daughter: "Which of these men do you want [to marry]?" She responded, "Both of them!" Rava said, "Then let me be the second one." (Bava Batra 12b)

Rav Hisda's daughter, a girl young enough to sit on her father's lap, is like a greedy child in an ice cream shop who wants both chocolate and vanilla. If given the choice between two men, she'll take them both! But Rava does not miss a beat. To the extent that he can still control his fate, he intercedes. He does not want to be the first of two men to marry Rav Hisda's daughter, which would mean either that he would die, or that they would divorce. Now it becomes clear how Rav Hisda's daughter could have known in advance that she would become Rava's wife. She always knew that she would remarry because she'd chosen Rava as a young girl, and so she is confident that her dormant womb will rally when she wishes to become pregnant again. In the margins of my copy of Yevamot, I gave her a thumbs-up.

In Yevamot, the emphasis is not just on marriage but also on having children, which is the first commandment in the Bible— to increase and multiply. The Talmud in Yevamot (61b) discusses a debate between Beit Hillel, who maintain that a man must have at least one son and one daughter to count as having fulfilled this commandment, and Beit Shammai, who maintain that a man must have two sons. All the sages agree, however, that fulfilling this commandment is so paramount that a man may even sell a Torah scroll so as to have enough money to have children. The Talmud then goes on to cite the case of Rav Sheshet (62b), who was childless because the classes taught by his teacher Rav Huna went on for too long. Rashi explains in his commentary on this page that Rav Huna did not allow for bathroom breaks, which affected his student's virility. But I wondered whether perhaps Rav Sheshet found himself staying so late in the study house that by the time he got home at night, his wife was already asleep. I, on the other hand, used to go to evening classes with the deliberate goal of staying out as late as possible before coming home to an empty house.

The tension between studying Torah and raising a family is dramatized in the figure of Ben Azzai, who captured my attention in a conversation about procreation in Yevamot (63b). Rabbi Eliezer asserts that anyone who does not engage in this commandment is considered as if he has committed murder, since the charge to procreate is juxtaposed in Genesis with the verse prohibiting bloodshed. Rabbi Yaakov then demurs that anyone who does not engage in this religious commandment is regarded as diminishing the image of God, since the charge to procreate is also juxtaposed with the verse about man being created in God's image.

At this point, Ben Azzai chimes in and declares that anyone who neglects the commandment to procreate is regarded as if he both commits murder *and* diminishes the image of God. The other sages leap up and lambast Ben Azzai for his hypocrisy: "Ben Azzai, there are those who preach and practice well, and those who practice well but do not preach well. But you—you preach well but do not practice what you preach!" Presumably Ben Azzai himself was unmarried, or at least he did not have children. And so he can offer only a faltering defense: "What can I do? My soul desires Torah. The world can be sustained by others."

On those nights when I walked back from class alone while all my friends with kids were ensconced at home, I sometimes pretended that I, like Ben Azzai, had made a conscious choice. Certainly I had far more time to study Torah than I would if I were saddled with the responsibility of raising a family. I enjoyed waking up early every morning and rushing out the door to my daf yomi class, and then coming home late after attending evening lectures. At the same time, I can't help but wish that I'd known, back then, that it was just a temporary stage of life. If only I, like Rav Hisda's daughter, had sat on my father's lap as a young girl and hand-picked my two husbands. Then perhaps I wouldn't have felt a flutter in my womb each time I went out among the streets and by-ways of Jerusalem, looking despairingly at the thousands of male humans in search of my Frog. All herring and mackerel, it seemed.

KETUBOT

≈

I Am a Jewish Man

THE ALTERNATIVE TO BEING SINGLE WAS BEING MAR-
ried, but the Talmudic view of marriage, too, leaves much to be
desired. Tractate Ketubot deals with the laws related to married
life and the responsibilities stipulated in the *ketubah*, the marriage contract. In practice, though, much of the Talmudic discussion is focused on the valuing (and devaluing) of women. The
sages consider the financial aspects of marriage, a transaction in
which a man acquires a wife for a specific sum of money. That
sum depends on whether the woman is a virgin at the time of
betrothal. Virginity is a key theme of the first chapter of Ketubot,
since a husband may claim to have discovered that the woman
he married was not in fact a virgin and therefore the transaction
was made under false pretenses. It may emerge that the woman
had not had intercourse but had suffered an injury that ruptured
her internally, in which case the rabbis debate whether she, like
any nonvirgin, is acquired for a discount. In any case, all women—
whether virginal or not—were expected to move from their
father's home directly to their husband's home, with all their

property transferred from one man to the other. I couldn't help but wonder how I fit into this scheme, as an independent woman in Jerusalem living in a room of my own.

And thus my thoughts turned to Virginia Woolf, who tried to find answers to her own questions about femininity in the books about women's history lining the walls of the British Museum. Examining the card catalogue, Woolf found herself marveling at just how many books were written by men about women: "Why are women, judging from this catalogue, so much more interesting to men than men are to women? A very curious fact it seemed, and my mind wandered to picture the lives of men who spend their time in writing books about women ... it was flattering, vaguely, to feel oneself the object of such attention," she writes in *A Room of One's Own*.[10] And yet Woolf was not interested in books written by men with their distorted portraits of women; she wanted to know how women could write more books themselves, and what they would need in order to do so. Like Woolf, I was flattered, vaguely, to find that women were objects of such great interest to the rabbis, who devoted all of Seder Nashim—a full sixth of the Talmud—to their affairs. But when I read through tractate Ketubot I identified not with the women whose dowries were being negotiated but with the men who were doing the negotiating.

After *A Room of One's Own*, I returned to Thomas Laqueur's *Making Sex*, a book I had first read ten years earlier when I was a student in Cambridge, strolling through the same green courts and quadrangles that Virginia Woolf describes. Laqueur writes about the fluidity of sex as an interpretive category, arguing that much of what we regard as fixed was not always so. Today we are used to thinking of the body in terms of two sexes—we view these biological distinctions as "real" and uncontestable, although we recognize that gender—the psychological, emotional, and social qualities that make us male and female—are socially constructed. But Laqueur shows that this is a very modern view; for much of human history, the cultural categories of gender were assumed to be real, whereas physical sex was conventional and subject to change. To be a man or woman implied a certain social rank and cultural role rather than a biological reality. Women were regarded as inferior manifestations of men rather than as a different category altogether, with female genital anatomy thought to be an involution of male anatomy. It was only in the Enlightenment that a biology of hierarchy (men as superior to women) gave way to a biology of incommensurability (men are different from women). Although in the Bible the first woman is described as "a helpmate opposite him," Laqueur contends that it was not until centuries later that women became, for the first time, the "opposite sex."

Laqueur inspired me to think differently about the historically contingent meanings of biology and gender. If what is fixed was not always so, then perhaps it was time to reevaluate my own relationship with sexual identity in Judaism. Perhaps a Jewish woman of the twenty-first century has more in common with a Jewish man of rabbinic times than with his wife—insofar as one can identify with Talmudic men without conspiring in the oppression of women. After all, women in the Talmud rarely owned property or lived independently, whereas I (and many women like me) earn a salary, have my own apartment, and participate fully in the social and political life of my community. I do not place a premium on virginity or on reproductive capacity; I value myself far more for the amount of Torah I have mastered. In another era, that would have made me a man.

To be sure, I identify with certain Talmudic men more than with their wives. I am more similar to Rabbi Hiya than to his wife, Yehudit, for instance. At the same time, though, I imagine I would make very different choices than Rabbi Hiya, who insisted that Yehudit bear him a third "bellyful" of twins even though the pain of birthing the first two sets nearly killed her (Yevamot 65b). Hopefully I'd be more sympathetic. Because, pardon the anachronism, but if I were a Jewish man living in Talmudic times, I'd like to think I'd have also been a feminist.

ॐ

"A woman must have money and a room of her own if she is to write fiction"—this is Woolf's central thesis, though it applies to Talmud study as well. In order to study Talmud, a woman must have money to buy books and a place to sit and learn without interruption. But ironically, for modern women like myself who wish to study Talmud, it is often not finding a room of one's own that is so problematic, but carving out space in the public sphere. We women can learn all the Talmud we'd like behind closed doors, with all the websites and podcasts in the world at our disposal. But when we bring our volumes of Talmud out into the open, we often run into trouble.

I discovered this for myself when I once again tried to learn Torah on an airplane. Intent on my study, I was not amused when a man sitting a few rows back tried to attract my attention.

"Brovender's or Drisha?"

This was his pick-up line, a reference to two major institutions of women's learning, one in Jerusalem (where I was flying to) and one in New York (where I was flying back from, via Frankfurt). I looked up from my volume of Talmud to find a tall man with a sleek mane of black curls standing next to my aisle seat, peering down at me with a curious half smile. He was about my age, dressed in jeans and a T-shirt, and he pointed to my book. "Where do you learn?"

I sensed immediately that my observer was way too cool and slick for my taste—his T-shirt said WANTED in big letters, which he decidedly was not. Moreover, I had just finished the third chapter of Ketubot, which discusses the punishment for seduction and rape. If a woman is seduced consensually or raped, the perpetrator has to pay her father a fine for his crime; the fine is higher for rape, since the rapist must also pay for the pain he inflicted. The rapist is additionally required to "drink from his vessel" (Ketubot 39a), that is, to marry his victim—even if she is lame or blind or afflicted with a skin disease. I wondered if any of this would interest the man speaking to me, who went on to share his name and his background: Elad was a *chozer b'she'elah*, a person who grew up religious but decided to throw out the Torah he learned as a baby with the ritual bath water. He left Jerusalem and moved to New York, where he was spending most of his time, as he put it, "bumming around."

"I'm in this inheritance battle with my siblings—my father died two years ago, and left us a hundred thousand dollars. We've spent over a million arguing about it." He tells me this proudly, checking to see if I am impressed by the sums of money he quotes. I am trying to pay attention, but my mind wanders when he says inheritance. Was it *karka* or *m'taltelin*, land or moveable property? If his father had left a widow, would she have gotten first dibs? Are his sisters and brothers both equally entitled to their father's possessions? What if his sisters are married? These were the very issues the Talmud considers on Ketubot 49b, the page I had open before me.

"You're lucky your father left you anything," I tell Elad, who is my unwelcome interlocutor if not yet my seducer. "He could have been a white crow." Elad leans over my seat to look at the page. The rabbis are discussing a law voted upon in Usha stating that a father is obligated to feed his sons and daughters when they are young. Is this the halachah, or not? Rabbi Yehuda seems certain that it is: "Will a crocodile have babies and cast them on to the whole village?" In other words, a person cannot churn out babies and expect the community to take care of them. Rav Hisda agrees: "If a father were to refuse to feed his children, the townspeople should turn over a mortar for him to stand on and call out, 'The crow loves his children, but this man does not.'" And how do we know that the crow loves his children, asks the Talmud? After all, doesn't the Bible say, "[God] gives bread to beasts, and to crows who cry out" (Psalms 147:9)? If God has to feed crows, then surely their parents are not taking care of them! *La kashya*, says the Talmud—it's not a difficulty. Rav Hisda was referring to black crows, who feed their young, whereas the biblical verse was referring to white crows, who do not. Elad follows along, but he does not look happy. He still wants to impress me, and he can see that it is going to be a challenge.

"I wrote a book, you know," he tells me. "Maybe I can show it to you, since you work with books?" This line figures in all the dreams and nightmares of anyone who works in the publishing industry. Elad scurries off to fetch his book from his seat some rows back, and my companion to the left, an American man in his sixties who has already told me that he runs a shipping business in Italy, raises his eyebrows. "That guy likes you," he says, followed by: "Jewish men are like Italian men—very horny, you know." I attempt a half smile. "Save me," I plead. I think of the halachic distinction between a woman who is seduced in a field, where it is possible that she cried out for help and no one heard her, and a woman who is seduced in a town, where surely someone would have heard. An airplane is more like a town than a field, I reason—let it be known that I cried for help.

Elad returns with an elegant black leather-bound volume that was clearly self-published. As with most Israeli books, the pages are too white, and I squint under the cabin lights. The book, a commentary on the Torah, is entitled the *Klil Tiferet*, "because my last name is Klil. This is what I call myself as a commentator. I was feeling bored, and so I wrote this book." He points out a few passages that he wants me to read—all the sections on women. (A common fallacy: if I am female, then surely it will be the parts in a book that are about women that will most speak to me.) While I squint at his pages, he tries to do business with my seatmate.

Argh, I requested an aisle seat for this very reason—there's nothing worse than sitting between two big talkers! I can generally get through four pages of Talmud on a transatlantic flight, but not with all these distractions. . . .

After ten minutes of feigning interest in the *Klil Tiferet* (the commentary, not the commentator), I am saved by the Lufthansa flight attendant and her duty-free cart. "Excuse me," she tells him. "We're about to begin serving dinner. I must ask you to return to your seat." Elad borrows my pencil to scrawl his phone number in the top margin of my Talmud, right above the title of the chapter: *Na'ara She-nitpat'ta*, the woman who is seduced. He's on a different connecting flight, but he urges me to call him when I get to Jerusalem. "We'll hang out," he tells me. "Don't worry, I have nothing to do anyway." By then, I would fortunately be back home in my room of one's own. In the meantime, I open my volume of Talmud and try to plow on.

☙

In exploring the subject of women and fiction, Woolf considers how women have figured in the fiction written about them by men. She points out that although we know very little about historical women—how women lived on a daily basis—fiction teems with colorful, larger-than-life female heroines, from Cleopatra to Emma Bovary. The contrast, she notes, is staggering: "Some of the most inspired words, some of the most profound thoughts in literature fall from her lips; in real life she could hardly read, could scarcely spell, and was the property of her husband."[11] Woolf contends that if we knew about women only from fiction, we would imagine them to be people "of the utmost importance; very various; heroic and mean; splendid and sordid; infinitely beautiful and hideous in the extreme; as great as a man; some think even greater."[12]

Woolf's analysis applies to Talmudic women as well. Whereas the women discussed in the legal sources in Ketubot are regarded as the property of their husbands, the heroines of the tractate's literary stories "burnt like beacons," to quote Woolf.[13] These are surely not historical women, but products of the rabbinic imagination—which makes them arguably only that much more remarkable. There is, for instance, the brazen woman who dupes her suitors and marries a man of her own choosing. I penned this limerick in her honor (Ketubot 22a):

A beautiful maiden-girl said
To the suitors who flocked, "But I'm wed!"
And once every last dope
Had abandoned all hope
She married her heart's choice instead.

Another heroine who inspired me with her pluck appears in the context of a Talmudic discussion about how much wine a woman should be permitted to drink (Ketubot 65a). This question is relevant in disputes about alimony: if a woman was used to receiving a certain allotment of wine from her husband, does the court continue to allot that same amount of wine to her after her husband's death? In this story, Homa, the widow of Abayey, comes to court after her husband's death to secure her alimony payments. The presiding judge, Rava, also happens to have been Abayey's study partner, and the Talmud pits Abayey's study partner and his wife passionately against each other, as I tried to dramatize in the following sonnet:

Abayey's wife, named Homa, came to court
She barked, "Dole out my food!" So Rava did.
She then said, "Next my wine—now be a sport."
Fair Rava said, "I can't do as you bid."

"But hubby dear served wine in glasses tall!
How tall, you ask? I'll show you." Homa raised

Her hands above her head; her sleeves did fall
Revealing shoulders bright. So Rava gazed.

Quick, quick ran Rava home, his loins aflame
And laid his wife to bed. She gasped: "Explain!
Who was in court?" "Er . . . Homa was her name."
His wife's eyes flashed in envy, rage, disdain.

So Rava's wife beat Homa to the ground:
"You've killed three men," she screamed. "Now leave this town!"

Rava's wife accuses Homa of being a murderous woman—a reference to the fact that Homa had been widowed three times. And
there the story ends, bringing the curtain down on the widow
who seduced her late husband's study partner and the jilted wife
bent on revenge.

Such a closing scene, with its close-up of two women, is rare
in the Talmud—even rarer than the "Chloe liked Olivia" plot
that Virginia Woolf was surprised to discover on the shelves of
the British Museum. Woolf laments how frequently male writers
depict the relationships between women as contentious, and suggests to her audience that they write about female friendship instead. But I enjoyed getting to know these feisty heroines. Just as
Homa's arm casts a ray of light in the courtroom, her story provides a bright contrast to the legal discussions that dominate this
tractate, in which women are spoken about but rarely given voice.

ᗬ

My study of Ketubot was, against all odds, an empowering experience. One morning I went jogging while listening to a daf yomi
recording and was saved by the page of Talmud I was learning. I
was on the road to Ramat Rachel, a kibbutz hotel at the southern
edge of Jerusalem that overlooks Bethlehem and the Judean hills.

Usually when I ran that route, I went no farther than the giant statue of the matriarch Rachel, who stands tall and proud with two little children clinging to the hem of her skirt. The base of the statue bears an inscription from the book of Jeremiah: "And the children shall return to their borders" (31:16), a prophetic vision of a time when Jacob's sons will be restored to their land. At this point, I would pause for a moment to read those words about returning, and then turn around and head back home.

On that particular morning, however, I decided to continue onward and head into the fields stretching beyond the hotel, which contain two hundred olive trees planted in parallel rows. Part of me knew I was being a little daring in running in a deserted field on the outskirts of town, but I was engrossed in daf yomi and light on my feet, and I threw caution to the wind. As I ran I learned about Rabbi Yehoshua ben Levi, who would sit and study Torah with lepers, unafraid of contagion. He is mentioned in Ketubot (77b) in the context of the Talmud's discussion of cases in which a man is forced to give his wife a divorce. If the man has a repulsive skin disease, a woman cannot be expected to stay married to him, and therefore the rabbinical court may force him to divorce her and set her free. The mention of skin disease leads to a discussion of the lengths to which various rabbis would go to avoid all contact with those who suffered from ra'atan, a terrible malady associated with leprosy: Rabbi Yohanan cautioned people to stay away from the flies that had come near the afflicted, Rabbi Zeyra never sat downwind from them, and Rabbi Ami and Rabbi Assi never ate any of the eggs that came from the alleyways where these lepers lived. In contrast, we are told, Rabbi Yehoshua ben Levi was not afraid to sit among them.

I was imagining Rabbi Yehoshua ben Levi studying with the lepers when all of a sudden I heard the sound of several dogs barking in the distance, all looking angrily in my direction. I kept running, but the dogs only came closer. They barked louder and came closer still. Soon I was surrounded by eight ferocious dogs at waist level, all barking fiercely and running alongside me.

Though I was terrified, I knew it was important that I not show the dogs my fear. I thought about a scene in a Maisie Dobbs novel, in which the British sleuth thinks she is alone in an abandoned barn when all of a sudden a threatening dog rears its head. Maisie, through intense powers of concentration, manages to calm her whole body so that the dog senses her fearlessness and backs off. If only I can stay calm like Maisie, I thought, I'll be OK. Then my thoughts drifted to more frightful literary canines, the terrifying black dogs of Ian McEwan's eponymous novel. I shivered to think of June Tremaine's nightmarish encounter with those savage bloodthirsty beasts in the French countryside in the months after World War II. Unlike Maisie, I had no way of calming myself down, and unlike June, I did not have a knife in my pocket. My literary imagination could distract me for only so long; how was I going to ward off the very real dogs that were surrounding me at that moment?

The Ketubot recording was still playing in my ears; just as I had not thought to stop running, I also did not think to take off my headphones. I learned that Rabbi Yehoshua ben Levi would justify his risky behavior by invoking a verse from Proverbs: "A beloved doe, a graceful mountain goat" (Proverbs 5:19). When people asked him how he dared get so close to the lepers, he would respond, "If Torah graces those who learn it, will it not also protect me?" (Ketubot 77b). As the dogs ran around me, I recited Ben Levi's words to myself again and again: "If Torah graces those who learn it, will it not also protect me?"

Somehow inside me I sensed that as long as daf yomi kept playing in my ears, I would come out of this situation unscathed. I thought about King David, who learned that he was destined to die on the Sabbath and therefore spent every Shabbat studying Torah; so long as he was learning, the Angel of Death was unable to overtake him (Shabbat 30b). I thought, too, about the Talmud in Sotah (21a), which interprets the verse "When you walk it will guide you" (Proverbs 6:22) to mean that Torah protects us wherever we walk in this world. Is Torah not a tree of life to those who hold fast to it? The olive trees around me swayed in the breeze, as if nodding in agreement.

Just as I was running out of sources about the protective power of Torah, I came to the main road at the edge of the field and saw a truck in the distance. I did not want to cry out lest I provoke the dogs, but I began waving my hands wildly in the air, and the driver turned in my direction. The dogs, seeing the approaching truck, immediately dispersed, their barks growing fainter and their heads hanging low in defeat. I thanked the driver for rescuing me, but I, like Yehoshua ben Levi, knew that Torah was the true source of my salvation.

As a person who learned on the go, I soon realized that the symbol of my independence was less a room of my own than a place to store all my books. Jerusalem has many libraries but nothing that rivals the British Museum, and so I had no choice but to amass my own collection. This proved a challenge given how often I moved. For years I kept my books in cardboard boxes, unpacking what I could. I piled books in my closet, in the backs of my kitchen cupboards, under my bed, and along my windowsills, but inevitably I had to keep at least four or five boxes unopened. Each time I needed to find a particular volume to reference, I would empty several boxes quickly and haphazardly without always bothering to put everything back properly—so many of my books lay strewn across piles of boxes and spilled across the floor.

I'd considered giving away some books, but I'd written in almost all of them, so the thought of parting was unbearable. Every volume of Talmud that I have studied is marked up in pencil with the date I learned each page scrawled on top, a summary of each section jotted in the margins, important cross-references circled, and favorite passages underlined. (A friend once looked at the tattered spines and asked me if I'd bought my volumes of Talmud used. "No," I responded proudly. "I used them!") My poetry books contain notes like "devouring lover with eyes," "death of hope," and "no second chance," which I rely on to help me choose the right poem to match—or challenge—the various emotional states of myself and my friends. And in my novels, my favorite passages are marked in pen and often indexed by page number in the back. While I could give away my copy of Ian McEwan's *The Child in Time*, say, and buy a new one someday, it would be frustrating to have to go through the whole book for the sake of that gorgeous passage about what it means to come to know a loved one's habits. This is true, too, of the descriptions of unrequited love in Alexander McCall Smith's *Sunday Philosophy Club*, and the Seltzer Equilibrium calculations in Rebecca Goldstein's *36 Arguments for the Existence of God*, and the Costco section of Dara Horn's *In the Image*—to give just a few examples.

Moreover, the more time passed, the more books I accumulated. When I first moved to Israel, I was worried that I would not be able to find easy access to English-language books. During my last few months in New York, while finishing off a third year at Random House, I had nightmares about endless Shabbat afternoons in the holy land with nothing to read. To ward off disaster, I raided the Random House book room and mailed two boxes of books to Jerusalem, hoping that these would sustain me until a friend would visit and bring reinforcements. (I joked that like the Israelites leaving Egypt, I left Random House "with multitudinous possessions.") Then, when I began working at the literary agency, I started bringing home any books we were unable to sell to Israeli publishers. It was not long before the Israeli branch of my personal library had nearly doubled.

In spite of owning a veritable library branch in this country, I was still not an Israeli citizen. By the time I reached tractate Ketubot, I had been living in Israel for three years. At some point my boss told me that she couldn't keep paying my salary if I remained on a work visa. I had learned from Virginia Woolf the importance of a steady income, and so I had no choice but to head over to the Ministry of the Interior and submit my application as a member of the nation that for millennia was looking for a country of its own. It seemed appropriate that while waiting for the clerk to announce my turn, I sat learning the final pages of Ketubot, which are about the importance of making one's home in the land of Israel.

The final mishnah of the tractate (110b) teaches that one member of a married couple may force the other to move to the land of Israel, but neither may force the other to leave. It does not matter whether it is the woman or the man who wants to live in Israel; this spouse always has the upper hand. The Talmud includes a series of hyperbolic statements in praise of living in the land, including, "Anyone who lives in the land of Israel is like someone who has a God; anyone who does not live in the land of Israel is like someone who is godless." These statements are followed by stories about Talmudic rabbis who so fervently desired to live in the land of Israel that they went to extraordinary lengths to do so. Rabbi Zeyra, for instance, could not bear to wait for the ferry to take him there, so he grabbed on to a tree branch and swung across the river. (Presumably he did not have very far to go.) Once they arrived, Rabbi Abba kissed the cliffs of Akko, and Rabbi Hanina repaired the roads. (The sidewalks of Jerusalem are in dire need of his services.) Unfortunately, none of the rabbis invested in improving Israeli bureaucracy, which was why my naturalization process, though relatively smooth, nonetheless entailed quite a few long afternoons of waiting.

Eventually I left the ministry with my Israeli identity card and called my mother in New York to share the good news: "I'm an Israeli citizen!" I announced. "Mazel tov!" she responded, unaware that I had had any intention of making *aliyah*. "What will you do to celebrate?"

I thought about her question for a moment. Aliyah, Hebrew for "ascent," is the term used for moving to Israel, which is regarded as an upward journey. But I did not regard my aliyah as something momentous. It was not the fulfillment of a lifelong dream; until I met Paul, I never even considered moving to Israel. And even once I did, I did not think of myself as having moved to Israel, but rather to Jerusalem. I am not a political animal; I was drawn to the Torah that comes forth from Zion. But then I had an idea. I would invest in bookcases! This seemed like the most appropriate way to celebrate my Israeli citizenship. After all, I had not felt ready to buy and build hardwood bookcases until I was committed to calling Israel my home; and conversely, I could not feel fully rooted in a place until my books were properly organized and displayed. And so shortly after I made aliyah, I spent a few late winter afternoons wandering from store to store in the industrial area of Talpiot comparing models. I finally found what I was looking for at Ace Kneh U'vneh, a store whose rhyming name (especially when compared to its alliterative English equivalent "buy and build") I loved almost as much as its furniture. The bookcases were made of a material that the store catalogue referred to as *book*, which is Hebrew for beech. So I bought and built (along with a friend and her trusty toolkit), and then I embarked on the more difficult project of arranging my books on my shelves.

In arranging my books, I tried to be as methodical as possible. My Steinsaltz Talmud volumes all went on the top shelves, along with any related reference books. Another shelf was reserved for those teachers who'd inspired me (through their classes or their texts) since moving to Israel: Avivah Zornberg (whose classes on the weekly Torah portion I attended devotedly), Ruth Calderon (whose book about Talmudic stories I went on to translate), and Rabbi Benny Lau (whose classes I attended and whose books, too, I eventually translated). Poetry (Hebrew, English, and bizarre hybrids of the two like E. E. Cummings in a language that knows no capitals and no vowels) were all situated at eye level, so they could flash immediately on the outward eye. Nonfiction books relating to the history of science (most of them ordered from academic presses through my literary agency account under the pretext of trying to sell them to Israeli publishers) were shelved together, including books on leprosy in premodern science and mesmerism in Victorian Britain. On the bottom shelf, where no one was likely to bend down and look, I hid all the books I was embarrassed to own: *Vegan with a Vengeance, The No-Gym Workout, How to Behave in Dating and Sex*, and the ones I can't even mention.

In the glory of late-night arranging and rearranging there was one moment of panic, when I realized that I had grouped my various prayer books with the Everyman poetry series simply because they were all the same height. I thought of my favorite part of Amos Oz's *A Tale of Love and Darkness* when the author relates how, at age six, his father cleared a space for him on his bookcases and let him put his own books there: "It was an initiation rite, a coming of age: anyone whose books are standing upright is no longer a child, he is a man." Oz describes how, in an effort to conserve space, he arranged his books by height. That night, he was made aware of his error: "Father came home from work, cast a shocked glance toward my bookshelf, and then, in total silence, gave me a long hard look that I shall never forget: It was a look of contempt, of bitter disappointment beyond anything that could be expressed in words, almost a look of utter genetic despair. Finally he hissed at me with pursed lips: 'Have you gone completely crazy? Arranging your books by height? Have you mistaken your books for soldiers?'"[14] I felt like Oz's father, Arieh Klausner, was glaring at me from his position on the top shelf—had I gone completely crazy?

Still, I knew there was rhyme and reason to the organization of my poetry and nonfiction (respectively), and no shortage of imagination when it came to the fiction. I had one shelf for my dozens of novels by Israeli writers: Michal Govrin, Yael Hedaya, Meir Shalev, David Grossman, et cetera. I had another shelf for novels I had not yet read, and yet another shelf for books I had edited. And below them were two empty shelves, because now I had more space than ever before.

These two empty shelves served as a reminder that there was another bookcase, too, waiting to be bought and built. This is the bookcase that someday, God willing, I hoped to fill with the twelve gigantic boxes of books still sitting in my parents' basement on Long Island. These include classics from childhood and high school: the complete novels of Austen and the Brontës, all the Norton poetry and literature anthologies, and everything A. S. Byatt has written to date. There, too, are the rest of the books I took with me when I left Random House—each with the Knopf rough trim and the handsome Borzoi on the spine. I missed them all like dear long-distance friends: how often did I ache to reach out for one of them— to check if I am remembering a favorite passage correctly or reread those delicious final paragraphs that send shivers up my spine each time afresh. Now that I had made aliyah, I no longer experienced the longing for Zion that had been such a hallmark of the Jewish people for centuries. Instead, I cast my thoughts toward the diaspora as I pictured the books in my parents' basement, longing for the day when all the exiles would at last be ingathered.

❧

Once I owned bookcases, I went ahead and purchased a full set of the Talmud, which I had previously bought only tractate by tractate. The full thirty-seven volumes took up two entire shelves, but I did not always keep them together. Sometimes I would place tractate Ketubot next to *A Room of One's Own*, or I'd slip Yevamot next to *Lady Chatterley's Lover* and revel in all the creative possibilities that a Talmudic library of my own afforded. I thought about Virginia Woolf being turned away from the library at Oxbridge by the beadle who apprised her sternly, "Ladies are only admitted to the library if accompanied by a Fellow of the College or furnished with a letter of introduction."[15] I thought of the women who populate tractate Ketubot, who belonged to their husbands no matter how brazen and bold. Virginia Woolf and Homa looked down at me from their new perch on my bookshelves, and I could see that they were pleased.

NEDARIM / NAZIR

✺

Ascetic Aesthetics

AS A COLLEGE STUDENT I LOFTED MY BED HIGH ABOVE my desk so that I could never conveniently lie down in my dorm room, convinced that by doing so I would avoid the temptation to nap casually. Sleep was slothful, and the less I could get by on, the better. Regardless of when I went to bed, I set my alarm for 5:30 every morning; the alarm clock was on my desk, so I had to jump down to turn it off, by which point I had no energy to climb back up to the loft. Suffice it to say that the snooze button was not invented for people like me—or for the individuals who populate tractate Nedarim.

Nedarim deals with the laws of vowing, and most of the vows cited in the tractate involve denying oneself benefit from someone or something. All of these vows are voluntary rather than obligatory. A person elects to observe certain prohibitions, presumably in an effort to deepen his or her piety and religious commitment. The Talmudic rabbis speak of people who vow to deny themselves sexual pleasure, or to abstain from eating certain foods, or to refrain from enjoying the company of a specific person, to give just a few examples. The subsequent rabbinic discussion revolves around the extent and applicability of various vows: If a person vows not to eat meat, may he still eat grasshoppers and fish (54b)? May a man vow not to take any pleasure in sex with his wife (15b)? Can a person vow to do something that does not seem humanly possible, such as not to sleep for three days (15a)—as indeed I had tried to do?

For the most part the Talmud frowns upon the making of such vows. They are regarded as restrictive and binding, and they add on prohibitions beyond those already stipulated in the Torah. After all, aren't Jews limited enough in what they can eat and with whom they can sleep? Why take on additional strictures? The rabbis quote from the book of Ecclesiastes (5:4): "Better not to vow than to vow and not fulfill." They warn that every time a person takes a vow, the notebook recording all of his deeds is opened in heaven, and God reevaluates his fate more critically (22a). Far better, the Talmud seems to suggest, to live by the Torah's laws and leave it at that.

But ironically, even my study of daf yomi was a vow of sorts. The Talmud speaks in Nedarim of a person who pledges to wake up and learn a particular biblical book or Talmudic tractate, explaining that it is as if such a person has "made a great vow to the God of Israel" (8a). I take my daf yomi vow very seriously—if I can't learn first thing in the morning, then often I will lug my volume of Talmud around all day as a way of reminding myself to learn and ensuring that I feel saddled until I do. And I do not let myself go to bed until I have learned the day's daf. In general I thrive on daily commitments—from exercise to journal writing to word-a-day calendars. But once I take them on, I find it hard to break free.

If I had to trace the origins of my tendency to bind and commit myself, I'd have to go back to my early adolescence, to the period when I was living in my father's house—to invoke the Bible's distinction between a woman's vows made in her father's home and those made in her husband's home (Numbers 30:4–17). I suppose it began at my bat mitzvah, which coincided with the week we read the Torah portion Naso. I gave a speech about the Torah's discussion of the *nazir*, which appeared in my portion and is the subject of the eponymous next tractate in the Talmud. The nazir, as described in the Torah and elaborated upon at length in the Talmud, is a person who vows to take on a set of strictures that include refraining from drinking wine, shaving and haircutting, and coming into contact with the dead for a period of at least thirty days. These strictures are intended as a means of drawing closer to God and achieving a certain level of holiness.

In my bat mitzvah speech I focused on the biblical injunction that the nazir must bring a sin offering at the end of his period of abstention. At first it seems strange that someone who seeks to become more holy has to bring a sin offering. How can holiness be sinful? In tractate Nazir, Rabbi Elazar HaKapar considers this question: "What does it mean, 'And he shall make expiation for the sin that he incurred on the soul'? (Numbers 6:11). Against what soul did he sin? Rather, he sinned in that he distressed himself [by abstaining] from wine. And if one who distresses himself by abstaining only from wine is called a sinner, how much more so is one who abstains from all things a sinner!" (Nazir 19a). The rabbis did not regard Judaism as a religion of asceticism. We are expected to enjoy the delicious and pleasurable aspects of life—not in a greedy or hedonistic manner, but in a way that acknowledges and pays tribute to their divine source. We are not supposed to engage in self-denial, but to enrich ourselves with all that life has to offer. So I believed.

At the time, I was on the brink of adolescence, speaking from the elevated synagogue *bimah* in a navy blue polka-dot suit chosen by my mother, with my hair tied back in a bow I was sure was too big for my head. I had no idea how prescient my speech would prove when, just a few years later, I became ill with anorexia. It began when I was at the start of my sophomore year in college, sleeping on my lofted bed and rising before dawn. Initially I was not focused on losing weight; I simply became, like the nazir, obsessed with asceticism and determined to get by on less. I mused on the phonetic similarity between "ascetic" and "aesthetic," believing that through self-denial I could achieve a sort of delicate beauty. Even words like "svelte" and "petite" began to assume, in my mind, a positive valence. Soon I would begin to think of anorexia in this way as well, conjuring a snow-white princess who glided along in a winter fairyland, leaving no footprints.

Although I never stopped eating three meals a day, I severely restricted my diet and the range of foods I would eat. As the number of calories I consumed decreased with each passing week, food assumed more and more of a central role in my life. I drove myself to extremes of hunger so that during class I'd be fantasizing about a green apple in my backpack, counting down the minutes until the lecture would end and I could savor that first juicy bite. Late at night I'd push myself to stay awake until I was so hungry that I could not bear it anymore, at which point I'd surrender to sleep. One night I had to stay up very late to finish a paper due the next morning, but I was so hungry that I could barely sit upright at my desk. To help push me through the night, I lined up a row of Cheerios next to my keyboard and told myself that for each paragraph I wrote, I would eat one Cheerio. Ten Cheerios later, I collapsed into bed, vowing that I would skip breakfast as a sin offering for having eaten.

As September cooled to October and October chilled to November, I became increasingly manic. Intense hunger acted on me like a double espresso; I was wired, energized, alert, and increasingly charged. That semester I took on an especially difficult course load, adding a fifth class to the standard four required of undergraduates. I began waking up earlier than ever before, determined to fit as much into each day as possible. Each morning I'd arrive at the gym just as it opened and claim my treadmill; although I preferred to run outside, I could study on the exercise machines and thus be twice as efficient. I planned my whole day so that I'd never waste a minute: I called my parents while I got dressed in the morning, ate breakfast during my first class, jogged back to my dorm room for lunch, and ate dinner at my desk while checking e-mail. I was proud of my ability to squeeze so many activities into my day, much as I squeezed my body into smaller clothing sizes with each passing week.

By November I had lost so much weight that I had to wear four layers of clothing to stay warm, and my roommates grew concerned enough to refer me to the university health services. The next thing I knew I had been committed to the eating disorders ward of a hospital, catapulted from the Ivy League to the IV League, as I grimly quipped. There at last I had to face up to the image of who I had become. In one of the most oft-quoted stories in tractate Nazir (4b), the rabbis tell of a nazir from the south, a shepherd with "beautiful eyes, a fair countenance, and a head of curly locks." This nazir relates that one time, while drawing water for his sheep, he caught sight of his reflection in the well and was seized by his evil inclination. "Empty one," he said to himself, "why do you take such pride in a world that is not yours, when in the end you will become worms and maggots?" He realized that in becoming a nazir, he was priding himself in his capacity for self-denial, even though he was destined for the same fate as every other human being on this earth. The true achievement was not self-denial, but surrendering his pride and complacency and realizing that he was a human being who, like most everyone else, enjoys good wine, is susceptible to impurity, and needs a haircut and a shave every once in a while.

Of course, it was only later, when I became a survivor of anorexia—marked by its ravages and shaped by its torturous toll—that I could appreciate the parallels between the nazir and the anorexic, and the ironic significance of the words I'd spoken on my bat mitzvah morning. Like the anorexic, the nazir aspires to a certain level of self-perfection, believing that he or she can transcend ordinary needs and desires. The nazir looks scornfully upon drinking wine in the same way that the anorexic turns her nose down at food; she doesn't need it, or can at least get by without it, because she is in pursuit of a higher goal. That goal, whether it is holiness or thinness or some amalgamation of the two, remains ever elusive, because we are embodied flesh-and-blood human beings. And it entails far too many sacrifices along the way.

For months after I was released from the hospital, food continued to divide me from those I loved most. I told myself that my sisters could eat whatever they wanted because they were beautiful, whereas I had to compensate for my unattractiveness by beating my body to unnatural thinness until I almost broke. When I passed thin women on the street I turned my head wistfully, as if they must be in possession of the ultimate happiness. And when I ate too much I felt guilty and gluttonous. I remember one of the first times I finally felt full after many months of deprivation. The heaviness in my stomach seemed as unnatural as a malignant growth. Distressed and uncomfortable, I crawled into the corner of my dorm room and began shrieking in anger and frustration. I clutched desperately at my legs; I twisted the flesh on my arms; I covered my mouth and eyes in shame and felt terribly alone. It was a long time before I appreciated how full life could feel when I went back to breaking bread with those I loved.

People who know that I was once diagnosed with anorexia often ask me how I managed to recover. It is a hard question to answer, but the Talmud has furnished me with one helpful metaphor. The phrase the rabbis use for undoing a vow is *l'hatir*, which means "to untie." To get out of a vow is literally to untie oneself from the knots and strictures with which one was previously bound. Recovering from anorexia was a process of unbinding myself from all the rules that had previously shackled me, from the number of Cheerios I could eat to the number of miles I had to run. I have come very far from those terrifyingly manic days, but I still fight the tendency to overschedule myself and to get by with less food and less sleep. If recovery means living as if one had never been afflicted in the first place, then I don't believe it is possible to recover fully from anorexia. Like the vowers of tractates Nedarim and Nazir, I will always be drawn to commitment and self-denial. But I'd like to think that with time, I have learned to untie some of those strictures and loosen up.

SOTAH

~≈

A Still Unravished Bride

IN EXPLAINING WHY TRACTATES SOTAH AND NAZIR ARE juxtaposed in both the Torah and the Talmud, the rabbis remark that "anyone who witnesses the Sotah in her disgrace will vow to become a nazir and abstain from wine" (Sotah 2a). The rabbis seem to be suggesting that the disgrace of the *sotah*—the woman who is suspected of adultery—is so disturbing and demoralizing that onlookers would swear off wine lest they lose control and engage in extramarital affairs. In some sense, then, the nazir and the sotah are opposites: the former curbs his or her desires, whereas the latter gives in to them freely. Perhaps it is surprising, then, that in spite of my penchant for self-denial, I saw myself drawn to the sotah too.

To be sure, I would never want to be the sotah. The Bible (Numbers, chapter 5) explains that such a woman is brought to the Temple by her husband, who suspects her of straying. There the high priest uncovers her head and forces her to drink "bitter waters" in a fearsome trial by ordeal. If she is in fact guilty, the waters will cause her belly to swell and her thigh to sag, and she will become "a curse among her people." If she is innocent, her belly will instead become full with child. And so whether she is innocent or guilty, the fate of the sotah is inscribed on her body for all to see, transforming her from seductress to spectacle.

It is all too easy to point to the sotah as a prime example of all that is patriarchal and misogynistic about Judaism's biblical and rabbinic roots. Merely because a woman is suspected of adultery, she is publically humiliated by her husband and the all-male priesthood? But as the Talmud explains, the bitter waters that the sotah is forced to drink contain the name of God dissolved in ink. And so the sotah imbibes a sacred text, which is what I try to do as well when I study her tractate. The meaning of sotah is "one who turns," since the sotah is one who is suspected of turning astray. Today, though, more and more women are turning back to the traditional texts of Judaism and finding their place in them. In an era when no woman will be brought to the Temple as a suspected adulteress—the Talmud states on the opening page of the tractate that the ritual fell out of practice in the wake of the Temple's destruction—my study of tractate Sotah fills me with the hope that women will find other ways of being drawn to the sacred.

Rather than being outraged by the sotah, I am drawn to her tale. And who wouldn't be? In this tractate about suspicion and sexual transgression the sotah becomes the ultimate enchantress, like Keats's "La Belle Dame Sans Merci," a "faery's child" who seduces knights with her "wild wild eyes," fills them with nightmarish visions, and then leaves them "alone and palely loitering" on the cold hillside. Several passages of tractate Sotah are voyeuristic if not downright pornographic, so much so that I would peek ahead at the next day's page to determine in advance whether I'd feel comfortable attending the all-male daf yomi class at synagogue the next morning. I did not want to be the only woman in the room when the high priest undressed the woman such that "anyone who wants to see her could come see" (7b). And, oh, how the rabbis look on!

The undressing of the sotah is described in graphic detail. The Torah merely stipulates that the priest uncovers the woman's head, but the rabbis add that the priest dishevels her hair and exposes her breasts, "assuming they are not too lovely" (8a). (One has to wonder what qualifies the priest to make such an assessment.) He also seizes her clothes, removes her jewelry, and ties a coarse Egyptian rope just over her breasts, which suggests a form of bondage or sado-masochism but is explained more practically as a way of ensuring that all her clothes don't fall off. Crucially, the exposure of the sotah is only partial. But it is the very partial nature of undressing that is the source of its seductive power, as I know from a lifetime of reading romantic poetry and novels.

So many great literary seduction scenes involve acts of gradual undressing. Of course, there is a difference between being forcibly undressed and undressing voluntarily, and the sotah's humiliation is not to be minimized. But the effect on the spectators is not all that different. In Keats's "The Eve of St. Agnes," the virginal Madeleine undresses as her suitor Porphyro secretly gazes at her from the closet in her chamber, witnessing as she "loosens her fragrant bodice" so that "her rich attire creeps rustling to her knees." We do not know what body parts become exposed; we are told only of the unclasped jewels, the hair freed of its pearls, and the clothes that fall to the floor, leaving Madeleine "half-hidden, like a mermaid in sea-weed." Elaborate sartorial detail is marshaled as a form of restraint, and we, like Porphyro, are in Madeleine's thrall. This is true, too, of Billy Collins's "Taking off Emily Dickinson's Clothes," where the poet imagines himself alone with the great nineteenth-century poetess in Amherst and reports that he "proceeded like a polar explorer / . . . sailing toward the iceberg of her nakedness."[16] Dickinson's nakedness is the speaker's ultimate destination, but the poem is more preoccupied with the journey there. And then there is Robert Herrick's "Upon Julia's

Clothes," where the poet is seduced not by Julia's bare flesh but by "the liquefaction of her clothes."

Notably none of the women in these poems undresses completely, presumably because total nakedness is far less sexy. The rabbis in Sotah (10a) discuss another classic literary seduction story in which the biblical figure of Tamar takes off her widow's garb and dresses as a prostitute, so that she might trick her father-in-law Judah into sleeping with her. She then presents him with evidence of what he did—the seal, cord, and staff she took as pledge that he would pay—and traps him into admitting his wrongdoing.

Clothes are a way of deceiving and tricking, as Tamar knew all too well. Perhaps it should not be surprising that clothes play such a role in seduction because seduction, too, necessarily involves duplicity. To seduce is to play a game of revelation and concealment; it is to alternately expose and then hide, always denying total transparency. But therein lies the rub, because if there is something that you are hiding, then you cannot be completely open. So long as you are alternately revealing and concealing, then you are not sharing everything with the other person. Thus seductiveness precludes intimacy.

The converse, I fear, is also true: intimacy precludes seductiveness. If you expose everything and keep nothing from the other person, you lose your allure. There is nothing seductive about a person who walks around naked all the time. And there is nothing exciting about a person who bares his soul from the outset.

As a person who values honesty and transparency in my relationships, I struggle with this balance between intimacy and seductiveness. I prefer to present who I am without makeup and without dissembling, with a take-it-or-leave-it attitude. I have no patience for playing games. But what is seduction if not a more sophisticated version of the classic games of childhood—show-and-tell, hide-and-seek, and catch? Gather around and peer in as I show you; look for me when I hide from you; catch me if you can. If I do not run and I do not hide, who will bother to come looking?

I feel this tension, too, when I write. My writing about the texts I study is deeply personal, baring truths about myself that I'd otherwise conceal. But I write because more than I seek to guard truth, I strive for beauty. When it comes to lived life, I am a deeply private person. But when it comes to written life—to life refracted through artistry—I unclasp the whalebone stays and turn away with lowered eyes as my loosened bodice rustles to the floor.

In the Talmudic text, too, the writing sometimes seems to be in service of beauty as much as—if not more than—it is in service of halachic truth. In the opening pages of Sotah, for instance, the rabbis discuss how much time a woman must have been secluded with a man in order for her husband to have legitimate grounds for suspecting her of adultery. Various rabbis suggest their own answers to this question, each of which is laden with sexual overtones (Sotah 4a). In perhaps the most Freudian response, Rabbi Eliezer says, "For the time it takes to encircle a date palm." Rabbi Akiva follows the phallic metaphor with an ovoid one: "For the time it takes to roast an egg." Rabbi Yehoshua has his own associations: "For the time it takes to mix a cup of wine," invoking the common Talmudic analogy between drinking and sex; elsewhere the rabbis teach that a man should not think of another woman during sex because "a man should not drink from one glass while his eyes are on another" (Nedarim 20a).

But perhaps the most suggestive answer of all is that of the sage known simply as Pleymo, who remarks, "For the time it takes to extend an arm into a basket and grab a loaf of bread." Bread, too, is frequently associated with sex in the Talmud. Later on that page we are told that "anyone who eats bread without first washing his hands—it is as if he had sex with a prostitute" (4b). Furthermore, snatching bread from a basket seems to suggest illicit activity, and the extended arm is surely also phallic. Perhaps because of these associations, Pleymo's response preoccupies the rabbis, who want to know whether the loaf of bread is hot or cold; whether it is densely or loosely packed in the bag; whether it is a fresh loaf or a stale one; whether it is made from wheat (which may slip from the hands) or from barley (which would not); whether it is soft or hard. This is clearly no ordinary loaf of bread.

The rabbis' X-rated discussion of the time in which a man and woman must be sequestered in order for there to be grounds for suspicion goes on for quite a while, certainly for longer than it takes to roast an egg or mix a cup of wine. The text unfolds as a sequence of metaphors that begins to seem more similar to a poem than to a halachic conversation—more beauty than truth. All of these metaphors are intended, perhaps, to refocus our attention away from the act itself, but ironically the metaphors are more suggestive than any description of intercourse could ever possibly be. And more erotic.

In her memoir *A Circle of Quiet*, Madeleine L'Engle laments that novelists are too explicit when it comes to sex. "If we've made love, we don't need to be told about it; if we haven't, a description of its physiological process isn't going to tell us anything. When the writer who is not afraid of the mysterious leaves something to the readers' imagination he is like the beautiful burlesque stripper who, with her diaphanous veil, added a sense of mystery to the human body." L'Engle says that one of the sexiest scenes she has ever read appears in *Madame Bovary*, where Emma and Leon get into a "carriage with drawn shades" that is seen driving through the streets "sealed tighter than a tomb and tossing like a ship."[17] The passion and potency of this scene lie not in what we can see but in what we can't. And so too with the sequestered sotah. It's hard to imagine that the rabbis were trying to write a great sex scene, but their diaphanous veils of metaphor are irresistibly seductive.

Even when resorting to metaphor, the sages do not leave the sotah alone for a moment. They are concerned that she might try to seduce her husband while they are traveling to the Temple for her trial, and once she arrives, they worry that she will entice the young priests working in the Temple. The sotah in the rabbinic imagination is a dangerous temptress who blows in like a hurricane with wild hair and lustful eyes, seducing everything in her wake.

Moreover, the seductiveness of the sotah seems to be contagious, because throughout the tractate the rabbis go on to describe several other scenes of lust, passion, and seduction, some of which border on the pornographic. We are told, for instance, that the biblical Joseph resisted the charms of his master Potiphar's wife by digging his nails in the ground so that his semen poured through his fingernails (36b). Torah, too, has seductive power in this tractate. Ben Azzai teaches that a man is obligated to teach his daughter Torah so that if she is rightfully accused of adultery and drinks the sotah waters, she will know that her Torah learning may delay her punishment. But Rabbi Eliezer offers a notorious dissenting opinion: "If a man teaches his daughter Torah, it is as if he has taught her promiscuity" (Sotah 20a). Their opinions seem to allow for only two possible types of women, both defined by their sexuality—one adulterous and the other promiscuous. Two pages later, the rabbis tell the story of a virgin who falls on her face and prays, "Master of the Universe! You created heaven and You created hell. You created the righteous, and You created the wicked. May it be Your will that men will not stumble on my account" (22a). Perhaps if she had learned some Torah, she might have had another dimension to her identity beyond her sexual appeal.

The rabbis go on to discuss the relationship between wisdom and promiscuity, playing on the Hebrew word *arum*, which means both "shrewdness" and "nakedness"; both terms appear in the story of the snake in Eden. This discussion reaches its climax with Rabbi Yossi ben Hanina's claim that "words of Torah can only be fully learned by one who makes himself naked before them" (21b). Rabbi Yossi is commonly understood as suggesting that in order to learn Torah deeply and fully, you need to strip yourself of any preconceived notions and start anew. But I'm not so sure. To me it seems that the most meaningful way to study Torah is by searching for the interconnections and resonances between Torah and the rest of one's reading, learning, and living. Torah cannot be studied in a vacuum. So I prefer to interpret Rabbi Yossi's statement as implying that to learn Torah, you have to be willing to make yourself vulnerable. You have to expose yourself, ripping your shirt to your breast and drawing on your most secret and shameful moments. You have to summon the courage to let the text resonate in the darkest recesses of your soul, in the hope that the text will illuminate your soul, and your soul in turn will illuminate the text.

My learning and writing have always been very intimate experiences. Rarely am I indifferent to the passage of Talmud I am learning. I cannot help but engage the text because the text engages me. At several points in the Talmud the rabbis interpret the verse "Moses commanded Torah, an inheritance for the congregation of Jacob" (Deuteronomy 33:4) as reading not "inheritance" (*morasha*) but "an engaged woman" (*m'orasa*). For the congregation of Jacob—the people of Israel—Torah is like an engaged woman, a "still unravished bride," as Keats would have it. There is always more to tease out, always more to be revealed.

GITTIN

~∿~

Writing Divorce

TRACTATE GITTIN, WHICH DEALS WITH THE LAWS OF divorce, takes its name from the plural of *get*, the rabbinic term for a divorce document given by husband to wife. Though a wife may sue for divorce in a rabbinic court, it is only a man who may give his wife a get. In the Bible this document is known as a *sefer keritut*, literally "a book of severing" (Deuteronomy 24:1), which a husband writes and transfers to his wife if he wishes to sever their connection. And so to become divorced, one needs to write a book. Indeed, much of the focus in tractate Gittin is on the act of writing: What sorts of ink must be used to write a get? On what types of surfaces may it be written? Must the husband himself write the get? Need the get be personalized for a specific woman? Can it be written in advance with the names then filled in, like the games of Mad Libs we used to play as kids on long car trips? What if five *gittin* are all written on the same paper, and one set of witnesses signs below? Given all these concerns, the tractate may be read as a primer in how to write oneself out of a marriage, which is what I, too, tried to do: armed with a pen, a

blank journal, and a bewildered and broken heart, I set out to
write my way through divorce.

And here I must pause, and preface these words from my sefer keritut with an important caveat. Obviously Paul figures in
them prominently; how could he not? But I have no doubt that if
Paul were to write his version of this story—his sefer keritut—it
would read very differently, and it would ring just as true. When
it comes to "matters between him and her," as the Talmud puts it,
there is no objective truth; there is only faithfulness to the truth
as we remember it. I have no desire to speak ill of my first husband
but merely to narrate my own experience. To the extent that he
figures in that experience, I can only ask my readers to divorce the
real Paul from my account of him, and to read with a generous
and forgiving eye.

I, too, try to be generous and forgiving when I look back on
my journals from that period. Sadly, much of what I wrote during
the breakup of my marriage is incoherent because I wrote only
in the rawest, most painful moments, when I could barely hold a
steady hand to paper or see through the veil of tears. Sometimes I
simply made slash marks across the page, like the jagged lines of
the broken hearts I used to doodle in my middle school notebooks. I found it difficult to document specific conversations and
moments, perhaps because any form of writing is an attempt to
convert experience into art, and the ugliness of it all felt so remote
from anything artistic. I was also overcome by shame—ashamed
that my marriage had failed, ashamed that I had failed—and so I
did not want to be writing, but rather erasing this chapter of my
life. Can a get be written on a page covered with erasures? the rabbis ask. It seems to me a silly question. All divorce is written on
top of erasure. We try to write our love, but it doesn't come out
as we want, so we erase; then we try again to write our love, and
again we erase; until eventually some of us give up writing our
love, and instead we write a sefer keritut.

My own sefer keritut is made up of the memories I recorded

throughout the unraveling of our relationship, and not the American civil divorce proceeding, which was relatively smooth and amicable, or the transfer of the get itself, which took place rather anticlimactically in a cramped rabbi's office in the basement of a synagogue in New York City. It was in that same synagogue that my best friend got married two days before I received my get. In attendance at her wedding was the man I would marry four years later, in a future still impossible to imagine. At the time Daniel and I did not meet; I was so depressed that I could not even brush my hair or dress appropriately for the occasion, and he was on crutches after a terrible bike accident. I had given up on the dream of my life unfolding like a romantic novel, but God, it seemed, was already writing the next chapter. Only years later did I realize that my get, my best friend's wedding, and my eventual remarriage were so intimately juxtaposed, like the volumes of tractate Gittin and Kidushin leaning innocently against one another on my bookcase.

Instead of writing about that pokey synagogue basement where I received my get, I wrote about an afternoon flooded with light. It was an early spring day in Jerusalem, and I stood by the open door of the refrigerator cleaning for Pesach. I pulled out a half-rotten apple from the refrigerator and said to Paul, my husband of eight months, "Oh well, this apple looks pretty far gone. I suppose I'll just eat it and be done with it." He was sitting at the kitchen table with an open book, studying while eating, and he looked up at me with all the love drained from his face. "If you have so little respect for yourself that you're going to eat a rotten apple, how am I supposed to respect you as my wife?" In synagogue just a few days later I would be chanting the Song of Songs, and I thought of a verse from the Bible's book of love poetry: "Like an apple tree among the trees of the forest, so is my beloved among the youths" (2:3). But here was I, prepared to eat rotten fruit, and therefore surely not fit to be the apple of anyone's eye.

I wrote, too, about our bicycle trip to the Galilee earlier that spring, where we rode around the dazzling blue waters of the

Kinneret. We stayed in a youth hostel where they mistakenly put us in a room with bunk beds instead of a double bed, and Paul did not object. We biked for hours in the Galilean heat without speaking to each other, until we came to a rest stop and ate our pita and egg salad sandwiches. I wrapped up the remaining food in a plastic bag and tied it to the handlebar of my bike. He was bending over to tie his shoes, and he got up, saw the food tied to my bike, and said, "Let me check that you did that right." He inspected my handlebars. "No, not like that." He furrowed his brow and looked concerned, and though I should have known better, I asked what was bothering him. "You are so impractical, so irresponsible. If I can't trust you to tie our sandwiches securely to your bicycle, how can I possibly trust you with my children?" How *could* anyone trust me with children? I was so often lost in thought or swept up in flights of fancy; how could I presume to think I was grounded enough to be a mother, or even a wife? I felt that Paul was confirming my deepest fears about myself: that I was inadequate in some fundamental and irreparable way. "A person should never instill excessive fear in his house," we are told in Gittin (6b), and in the Talmud the word "house" is interchangeable with "wife." A person should not instill excessive fear in his wife, but already I was terrified that he would leave.

Ultimately we both left, because the end, when it came, was apocalyptic. Later I would learn it was just a small and easily contained brushfire that caused us to flee when we saw those flames in our backyard, but in the heat of the moment I ran and ran. I knew instinctively that one should run from a fire, and so I did, without realizing that it was my own hearth that was smoldering. The Talmud (Shabbat 115a) discusses what a person is permitted to save from a burning building on Shabbat, but at that moment I had no thought of saving anything except perhaps myself.

I wrote about that first night after I fled. Paul returned to our apartment, but I could not bear to go back. Instead I slept on the couch of a friend who lived in our neighborhood and had sensed, though he was discreet, that all was not well in our home. I knocked on his door, carrying nothing with me, and asked if I could stay over. Simon was and still is a dear friend, and he did not ask any questions. In his living room was a maroon couch made of faux velvet, very similar to the couch in my parents' house when I was growing up, and when I slept there it was like I had returned to the cocoon of my childhood, without any concerns or responsibilities. Several days passed in a blur. I rarely got up and did not distinguish day from night, hardly aware that the world outside continued to exist. I assume that Simon, kindhearted soul that he is, brought me food to eat. He definitely brought me a pen and a notebook, which is why I remember all of this.

About a week later, Simon suggested that I move to his spare bedroom, and getting up from that couch felt like getting up from shiva, the traditional seven-day period of mourning. I was mourning my marriage, which had seemed so full of promise less than a year earlier when we delighted in our newfound love for each other and in the romance of moving across the world together. I was mourning the direction I had thought my life was heading, which seemed a farce. And I was mourning that part of me that had been so innocent and hopeful, that part of me that believed I was writing my love story on clean and crisp white paper, that part of me that thought I would never want to go back and erase.

I wrote about that first Shabbat after I fled, during the Passover of my own exodus, when I was supposed to chant the Song of Songs in synagogue. I wondered how I would bear the incongruousness of singing the Bible's celebration of carefree and sensual love with my own heavy and hurting heart. "My beloved is mine, and I am his, who browses among the lilies" (2:16). Who was I to be a conduit for this expression of young, innocent love—I, who had been discarded like a plucked and wilted flower? But I did not want to renege on my responsibility to the congregation.

And so I resolved that I would sing these words not hopefully—the days of hope were over like autumn and gone like rain—but defiantly, fighting to keep my voice steady and to hold back the tide of tears. "Whither has your beloved gone, O fairest of women? Whither has your beloved turned?" (6:1). I held my head high and chanted these words as if daring Paul to return. "My beloved has gone down to his garden, to the bed of spices, to pick lilies" (6:2).

At some point Simon connected me to Andrea, who became my running partner and who brought daf yomi into my life. He also took me with him to the library every day, which gave me a place to go, even if I was only pretending that I could concentrate on work. I don't know how Simon realized what would be best for me during that raw and terrible time, but it seems inherent in his nature. A few years ago a friend sent me a poem she had written called "The Edge of Kindness," imagining kindness as an island that extends as far as the eye can see but surely must have borders, and perhaps even precipitous ones. I read the poem and thought of Simon. I have sailed on the seas of his kindness for innumerable nautical miles, like a sixteenth-century explorer searching for the edge of the earth, and I have never come close to falling off.

Simon encouraged me to keep writing. He also encouraged me to focus on work, and I tried to return to the book I was editing. The book dealt extensively with the section of tractate Gittin known as *aggadot haHurban*, the stories related to the Temple's destruction. The Temple in the Talmud is known as *bayit*, a home, since it was the home for God's presence among the people of Israel. The destruction of the Temple, *hurban haBayit*, is also the destruction of the home, and so many of the tales in this story cycle, which follow one another consecutively and span three pages of Talmud, deal with the devastation to Jewish family life: a wedding pillaged by Roman soldiers; a man who tried to divorce his new wife by falsely accusing her of sleeping with his friends at his wedding celebration; a brother and sister kidnapped by two separate masters and then forced to marry one another.

In perhaps the most moving tale, the Talmud tells of a carpenter's apprentice who falls in love with the wife of his master (58a). When the carpenter falls on hard times and needs to borrow money from his apprentice, the apprentice insists that his master send his wife to him as his bond. The master obliges. But then the apprentice gives the master grounds to suspect his wife of infidelity, and he suggests that he loan his master money to divorce his wife. The master accepts and reluctantly divorces his wife, who remains living with the apprentice. When the master cannot repay his debt, the cruel and conniving apprentice suggests that the master come work for him to pay it off. "So they [the apprentice and his new wife] used to sit and eat and drink while he waited on them, and tears used to fall from his [the master's] eyes and drop into their cups. From that hour the decree [of the Temple's destruction] was sealed." The carpenter's apprentice, who was supposed to learn from his master how to build homes, instead destroyed the home of his master. And because of the home he wrecked, God's sacred home was destroyed as well.

The stories of the Temple's destruction in tractate Gittin are filled with tears and pathos, and as such they are anomalous in this tractate, which is otherwise preoccupied with technicalities. Gittin is much more about the "how" of divorce than the "why" of divorce. We learn about how a get is written, signed, folded, and transferred from one spouse to another, but there is almost no discussion about why a couple might get divorced, what sort of emotions might be involved, or how the matter can be handled most sensitively. But then on the last page of the tractate, after ninety pages of technical detail, we return momentarily to the emotional plane with one arresting line: "When a man divorces his first wife, even the altar sheds tears" (90b). Tractate Gittin is a reminder that we weep for the destruction of the Temple, but the Temple also weeps for the destruction of the Jewish family. The get itself is a dry formula, with the same wording used for every couple. But like the pages of my journals from that time, each get is stained with someone's tears, and there is weeping in God's house, too.

KIDUSHIN

≈

Toward a Theory of Romantic Love

Whereas Gittin is about how to get rid of a wife, Kidushin is about how to acquire one. A man acquires a woman, and never the other way around, as the Talmud tells us, "because it is the nature of a man to pursue a woman, and not the nature of a woman to pursue a man" (2b). The Talmud illustrates this principle by means of a parable. "It is like a man who has lost something. Who looks for whom? The owner looks for his lost item." That is, Adam lost his rib when God removed it to create woman; thus every Adam spends his life looking for his missing Eve. We women are like the wedges in Shel Silverstein's children's book *The Missing Piece*, waiting for the right circle to roll by and trying not to let our edges soften too much in the interim.

As a teenager, though, I resolved that I would not spend my life waiting around. I grew up quoting Anne of Green Gables ("Oh Gil, I don't want diamond sunbursts and marble halls. I just want you!") and Catherine Earnshaw ("My love for Heathcliff resembles the eternal rocks beneath—a source of little visible delight, but necessary"). Somewhat embarrassingly, my earliest ideas about romance were forged in the fiery furnace of Colleen McCullough's *The Thorn Birds*; I can still picture the bright orange cover of the mass-market paperback I placed within the open math textbook on my lap, my knees tilted up toward my chest so I could sneak a few pages of reading during class. One junior high school summer, a few weeks after I had finished the novel, my mother and I stayed up past midnight watching the eight-hour TV miniseries adaptation. I was enchanted by the grand panoramic views of the Australian outback, the soft silk Ashes of Roses gown against Meggie's flaming red hair, and the sublime melancholy of the music that would run through my head all summer long. That was the summer of my first boyfriend, and though I did not take the book with me to camp, I had already memorized the first paragraph:

> There is a legend about a bird which sings just once in its life, more sweetly than any other creature on the face of the earth. From the moment it leaves the nest it searches for a thorn tree, and does not rest until it has found one. Then, singing among the savage branches, it impales itself upon the longest, sharpest spine. And, dying, it rises above its own agony to out-carol the lark and the nightingale. One superlative song, existence the price. But the whole world stills to listen, and God in His heaven smiles. For the best is only bought at the price of great pain . . . or so says the legend.[18]

This passage was my credo of romantic love, a statement of everything I believed about the human heart. I was determined that I would love just once, but that it would be a grand and majestic love that would demand every fiber of my being. I was sure that this love would be painful—deeply, agonizingly, heart-wrenchingly painful—but that the depths of pain would be matched by heights of ecstasy. I would put the thorn in my breast and perhaps I would die in so doing, but still I would do it.

Throughout high school I collected the most beautiful literary passages I could find about romantic love and copied them down into an onion-skin notebook. Although I was an Eve rather than an Adam, I was prepared to do my part and declare, with Kenneth Koch: "I love you as a sheriff searches for a walnut / That will solve a murder case unsolved for years."[19] When I thought I had found someone worthy of loving, I would fall upon him hopelessly and passionately, leaving the poor young man feeling bewildered if not beleaguered. Often bored in class, I wrote love letters and sonnets on the blank back pages of my spiral notebooks. I never tore out the pages or showed them to anyone, certainly not to the one to whom they were addressed. I specialized in unrequited love, or "Love without hope," as Robert Graves termed it in a poem about a bird catcher in love with the squire's daughter. When the bird catcher tips his hat to greet her, he inadvertently sets the imprisoned birds free, and they all swarm around her head singing.[20] Like the young bird catcher, I became a fool for love, whether it was the love of the non-Jewish boy who lived around the corner, my high school English teacher, or Gilbert Blythe himself—in ascending degrees of implausibility. Needless to say, I never caught any birds.

I wonder how the rabbis of the Talmud would feel about all the energy I invested in my unrequited passions. In Kidushin (40b) the sages debate the relative merits of study and action: is it better to spend one's days learning Torah or performing good deeds in the world? They ultimately side with Rabbi Akiva that study is greater, because study leads to action. I suspect that the rabbis would have told me that all my pining was fine, so long as it led to an actual romantic relationship—which in my case it rarely did. Or, as Shakespeare would have it, "The expense of spirit in a waste of shame is lust in action, and 'til action, lust is perjured, murderous, bloody, full of blame."

With time I developed a more sober view of romantic love. When I finally began healing from my divorce, I hoped that I would not love only once; I realized that there were multiple men with whom I could imagine leading a happy life. I also began to appreciate the range of different relationships that seemed to work, even against all odds. One of my college friends married a professor fifteen years her senior; another married a much younger undergraduate whom she had met while teaching abroad. My aunt, recently widowed, married a widower who had been her sweetheart in summer camp thirty years earlier. It was impossible to know in advance for whom one was searching; I could only pray for the ability to recognize the right person when I saw him.

After my divorce, too, I came to realize that the right person is not always the person who seemed so right initially. The second chapter of Kidushin deals largely with betrothals that take place under false pretenses. A man may betroth a woman on condition that she has no "blemishes," and then discover that in fact she has blemishes; if so, she is not in fact betrothed to him (50a). According to the rabbis, these blemishes include a scar from a dog bite, or too much cleavage, or a husky voice. At the same time, though, the rabbis teach in the same chapter that "it is forbidden for a man to betroth a woman without first seeing her, lest he see in her something repulsive and be repulsed by her, since the Torah says, 'love your neighbor as yourself'" (41a). That is, a man should not find out too late that he married a woman he cannot find attractive. If only this lesson had been internalized by the hero of Hawthorne's story *The Birthmark*, a scientist who cannot bear the birthmark on his wife's cheek. Finally she agrees to let him remove it, and she dies from the potion he makes her drink. I sometimes think that Paul married me on condition that I had no blemishes—that is, on condition that he not find anything he did not like. When things grew tough, we responded very differently: I felt that we had committed to one another unconditionally, and so we would find a way to work through our difficulties; he felt that the difficulties—the blemishes—undermined the commitment itself.

When I realized, painfully, that the same person who swept me off my feet could pull the rug out from under me, I became more skeptical about romantic love. I knew what it felt like to be completely smitten, and I looked on with raised eyebrows as various friends fell passionately in love and told me all about it. Each time another friend gushed about a new relationship, I thought of Wendy Cope's poem "The Orange." Cope describes those glowing first moments of romantic love, in which even the most ordinary pleasures, like a huge orange shared among friends at lunchtime, make us smile and laugh.

Popular psychology holds that when we first fall in love, the brain releases neurotransmitters that contribute to increased energy, rapid pulse, a sense of heightened perception, and a more positive outlook on life. And indeed, the Talmud in Kidushin (81a) relates several stories of rabbis who acquire superhuman strength upon falling in love. For instance, Rabbi Amram hosted a group of beautiful women following their redemption from captivity. Lest he be tempted to approach them, he asked the sages to remove the ladder leading up to their attic room. One day one of the women passed by the opening to the attic, casting a radiant beam of light. Upon seeing her splendor Rabbi Amram ran and moved the ladder back in place, even though it was so heavy that it ordinarily required ten men to lift it. Fortunately he managed to subdue his evil inclination by yelling "Fire!" when he was halfway up the ladder, such that all the sages rushed in and he was saved from temptation. In another story, Satan appeared to Rabbi Akiva in the form of a beautiful woman perched at the top of a palm tree. Desperate to reach her, Rabbi Akiva managed to leap halfway up the tree. He was saved just in time when Satan revealed his true identity. A similar story is told about Rabbi Meir, who spotted a beautiful woman (again, Satan in disguise) across the river. When no ferry came, he swung from a rope and forded the river. He too was spared.

As both the psychologists and the rabbis would have it, then, romantic love is not just an intense emotional experience, but a somatic one as well. Our body chemistry shifts when we fall in love—we become almost like superheroes, or like the biblical Jacob, able to roll a heavy stone off the mouth of a well with Rachel looking on. I think of it as the orange stage of love—that stage when the whole world seems aglow with possibility and ordinary things are infused with the thrill of being alive. Sadly, though, it is often just that—a stage. The glow fades, and the succulent fruit is no more.

And so gradually I adopted a different credo of romantic love, one that seemed more true to the reality of my own loving and losing. Instead of Colleen McCullough's *The Thorn Birds*, I identified with Jack Gilbert's "Waiting and Finding," a poem about a boy in a kindergarten music class who wants to play the exotic red and gold tom-toms but finds himself instead stuck playing the ordinary triangle. Unlike the tom-toms, the triangle is not played continuously; it is struck only every so often, and then it reverberates and fades out until the time comes to strike it again. Still, the boy finds that it is the sound of the triangle that stays with him because it teaches him that love is something that we spend our lives finding, then losing, and then waiting to find again. During those loveless stretches, we must live, as Gilbert puts it, "silent in the middle of the world's music. Waiting for the best to come again."[21]

According to Gilbert there is no one superlative song of the thorn birds, but rather a series of cacophonous rehearsals in which everybody tries to learn how to play their part, and most of us never get it exactly right. The romance of romantic love lies not in its unique, once-in-a-lifetime quality but in the guaranteed fading out and return. Love thus has poetry in the same way that a sunset has poetry: the color streaks across the sky as the light fades, but then the sun always rises.

For the thorn birds, life ends when the song dies. But Gilbert's poem is a reminder that life goes on in periods of silence.

We wait and wait, and then perhaps we find. In this sense, we are all on a quest like Adam. But what we are searching for is not our one and only missing piece but rather another opportunity to fall in love, to savor the orange, to strike the perfect shimmering note on the triangle. We are waiting for the best to come—again.

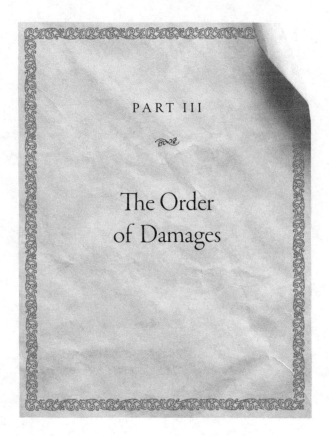

PART III

The Order
of Damages

BAVA KAMA / BAVA METZIA / BAVA BATRA

∽❧

Suspended in a Miracle

I MET, DATED, AND MARRIED MY HUSBAND DANIEL against the backdrop of my learning of Bava Kama, Bava Metzia, and Bava Batra. These tractates—originally one long tractate that was subsequently subdivided—contain the core of the Talmud's discussion of civil law, specifically how people interact with one another and share space: What happens if my ox falls into your pit? Or if I rent out the second story of my home to you, and it collapses? Or if you open up a shop near my home and the noise keeps me up at night? As I let Daniel more and more into my life, the Talmudic text became a primer for how to look out for the other: how to seek out that person who will become a lifelong partner, and how to look out for that person as dearly as—if not more dearly than—we look out for ourselves.

Even before I met Daniel, I struggled with how to look out for myself. At the beginning of Bava Kama we are taught that "a person is responsible for guarding his own body" (4a). That is, a person should take care not to harm others with his or her physical person. It is a skill I have had to master because I've spent most of my adult life walking through the world with a book, reading as I walk. Somehow I am able to see and assimilate the words on the page while also being aware of the bumps in the road, the shape of the cobblestones, and the telephone poles and traffic meters that interrupt the sidewalk. I have a friend who lost her vision a couple of years ago. She works with a "mobility instructor" to learn to memorize the paths she takes regularly, so that she will not trip or stumble. I am blessed with decent vision, but I can very much relate.

There is a science to reading while walking. It is easier with poetry than prose (the line breaks provide a natural opportunity to look up), and with paperbacks rather than hardcovers (less weight to support), and with larger-print books (less squinting). But at this point there is almost no book I wouldn't take with me on the road, and I would never, ever leave the house without something to read. When I first moved to Jerusalem, I spent Shabbat afternoons taking walks with the guidebook a close friend had given me, choosing a different route each time. Though sometimes I was too absorbed in the map or the illustrations to lift my head from the page and look at the building in front of my eyes, I tried to take in the stones as well as the stories. I discovered landmarks such as the "Dead Groom's House" on Jaffa Road, built in 1882 by the parents of a Christian Arab young man who died on the eve of his nuptials but whose parents decided to hold the ceremony nonetheless—dressing the dead groom in his festive garb and seating him next to his unsuspecting bride. (Today the building houses the Ministry of Health.)

Another week I visited the former leper hospital around the corner from my apartment. It was a building I'd passed hundreds of times, though I'd never before stopped at its gates to walk down the long stone pathway lined with overgrown trees leading to an abandoned but still striking stone edifice. The outside of the building bore the inscription *Jesus Hilfe*, German for "Jesus helps," on account of the Protestant missionaries who founded the hospital to heal and mission to the lepers of Jerusalem, who had formerly congregated as beggars at Zion Gate. I thought about Rabbi Yehoshua ben Levi, who studied Torah with the lepers, and I learned about his modern counterpart, Rabbi Aryeh Levin, who began visiting the lepers to study with them after he met a woman weeping at the Kotel—the last remaining wall of the Temple—for her afflicted son.

During the week, when I was too busy going about my daily business to do any touring, I was mostly oblivious to my surroundings because I was buried in other books unrelated to my environs. I read poetry in elevators, short stories in doctor's offices, and long novels while waiting in line at the post office or the supermarket, marking time not in minutes lost but in pages gained. Often I'd carry around all three in my bag just in case; the prospect of being caught stranded without a book to read was a fate equivalent in my mind to one of Dante's circles of hell.

Over time I developed a reputation in Jerusalem as the woman who reads and walks. One morning I went jogging as usual but failed to look where I was going and bumped into a pole. For the next few days I had a huge bruise on my forehead, and everywhere I went I was met with the same response, often from people I regarded as total strangers: "Oh, so you were reading while walking again!" I tried to defend myself, insisting that no, in this case I was jogging and there was no book in sight, but no one believed me. The Talmud (Bava Kama 32a) warns about the dangers of running recklessly: According to the opinion of the sage Issi bar Yehuda, if a person who is running and one who is walking collide and injure one another, it is the runner who is responsible for all damages because he is the one acting in a "changed" manner—that is, his behavior is different from the way that people ordinarily move through the world. However, Issi bar Yehuda qualifies that if one runs at twilight on the eve of the Sabbath, he is exempt from paying damages, because everyone is allowed to rush to get ready for Shabbat.

Fortunately I have never injured another person while running, or while reading and walking, for that matter. In this sense I am what is known in Bava Kama as a *shor tam*, an "innocent ox." A shor tam has never gored another animal or person before; it stands in contrast to a *shor mu'ad*, which has a history of goring and therefore incurs higher damages for its owner should it gore once again. Indeed, the only person I ever injured with my ambulatory derring-do is myself, but these minor injuries seem worth all the hundreds of extra pages I've managed to read in transit.

The one place in Jerusalem where I never take out my book is the shuk, the open-air marketplace where I do my food shopping. The shuk and the bus I ride home after shopping are two of the rare common spaces of Jerusalem, places where people from all sectors of society come into contact—from Haredi (ultra-Orthodox) Jews to Arabs to secular teenagers sporting tight black jeans and pierced belly buttons. In the shuk I jostle my fellow bag-laden shoppers as I lean over to choose the juiciest tomatoes, the spiciest olives, the warmest and crispest potato burekas. I follow my nose and eyes, enticed by the pungent-smelling cheeses and the cardamom-flavored Turkish coffee. The rabbis say that "one who eats in the shuk is like a dog" (Kidushin 40b), and Rashi explains in his commentary that such an individual lacks any sense of dignity. But sometimes I cannot resist—I reach into my bag and take out a pita so hot that the plastic bag encasing it has become clouded with steam, and I savor each bite. I buy my produce from two brothers I've gotten to know personally; each week we check in with one another as I lean in to examine their grapes or to pile juicy lemons in my bag. Then I make my way to the herb stall, owned by a religious man with a black *kippah* on his head who offers me his commentary on that week's Torah portion as I pick from his piles of fresh basil, parsley, mint, and lettuce leaves.

Finally I head to the dry goods stall run by a young Ethiopian family, where I buy quinoa, oatmeal, lentils, and beans in bulk, occasionally inquiring about a new grain that I don't recognize.

When I shop in the shuk, I must be fully conscious of everything around me, which is why I would never dare to read. I am careful to bury my wallet deep in the zippered compartment of my bag, since the shuk is notorious for rampant pickpocketing—an issue that is treated in Bava Kama (118b) in the chapter about various kinds of theft. In my left pocket I keep only the bills and coins I will need for my next few purchases; in my right pocket is my shopping list and a pen for crossing out each item I purchase. I type up and print out the shopping lists at home, working off a master list template that I modify and label by the name of that week's Torah portion: "Shuk list Noah," "Shuk list Lech Lecha," et cetera. I am not only careful about guarding my money but also about treading gingerly through the aisles filled with bags, carts, and discarded cardboard fruit and vegetable boxes. I try to keep my distance from the old, shrunken religious women in thin headscarves who drag their carts behind them without looking back, relying on their fellow shoppers to get out of their way. Every so often a lanky teenager comes rushing through the aisle carrying over his head a wooden tray stacked with hot, freshly baked pita, which he delivers to the nearest bakery stall. I marvel that he doesn't crash into any of the elderly ladies with their market carts, scattering oven-fresh pita on the floor.

The Talmud in Bava Kama brings several tales that involve accidental run-ins in the shuk and other public spaces. My favorite is the case of the camel laden with flax that passes by the door to a store where a candle is burning in the entryway (22a). The flax catches fire and the upper story of the store bursts into flame. Who is responsible, the owner of the camel or the owner of the store? The rabbis respond that if the candle was outside the entryway, then the store owner is responsible; if it was inside the store, then the camel owner is responsible. But Rabbi Yehuda grants that if the candle in question was a Chanukah candle, then the store owner is never implicated since he—like Issi bar Yehuda's runner who was rushing to prepare for Shabbat—was engaged in performing a *mitzvah*, a religious commandment.

I have had several such close encounters in the shuk, though thankfully none have involved camels or conflagration. All too often I find myself with my head in someone else's smelly armpit, or I look down to see that my feet are straddling another shopper's bag of carrots. Even so, I would choose the shuk over the supermarket any day. I take pleasure in knowing the people from whom I buy my produce and feeling like they are a part of my life. I also enjoy noticing which fruits come in and out of season as prices grow successively lower and then mount again. Each year I wait until the strawberries stacked in heaps that reach my shoulders are sold for four shekels a kilo, and then I watch the vendor shovel them into a plastic container with a dustpan. I look out for the first apricots in May, the first pomegranates in August, and the first green clementines in September that turn increasingly yellow as the fall sets in.

At the shuk I buy as much produce as I can carry, and when I cannot manage to lift another kilo, I hobble to the bus stop. By this point my shoulders are aching and I have red streaks across my palms where the handles of my bags have dug into my skin. I place the bags down at the bus stop, my feet encircled by my purchases as I wait to board the crowded bus, elbowed by other tired shoppers who try to cut ahead of me.

The buses in Jerusalem, like the shuk, offer another opportunity to come into contact with a wide swath of society. While the public buses in the more religious neighborhoods of the city are segregated, with men in front and women in back, I am free to sit wherever I want on the bus home from the shuk. That said, I often get strange looks from the Haredi men standing near me when I practice my Torah reading for the coming Shabbat. I chant from the Torah in synagogue almost every week and carry around photocopies of the portion I am learning folded into my pocket for easy access whenever I have a free minute. But Haredim do not believe in gender egalitarianism in prayer, or in women singing in public, since a woman's voice is thought to be provocative. I try to sit down next to someone who won't mind my quiet chanting, though it's hard to predict who will be an accommodating seatmate. Once I decided that I'd rather put my bags on my seat than sit down myself; it would be easier not to have to reach down again than to sit comfortably for the ride. The querulous, hectoring old lady sitting next to me would have none of it: "You can't take up a seat just for your bags," she insisted, lowering them to the floor herself. "But it's my seat," I protested. "I'm just electing not to sit in it." Don't I have as much of a right as anyone else to one seat in the public domain, however I may choose to use it? This is not a case that comes up among the property laws discussed in Bava Kama, but it seems like it would fit right in.

※

It was from shopping in the shuk that I learned how to share public space while still looking out for myself; and it was from my relationship with Daniel that I learned how to share intimate space while continuing to honor my own emotional vulnerabilities. I can't really say when Daniel and I first met, since it was less a proper meeting than an experience of inhabiting the same space for one evening a week over the course of the many months that we were both in Avivah Zornberg's class on the weekly Torah portion. The class, which I had been attending for years, was a lifeline for me. Zornberg is not just a brilliant reader of texts but also a kind, compassionate human being who seeks out the spark of God in every single person with whom she crosses paths. Whenever she speaks, I feel like she is addressing her words directly to me, as if I am the only person in the room. Perhaps that is the reason I never noticed Daniel, who was apparently sitting just a few seats over and trying to catch my eye for several weeks.

Daniel claims he first noticed me when I quoted from Blake's "Tyger, Tyger" in class, a poem our teacher invoked to describe how the tranquility of the biblical patriarch Jacob was interrupted by the agitation of his son Joseph. When called upon, I recited the poem in full, apparently twisting the sinews of Daniel's heart. From the outset our courtship revolved around poetry, and it was for a long time an epistolary romance: Daniel e-mailed me selections from the poems he was analyzing in his PhD dissertation, and I wrote back analyzing his analyses until we had taken each poem thoroughly apart. But when Daniel grew so bold as to send me Byron's "She Walks in Beauty," I demurely refrained from comment, afraid of being too explicit about what was in fact unfolding between us—"the smiles that win, the tints that glow."

The Talmud in Bava Kama (41b) relates that the sage Shimon HaAmsuni was famous for coming up with an exegetical interpretation of every word in the Torah, even the most insignificant word *et*, which is essentially a grammatical placeholder. But then he came to the verse that begins with the word "et" and reads, "[Et] the Lord your God you must fear." Here he did not offer any interpretation, since the point of this verse is that one should fear only God, and nothing else. His students questioned how he could throw away his life's work, and he responded, "My students—just as I receive merit for exegesis [*drisha*], so too will I receive merit for refraining from exegesis [*prisha*]." I trusted that Daniel appreciated our correspondence even when I demurred to comment.

Throughout our courtship I was generally the reserved one, the hesitant one—as exhilarated as I was terrified about striking that perfect, shimmering note again. At one point I came to a Talmudic legal discussion about whether one may use dye made out of the bark of trees grown during the sabbatical year, when it is forbidden to derive benefit from anything that grows from the land. The rabbis explain that the laws of the sabbatical year apply only to items that provide benefit when they are consumed. When the pigment is removed from these dyes in the boiling process, anything that remains is useless, so they are considered used up and hence forbidden during the sabbatical year (Bava Kama 101b). It was a dry legal passage, but I bristled. I wanted us to keep discovering each other, to continually animate and never exhaust one another. Daniel assured me that the more we got to know each other, the more we would want to know—our colors would keep blending to form ever-brighter and more variegated hues, and our love would not be a sealed vat but an ever-flowing fountain.

After we'd been dating for a couple of months, I convinced Daniel to take up daf yomi with Bava Metzia. He began joining me at the morning daf yomi classes I was then attending at a local synagogue, though we always made sure to stagger our entries so that it would not appear as if we were arriving together at 6:15 a.m. Apparently this was OK, since the Talmud in Bava Metzia teaches that "when it comes to these three things, a person is permitted to deviate from the truth: his tractate, his bed, and his inn" (23b). That is, a person can lie about whether he has learned a particular tractate, and he can lie about the bed or inn where he slept the previous night. At least Daniel and I were transparent about our tractates.

☙

The opening chapters of Bava Metzia deal with the laws of returning lost objects. When is the finder obligated to return the lost item and to what lengths must he go to do so? Daniel, early on, decided that I was his missing piece, and he was bold enough to tell me so. But I had only recently broken up with Omri, whom I'd dated for even longer than I'd been married to Paul. After two failed relationships, I was more interested in the lost rings of figs described in the first chapter of Bava Metzia than in finding the person who

might or might not have walked off with one of my ribs. The opening pages of Bava Metzia present the rabbinic principle that the
burden of proof is on the person who wants something in his
fellow's possession (2b). After several months of dating, Daniel
wanted my consent in marriage, but I still needed to be convinced.

Looking back, I can see now that I gave him quite a hard
time. Painstakingly protective of my privacy, I never wanted us
to be seen in public. I was falling in love in spite of myself, and I
thought of our relationship as a fragile butterfly with fluttering
wings that I wished to keep cupped in my hands. I worried that
the harsh light of other people's gazes might damage or still those
dazzling wings, and I was terrified of suddenly being deprived
of all the beauty that seemed to have blessedly and unexpectedly
flown into my life. I suspect the Talmudic sages would have
understood. In a discussion of the importance of storing one's
money in a safe and secure place, Rabbi Yitzhak comments, "Blessing is only found in that which is hidden from the eye" (Bava Batra 42a), quoting a biblical verse about God blessing his people's
storehouses. Daniel was my newfound treasure, and for just a
little while longer, I wished to keep our relationship a secret. And
so although we were "going out," most of our dates consisted of
reading poetry together in the private domain of one of our apartments.

The first time Daniel came to visit me he brought me a bag of
dates that he'd purchased in the shuk, which was, as it turned
out, where he shopped as well. He was making fun (and making
pun) of the fact that I had never agreed to properly date him, but
I thought of one of my favorite contemporary poems, Edward
Hirsch's "Dates," about the symbolism of the date in ancient and
medieval Jewish and Arabic traditions. I read the poem aloud to
Daniel that evening, savoring my favorite images as I licked the
sticky sweetness off my fingers: Hirsch writes that when God ban-
ished Adam from Paradise, he ordered him to uproot the date

palm, and so Adam replanted it in Mecca. "Thus is the bitter made sweet again."[22] I wondered if my own heart of palm could be replanted in new soil, and if it would blossom yet again.

༭

Daniel later told me that he mistook me for a painfully shy recluse like Emily Dickinson. As was characteristic of our poetic and Talmudic exchanges, I responded by invoking the first chapter of Bava Batra, which we had just begun learning. I was not a recluse, I told him, but I believed in *hezek re'iya*. Hezek re'iya, which literally means "the damage of seeing," refers to the notion that the invasion of privacy caused by looking at someone else's property is tantamount to physical damage. The term comes up in a discussion about two neighbors who argue over the construction of a fence. One would like the fence built so that the other cannot see into his yard, but the other does not want his yard divided. Is the first neighbor legally authorized to force the second to agree to the fence? Those rabbis who support the notion that hezek re'iya constitutes a real form of damage agree that a person can legally prevent his neighbor from gazing into his property by forcing him to agree to the construction of a fence. On the opposite side of the divide are those rabbis who argue that the damage of being seen is not real damage, and therefore the individual who desires privacy cannot force the fence upon his neighbor. Ultimately, the Talmud concludes that yes, the damage of being seen constitutes a very real form of damage, and people have the right to protect their own privacy.

I can trace my own sensitivity to hezek re'iya back very far, to my early childhood as a rabbi's daughter, growing up in a house on the synagogue property. Although we had a fence separating our yard from the synagogue, anyone who drove into the parking lot could always look into our windows. My parents were vigilant about drawing the shades at night and keeping the front yard neat. In synagogue, too, my siblings and I had to be on our best behavior because our parents insisted that our actions set an example for others. We felt the eyes of the community upon us at all times, an experience epitomized by one unforgettable weekend in which my parents declared that we were having a "Shabbat in." My father had the Shabbat off, but my parents did not feel like traveling. Nor did they want anyone to know that we were home. So we drew the shades, parked the cars in the garage, and spent Shabbat in Secret Annex mode, praying and eating together without leaving the house.

From an early age, my siblings and I learned never to reveal more than we needed to about our family. If someone called to speak to the rabbi, we were supposed to say, "I'm sorry, he can't come to the phone right now," and not that he wasn't home, and certainly not that he was at Mrs. Knecht's funeral or at the supermarket buying more paper towels. My parents are warm and welcoming hosts, as everyone who knows them will attest, but they instilled in each of us the value of privacy. For me it has become second nature. I eschew social media and group e-mails, preferring to communicate with one person at a time. My journal seems a more appropriate repository for my reflections than my Facebook "status," and I care that my personal space remain just that.

And so for as long as possible I kept my relationship with Daniel a private affair. If I referred to him it was only casually, as a summer fling, which was of course what I most feared. When my mother came to Israel on a business trip two months after we'd begun dating, I hinted that I was seeing someone, but didn't elaborate. On her last afternoon in Jerusalem, I reluctantly agreed to let her meet him, but only briefly—I deliberately waited until Daniel was on his way to catch a bus out of town and asked if he'd stop by my apartment with just five minutes to spare. (I marvel that here, too, he indulged me, never once patting me on the shoulder and saying "Don't be a ninny"—which was what I surely deserved.) Since we kept our relationship just between us for so long, it was only later that we discovered how intimately connected our families already were—my brother had gone to camp with his sister, my sister had gone to college with his brother, and my other sister belonged to the same campus community where Daniel had gone to graduate school.

With so much else to talk about, Daniel and I never engaged in Jewish geography—a game I try to avoid. When I introduce myself, I generally offer only my first name unless pressed; in the circles in which I travel, most of the people I meet are likely to know at least one member of my immediate family. It seems far more likely to be known than unknown in a world of increasing interconnectedness, and I would like to be free to introduce myself on my own terms. Early in our relationship Daniel and I read Whitman's poem about the "noiseless patient spider" standing isolated on a promontory, launching "filament, filament, filament out of itself, ever unreeling them, ever tirelessly speeding them."[23] I wanted that gossamer thread I was flinging to catch, but I was not yet ready to get caught up in an elaborate web of social networks.

Living in Jerusalem, I knew all too well that it is impossible to share something with a friend and expect it to stay a secret, because as the Talmud states in Bava Batra (28b), "Your friend has a friend, and your friend's friend has a friend." The Jerusalem I inhabit is less a city than a small village of overlapping social circles in which everyone knows (and talks about) one another. The street where I work, Emek Refaim, is lined with a dozen small cafes with glass storefronts, and anyone who walks by can see everyone inside. When I walk down this street, I am conscious of all the pairs of eyes that might possibly be upon me at any moment. Were I to sit in the windows of one of those cafes with Daniel, I was convinced that half the city would know, within moments, that we were together. And the city was not even the limit, because Jerusalem is one of the most popular tourist destinations of Jews the world over. I am constantly running into people from earlier stages of my life: a classmate from my Jewish day school, an acquaintance from Harvard Hillel, an old friend from the Upper West Side. *Everyone passes through Jerusalem*, as a friend once joked in the refrain of a sestina.

Of course, the other side of the coin is that sometimes being seen is deeply affirming. Part of what made me feel most at home in Jerusalem was the number of familiar faces I spotted whenever I walked down Emek Refaim. The name of the street literally means "The Valley of the Ghosts," though for me it has generally been a pleasant haunting. At the time I followed a rather predictable schedule, and so each day I'd see many of the same faces—the fellow 6:00 a.m. joggers, always at the same part of the jogging path at the same time each day; the mothers pushing their kids in strollers to preschool just when I was coming back from my daf yomi class; the owner of the stationery store who walked down my street each morning on his way to work. And then there were my friends who lived in the neighborhood, whom I'd run into at the bakery on Friday mornings, or at the coffee shop in the afternoons, or at the bus stop. The brief exchanges of pleasantries with those I knew by name, and the smiles and nods from those I did not, contributed significantly to my sense that I was known, recognized, acknowledged.

Still, I did not want all those familiar faces to know and recognize and acknowledge Daniel's role in my life—at least not yet. First I needed to figure out just how much a part of each other's lives Daniel and I would become. To some extent that answer was figured out for me by Daniel's father, who was in faltering health and was determined to see his son happily wed. Seeking to honor his father, Daniel wanted to make it a fait accompli, whereas I was still on the fence. I loved Daniel, but how could I trust in his love for me? As we dated farther into Bava Batra, we came to the concept of the *shechiv mera*, a man who is on his deathbed. His words carry an authoritative weight that those of a younger, healthier man would not (Bava Batra 131a). I could not decide to marry on someone else's timetable, but at some point I was going to have to take a leap of faith.

When we got married less than a year after we'd met, it was a fearful and thrilling leap, and one that called to mind another tiger poem, Eliza Griswold's "Tigers," which describes two lovers standing at the edge of a precipice with tigers threatening them from above and below. As they cling to a vine at the edge of the cliff, they resolve, "Let us love one another and let go."[24] I told myself that there were tigers above and below; there was as much to fear if I did not marry Daniel as there was to fear if I did. There were no guarantees, but I could live my life based on either what I hoped would happen, or what I feared might happen. And so marrying Daniel was less an act of courage than an act of faith. When confronted with tigers above and below, I chose Griswold's pluck over Blake's terror.

Our wedding took place in New York and not Jerusalem because we thought it would be easier for Daniel's father, who walked him down the aisle. He was still strong enough—or perhaps invigorated enough by the magnitude of the moment—to leave his walker at the end of the synagogue aisle and lean on Daniel, who was supported by his mother on the other side. A marriage ceremony is traditionally regarded as a time of divine favor in which our prayers are more likely to be answered, as if the poles of the wedding canopy could pierce the heavens. I felt the gravity of the moment as I stood at Daniel's side, facing my father, who was conducting the ceremony. I prayed for Daniel's father, and I prayed for us, and I tried not to look past the edge of the canopy. There were nearly three hundred people in the room, and my knees were quaking.

I knew that I loved Daniel, and he had convinced me that he loved me. But such a public avowal of our love for one another seemed antithetical to my Dickinsonian sensibilities—I told Daniel that I would be very glad to celebrate our nuptials, but first I wanted to elope for a few years and make sure that it was really going to work.

"How can you know what will be with us?" I asked him. "Are you a prophet that you can see what the future holds?"

"No," he responded, "but you are a scholar of Torah, and a scholar is preferable to a prophet," he told me, quoting from Bava Batra (12a).

"Perhaps you'll tire of me," I pressed on, invoking a William Matthews poem we had read together.

The allusion was not lost on Daniel, who was quick to tell me that I was like a great city to him, or like a park that finds new ways to wear each flounce of light. "Soil doesn't tire of rain," he quoted right back at me just moments before he walked down the aisle.[25] He had the last word, and I could only follow him with my eyes and smile.

At the time we were almost at the end of Bava Batra, where the Mishnah (98b) teaches about a person who accepts a contract from a friend to build a wedding house for his son. In considering the minimum size of house that is acceptable for this purpose, the rabbis draw an analogy to the Temple, which is often used as the model for other structures in rabbinic literature. Rabbi Hanina points out a contradiction between two different measurements of the Temple stated in two verses from the book of Kings—in one verse, the Holy of Holies is thirty cubits high; in another verse, it is twenty. The Talmud resolves this contradiction by explaining that one measurement refers to the height of the Holy of Holies from floor to ceiling, whereas the other measurement starts from the tops of the cherubs, which were ten cubits tall, and goes up to the ceiling. But why would one opt to measure from the tops of the cherubs rather than from the floor? The Talmud answers that this way of measuring comes to teach that all thirty cubits of the Holy of Holies were as empty as the uppermost twenty because the cherubs took up no physical space.

As the Talmud goes on to relate, the cherubs were "suspended in a miracle" (99a), hovering in spiritual space alone. This phrase spoke to me as someone who lives very much in my own head, walking through the world with my nose in a book and forgetting to turn off the stove until I come to the end of the chapter. Daniel has wide-ranging intellectual interests, but he also knows how to drive a car, change a tire, and unclog a drain. My fears notwithstanding, I felt fortunate to be joining my life with someone who shares my intellectual and spiritual depths but is also practical and down-to-earth. We would both fill our home with books, I trusted, but Daniel would be the one to ensure I did not burn it down.

The Talmud then explains that part of the miraculous positioning of the cherubs was due to the fact that their wingspans alone were equivalent to the entire width of the Holy of Holies. Where, then, were their bodies? The rabbis offer several possible answers: perhaps they stood on a diagonal, or perhaps they stood with their wings overlapping, or perhaps they stood with their wings protruding from the center of their backs like chickens. It is a delightfully whimsical passage, blending the profound and the particular, the momentous and the mundane—as marriage does, too. And it relates to questions of how to share space—how to make room for another person, and how to let another person into your space. That this space is the Holy of Holies is not incidental. I was privileged that Daniel was making room for me in his life. And although I was not without considerable trepidation as we stood on the precipice of our new life together, I remained hopeful that the wedding house we were building would always be a shared and sacred space.

SANHEDRIN

~≋~

Another Lifetime

I LEARNED TRACTATE SANHEDRIN DURING OUR FIRST
year of marriage, one of the happiest years I can remember. The
tractate focuses on the administration of justice in Jewish society,
including the composition of civil and criminal courts, the role of
the king and the judge, and the forms of capital punishment.
Friends joked with me that the Talmud's emphasis on the value of
compromise in judicial proceedings surely came in handy during
the first year of marriage, a time of learning to live together and
make sacrifices for the sake of each other. But it's not really true.
During our first year of marriage Daniel and I never argued, not
even once; having met and married relatively late in life, we were
both just so happy to have found that person whose needs we
would gladly accommodate. It was a blissful prelapsarian stage in
which, free of the stresses of raising children, we could simply enjoy the miracle of our togetherness—all the while learning about
stoning, hanging, decapitation, and the Talmud's other forms of
punishment for the most heinous of crimes.

We spent much of our first year of marriage studying Talmud

together. Neither of us enjoyed household chores, so we developed a system whereby one of us—generally Daniel—washed the dishes or cleaned the floor, while the other—generally me—read daf yomi aloud. This way, what might otherwise feel like a burden was lightened by the pleasures of Torah and togetherness. One night I read aloud to Daniel the Talmudic debate in the opening pages of Sanhedrin (6b) about whether absolute justice is possible in our imperfect world, a discussion that lays the theological foundation for the tractate. The Talmudic sage Rabbi Eliezer, the son of Rabbi Yose HaGlili, pits Moses against Aaron as straw men. Moses strove for absolute justice and lived by the motto, "Let the law cut through the mountain," believing that the iron rule of law could break through the dirt and stone of this world. Aaron, in contrast, was devoted to the pursuit of peace and advocated instead for compromise, settlement, and accommodation. Moses was a man of truth, but Aaron was a man of peace.

I'm not sure whom I side with in this debate, but Daniel, to be sure, is in Aaron's camp. He is not one to pick a fight or provoke, nor does he allow himself to go to bed angry. "When our love was strong," the Talmud states on the next page of Sanhedrin, quoting a folk proverb, "we could sleep on the tip of a sword. But now that our love is no longer strong, even a bed of sixty *amot* [the length of a forearm] is not wide enough for us" (7a). When we first got married, we slept on a mattress on the floor until we had time to buy a bed. It was only a bit more comfortable than the tip of a sword, but we hardly noticed.

I was, to a large extent, the same person I had been when I was married to Paul, but the dynamic between Daniel and me was completely different. A teacher once told me that the key to a happy marriage is the ability to recognize that the traits that drive you most crazy about your spouse are expressions of the very same traits you love most about him or her. It frustrated Daniel—as I'm sure it frustrated Paul—when I left the artichokes to boil for hours on end, so absorbed in my novel that I did not notice when the whole apartment began to smell like burnt vegetable matter because all the water had evaporated from the pot. But Daniel recognized that my carelessness is bound up in my passion and my ability to lose myself in something I love; that my rich intellectual life goes hand in hand with my disregard for practicalities; that the woman who can't be bothered to learn the art of makeup is the same woman who won't notice if the dishes were thoroughly cleaned or if the floor was swept after dinner. I may not tie the sandwiches to the handlebars properly, but I'll definitely have a great book of poetry in my backpack—one that we have both not read and can enjoy together even if our picnic lunch lies strewn by the roadside several kilometers back.

Daniel took my faults in stride and even jested about them, dancing around the kitchen with me while we waited for the pasta to boil (after I'd ruined the fish we were supposed to be eating), and graciously putting on earplugs when I practiced chanting my Torah reading aloud for a solid twenty minutes. He sent me e-mails in iambic pentameter, challenged me to identify his allusions to Yeats and Stevens, read copies of my best college papers and shared his with me. Endlessly creative in his affections, he called me by silly nicknames, surprised me with tickets to outdoor concerts of ancient liturgical poetry, and took me at dusk to see the Old City walls illuminated as if by magic lantern in a summer light festival.

Later we referred to that newlywed year as "another lifetime" because so much of what we did together became impossible once our children were born. Instead of a honeymoon, we went on long weekend trips to London (for a wedding) and Paris (to visit friends), coordinating our tourism with daf yomi. While we were in the Tower of London we studied Sanhedrin's laws about how a person is hanged, and at the Palais de Justice we reviewed the procedure for interrogating a witness. Back in Jerusalem we hosted Shabbat meals for various groups of friends featuring

Talmud-themed dishes such as Reish LaQuiche—a quiche named for the sage Reish Lakish, who sold himself as a gladiator in his youth but then reformed his ways and became a prominent Torah scholar—or a dessert consisting of a cup of pomegranate seeds in a glass that we introduced simply as "Rabbi Yohanan," since Rabbi Yohanan's beauty is compared to a glass of pomegranate seeds in the sunlight. Through it all, we attended the morning daf yomi classes together, where we gave nicknames to the various older men who comprised the rest of the class: "the bear," a warm and fuzzy man with a thick beard who asked all the best questions; "the dentist," who reminded us of Mr. Dussel from Anne Frank; and "the laureate," who resembled a classic portrait of Wordsworth. After class, we each headed to work, though I stopped first at the pool.

Beset now with a broken toe, I swam instead of jogging. I had first started swimming years earlier, when I'd broken my foot in the middle of tractate Yoma and needed a new form of exercise. I became a member of the Olympic-size swimming pool that was conveniently located on the ground floor of the office building that housed our literary agency; the window above my desk overlooked the pool, so I watched children careen down the twisty waterslide and land in the water with a delighted splash as I answered my e-mails.

The Talmud in Sanhedrin (17b) speaks of all the institutions that must exist in a particular city in order for a Torah scholar to live there. The first is a civil and criminal court, which explains why this discussion appears in tractate Sanhedrin. But there are nine others: a charity fund, a synagogue, a bathroom, a doctor, a bloodletter, a scribe, a butcher, a schoolteacher, and a public bath. The pool was my equivalent of the public bath; I could no sooner imagine living in a pool-less Jerusalem than in a city in which Torah study is not a preeminent value.

I couldn't figure out a way to study Talmud while swimming, but even in the pool, my mind was never empty. I left photocopied poems encased in a protective plastic sleeve at the edge of the pool and memorized them as I swam. There is something about the end-stopped nature of poetry (in which each line comes to an end at a fixed point) that is akin to swimming in a pool, where one has to turn around after each length. When I got to the edge of the pool, I stole a glance at the next line and then cut back under-water, stroking to the rhythm of the poem's meter reverberating in my head. This was how I memorized all of Edwin Arlington Robinson's "Eros Turannos," regaling Daniel after each swim with another stanza of the poem's stormy passion and aquatic imagery: "Though like waves breaking it may be, / Or like a changed famil-iar tree, / Or like a stairway to the sea, / Where down the blind are driven."[26]

Other days I reviewed the weekly Torah reading while swim-ming laps. The Torah is divided into fifty-four portions that are chanted each Shabbat of the year (and sometimes combined). Each portion is in turn divided into seven *aliyot*—the plural of aliyah, Hebrew for "ascent," since one person is called to ascend to the Torah for each aliyah. At the time I chanted at least one aliyah each Shabbat at my local egalitarian minyan. Daniel prayed elsewhere, at an Orthodox minyan down the street, but he over-heard me practicing all week long (earplugs notwithstanding). By the end of the week, I usually knew the aliyah more or less by heart and could chant it in my head underwater. I dreamed of inventing a pool that would enable me not just to review but also to learn my Torah reading while swimming. The pool would have seven lanes, one corresponding to each aliyah of that week's To-rah portion. (Torah reading is also known as *leyning*, from the Yiddish word for "reading," and so each lane would double as a *leyn*.) A series of overhead projectors would flash the words of each aliyah onto the bottom pool surface of each lane so that the swimmer could follow along as she made her way face-down through the water. This way, swimmers could choose their lanes according to what they were leyning.

I think about what the Talmudic sages would have made of my leyning pool. In Sanhedrin (101a) they teach that one should not recite biblical verses in secular contexts, lest Torah become regarded as something frivolous. The rabbis speak specifically of the Song of Songs, the Bible's book of erotic poetry, which they worry will become a mockery if read as anything other than sacred writ. I imagine the sages would have been none too pleased by my chanting Torah in a bathing suit in the Jerusalem public pool. Many waters cannot quench my reverence for Torah, I imagined myself reassuring them, nor can rivers or pools sweep it away.

⁓

The summer after we got married I had the chance to share my love of Torah with a group of American high school students when I took my first serious teaching job. I do not think of myself as a teacher. I tend to prefer to work in quiet solitude, alone in the library with a book I am reading, translating, or editing. But the Talmudic sages extol the value of teaching, asserting that one who learns but does not teach resembles a fragrant myrtle tree in the deserted wilderness (Rosh Hashanah 23a)—perhaps the rabbinic equivalent of the Buddhist koan about the tree falling in the forest with no one around. In Sanhedrin the sage Reish Lakish—the one for whom our Shabbat quiche was named—asserts that anyone who teaches his friend's child Torah is regarded as if he fashioned him (99b), since a person is shaped by the Torah he learns. And at the beginning of the next tractate, Makkot (10a), the Talmud cites Rabbi Yehuda HaNasi's oft-quoted assertion that he learned much from his teachers, even more from his colleagues, and most of all from his students—and I suppose this was true for me as well.

Though I had come prepared to teach Talmud, my students wanted to talk about existential religious questions. An elite group of high school juniors accepted to the summer program for their academic merit and intellectual aptitude, they would stay up all night arguing about God, faith, the divinity of the Torah, and the problem of theodicy. In the mornings, arriving at class exhausted and bleary-eyed, they pressed me to help them think it all through: If God exists, why is there so much evil in the world? What really happened on Mount Sinai? Do we have souls, and what happens to them after we die?

I listened patiently, taking the time to hear them out. My earnest and troubled students assumed that I had figured out all the answers for myself, because if I hadn't, how could I possibly concentrate on anything else? I tried to explain to them that yes, these were all good questions, but they no longer kept me up at night. It is not that when we grow up, we stop thinking critically, or that we miraculously find all the answers. But on some level, as Rilke puts it, we learn to live our way into the answers—in a way that does not stop us from going on with the rest of our lives.

Fortunately, though, I knew what to say in response because many of these questions are conveniently addressed at the end of tractate Sanhedrin (90a). Following on the heels of the Talmud's discussion of capital punishment, the final chapter of Sanhedrin discusses those sins that are so grave that they deny the individual a place in the world to come. These sins are primarily lapses of faith, including denying the divinity of the Torah and denying that the dead will be revived.

Invoking the Mishnah in Sanhedrin, I told my students that both the divinity of Torah and the revival of the dead are fundamental tenets of my own faith. I believe that Torah is divine. But for me this does not mean that God handed the entire Written and Oral Torah to Moses on Mount Sinai. Rather, Sinai is the human record of an encounter with God. As a human record, this document is historically contingent: it was written at a particular historical moment, and reflects the biases of its time. This record has had to be adapted to later generations, both to changing historical circumstances and to evolving theological understandings. Those adaptations are known as *midrash*—the creative commentary that reworks and retells the Bible so as to render it ever relevant.

In high school my students had surely learned, as I had, about the difference between natural numbers and rational numbers. Natural numbers are integers: 1, 2, 3, etc. Rational numbers are the decimals in between, including 1.1, 1.12, 1.23378. Both sets are infinite, but only the rational numbers are infinitely dense, meaning that there are an infinite number of rational numbers between any two natural numbers. Torah and midrash are similar. Between any two words—or occasionally even letters—in the Torah, there are an infinite number of *midrashim*, or reinterpretations, that are possible. The Talmud in Sanhedrin captures this notion in an exegetical reading of a verse from Jeremiah (23:29): "Behold My word is like fire—declares the Lord—and like a hammer that shatters rock." The sages comment, "Just as a hammer strikes innumerable sparks off the rock, so too does a single verse have many meanings" (Sanhedrin 34a). When studying and teaching Torah, we are meant to generate sparks.

And yet perhaps sometimes there can be too many sparks. The Talmud at the end of Sanhedrin (99a) explains that even someone who challenges the divinity of any single verse in the Torah is denied a place in the world to come. "Yes," said one of my students, "but what about the verse that calls my sexual practice an abomination?" I could identify with the impulse to deny certain verses; obviously there are parts of the Torah that are more problematic to a modern, egalitarian, pluralistic sensibility. Yet I see no reason to excise particular verses because midrash offers a ready alternative. Although there is a venerable midrashic tradition that must be taken into account, Torah is infinitely dense, and I have faith in our creative reading strategies. There is a fine line, I recognize, between extolling the creative possibilities of midrash and declaring that Torah can say anything we want it to. Even so, I believe too much in the former to allow the fear of the latter to hold me back.

My students, though, were not satisfied. "But how can you believe in the Torah when it has been so clearly contradicted by modern science? Aren't the miracles of the Bible scientifically impossible?" I told them that I did not experience this tension, because religion and science belong to two separate realms. We can look to science to answer how the world was created and to religion to answer why the world was created. Science can say if the universe is expanding or contracting, but only religion can inspire us to connect to other people in meaningful ways so that the universe does not seem so vast and lonely. I do not question my faith or subject it to rigorous scientific analysis because the proof is in the pudding, or in the Shabbat noodle kugel: my life is richer and more meaningful because I am in an ongoing relationship with God. I perform *mitzvot*—religious commandments— because they are a way of engaging in that relationship. A mitzvah is an opportunity to encounter the divine. Saying a blessing before eating is a way of involving God in the meal, and praying in the morning is a way of infusing the day with holiness. Whenever possible, I try not to pass up those opportunities. Granted, not every mitzvah offers an obvious path to God, but I have enough faith in the system as a whole to suspend my doubt about some of its particulars.

Perhaps there is an element of blind faith involved, but I believe that the more I live my life in accordance with God's commandments, the more I will feel God's presence. Conversely, the more I doubt and question and run away from the tradition, the farther away God will seem. And so just as each morning I wake up and lift up the shades to let the sun stream in to my bedroom, I also try, each day, to open the gates of my heart and let God in.

☙

The other lapse of faith identified in Sanhedrin as being so grave as to deny a person a place in the world to come is the sin of saying that there is no basis in the Torah for the notion of the revival of the dead. As the Talmud explains, this is a case of the punishment fitting the crime; surely any person who does not believe in an afterlife in which the dead will be revived should be denied a place in that afterlife.

Although the Bible makes no mention of an afterlife, rabbinic tradition refers to an end of days in which the Messiah will come and the dead will be revived. Perhaps the revival of the dead is simply another way of saying that what we see is not all we get. Given all the injustice and oppression in our world—given all the bad things that happen to good people, to paraphrase the title of a book that was on my father's bookshelf when we were growing up—I must believe that there is another realm in which the scales of justice are recalibrated. At the same time, this does not absolve me of the responsibility to pursue justice in this world. I think of the messianic era as more of a challenge to humanity to pursue our ideals than as a divine promise that these ideals will someday be realized. And it seems that the Talmud does not disagree, at least according to one rather fabulous story in tractate Sanhedrin (98a).

The Talmud relates that Rabbi Yehoshua ben Levi once asked the prophet Elijah when the Messiah would arrive. "Ask him," said Elijah, and he directed Rabbi Yehoshua ben Levi to the gates of Rome, where the Messiah sat among the sick and wretched changing the bandages on their wounds. Rabbi Yehoshua ben Levi dutifully set off for Rome, where the Messiah told him that he would come "today." Rabbi Yehoshua ben Levi returned to Elijah and told him that the Messiah had promised to come that day, but had not held true to his promise. Elijah explained that the Messiah was in fact quoting a verse from Psalms: "Today, if you will heed His voice" (Psalms 95:7). That is, the Messiah will come the very same day that people do God's work in the world. This work seems to involve sitting among the sick and wretched at the gates of the city and the margins of society, helping them find healing. The notion of the Messiah, then, is a metaphor for the redeemed world to which we aspire. The world will not be redeemed when the Messiah comes; rather, the Messiah will come when we redeem the world.

The modern Israeli philosopher Yeshayahu Leibovitz wrote that a false Messiah is any Messiah who has already come. The messianic era is an aspiration and an ideal, rather than a stage of history. And so I strive to do my small part to hasten the Messiah, a charge I associate with recognizing and respecting the common humanity of all my fellow human beings. The Mishnah (Sanhedrin 37a) teaches that all coins are minted using a single stamp and come out identical to one another, but all human beings are created according to the same template as Adam, and yet no two people are identical. For this reason, says the Mishnah, anyone who destroys a single human life is regarded as if he has destroyed an entire world, and anyone who saves a human life is as if he has saved an entire world. By the same token, every human being can say, "The world was created for me." Each person alone is sufficient grounds to create the world, and no one may say, as we learn later in Sanhedrin, "My blood is redder than yours" (74a).

It is not by chance that these issues arise in tractate Sanhedrin, with its discussion of when capital punishment is warranted. According to the rabbis, respect for the inalienable human dignity endowed by the divine image in which all humans are created does not invalidate the justness of capital punishment. Trying to balance the two values, the rabbis go to great lengths to preserve the integrity of the human body even while administering capital punishment. The punishment of burning, for instance, involves pouring hot lead down the throat of the condemned while leaving the exterior of the body intact.

When I think about the implications of being created in the image of God, I am reminded of the class pictures we used to take in elementary school every year. The photographer first took a picture of the entire class, and then each student was called in for an individual portrait. Before taking the individual shot, the photographer directed his assistant to try out various backgrounds to achieve the ideal contrast. First they hung up a white curtain behind me, but it made me look too pale. Next they tried red, but that clashed with my pink dress. Then they tried a light blue, and the photographer decided that yes, this was the best background for me. I came to realize that not everyone looks beautiful against every background, and not everyone shines in every context. But each person contains a spark of the divine, and so I retain the faith that for each person there is a context in which he would stand out. Even if I never see that person in that context, I try to treat him with respect and dignity because I am confident that such a context exists. My belief in the divine spark in every human being is a direct corollary of my belief in God, and it is just as fundamental to my faith.

The challenge of constantly bearing in mind the dignity and integrity of a fellow human being is, in a sense, the essence of marriage. I used to think of marriage as a goal to be attained, but now I recognize that the ideal marriage, like Leibovitz's Messiah, is a lifelong aspiration. This is certainly the case for Daniel and me. Our rapturous first year together was followed by significant challenges, but I remain grateful to God for the opportunity to build my life with such a wonderful human being. Indeed, the mere fact that we have merited to spend our life together seems proof of divine providence.

Ultimately I believe in God because I cannot live my life any other way. True, I can't prove the existence of God in a way that would satisfy all my teenage summer students. Likewise, I cannot explain why following each and every commandment has the effect of making me a better person and the world a better place. But the totality of living a life infused with reverence for God and the study of God's Torah has enriched me in ways I can only begin to fathom, and in life's most joyous and wondrous moments it seems impossible to conceive of a world without divinity. I do not know if this is sufficient to merit me a place in the world to come, but it is certainly sufficient to inspire me each day anew to make a place for God in this world.

MAKKOT / SHEVUOT

～❧

Sarah Ivreinu

TRACTATES MAKKOT AND SHEVUOT CONTINUE SANHEDRIN'S discussion of courtroom procedure, focusing specifically on the testimony of witnesses and the punishment for capital crimes. At the end of tractate Makkot (24b) the Talmud describes an arresting scene in which four rabbis are ascending to Jerusalem in the wake of the Temple's destruction. When they arrive at Mt. Scopus, which overlooks the city, they rip their clothes in mourning. Then, when they advance to the Temple Mount, they espy a fox scampering out of the Holy of Holies. Three of the rabbis begin to cry, but Rabbi Akiva instead bursts out in laughter. "Why are you laughing?" the other three ask him. "Why are you crying?" Rabbi Akiva responds.

The three rabbis explain the obvious reason for their tears—the holy site of connection between God and Israel has been ravaged. Rabbi Akiva, in turn, explains that he is laughing because he is reminded of a verse from Isaiah (8:2) in which the prophet calls upon two witnesses, Uriah and Zechariah. Uriah, who lived during the First Temple period, offered a prophecy of doom and destruction: "Zion shall be plowed as a field, and Jerusalem shall become heaps of ruins" (Micah 3:12). Zechariah, in contrast, offered a prophecy of hope: "There shall yet be old men and women in the squares of Jerusalem, each with a staff in his hand because of great age. And the streets of the city shall be crowded with boys and girls playing" (Zechariah 8:4). According to Rabbi Akiva, Isaiah's conjoining of the prophecies of Uriah and Zechariah suggests that the latter is dependent on the former: until Zion is plowed, Jerusalem cannot experience a renaissance. And so now that Uriah's prophecy of doom has been fulfilled, Rabbi Akiva is confident that Zechariah's prophecy of hope will come true as well.

Rabbi Akiva's optimism reminds me of my dear friend Sarah Ivreinu, "Sarah our blind one," as I came to refer to her. I met Sarah while volunteering for a charitable organization that matches young visitors with the elderly and homebound. Sarah, in point of fact, is neither. In spite of her blindness, she maintains quite an active lifestyle: she volunteers as a receptionist in an office in town, attends regular classes and lectures, and shops every Thursday with a friend in the shuk, where I would occasionally run into her.

For about four years—from shortly after my divorce until a year after our son was born—I visited with Sarah every Wednesday afternoon, rain or shine. We met on the sidewalk outside her apartment in a run-down neighborhood at the edge of the city. From there we set off on a walk together through the local streets, ending up at the same shady green bench (although she is blind, she always insisted that we sit only on green benches) where we rested our legs before I accompanied her back home again, chatting all the while. Sarah, who came to Israel from Persia as a young child, is from a different world than I—she is deeply religious (there are days when I look at what I am not wearing and thank my lucky stars that she can't see me), extremely superstitious, terrified of anyone who is not Jewish, and utterly unaware of many of the pleasures I take for granted. I once brought her

Victoria's Secret scented body lotion as a present from America, and when I helped her rub it on her hands she looked at me as if she had died and gone to heaven. Another day, when it was too rainy to walk, I took her out for coffee at her local pizza parlor, and she played with the plastic spoon that came with her coffee and asked me if I thought anyone would mind if she kept it as a souvenir.

Sarah was my therapist during those four years, though I'm not even sure she knows what a therapist is. In the wake of my divorce, friends and family members encouraged me to seek professional help, but I was resistant. I am dubious of the efficacy of therapy for me. It seems to entail a pledge of honesty that I have a hard time keeping. I am, by nature, a storyteller; when I chronicle the past I inevitably craft it. And so I don't think I could commit to speaking truthfully in a therapeutic context—let alone in a courtroom.

The Talmud in Shevuot explains that the courts go according to what a witness says rather than what a witness means to say. For instance, the rabbis consider the case of a witness who swears to have seen a "camel flying through the air." Ravina suggests that perhaps this witness saw a large bird, and called it a camel. The other rabbis respond that we follow a person's "mouth," not his "mind" (29a). But what about therapy, where the mouth is supposed to be a means of giving voice to the contents of the mind? I worried about all of the uncertainty that therapy seems to entail. A therapist is not like an eye doctor who gives a vision test and a prescription for glasses; with therapy, the test questions are ongoing, the prescriptions are vague, and often the world looks even blurrier as time goes on.

The Talmud then considers the question of whether women may serve as witnesses (30a), resolving that they may not. The Rabbis invoke a verse from Psalms (45:14): "The honor of a king's daughter is within"; so too should all women confine themselves as much as possible to private spaces. But Sarah bore witness to everything that went on in my life, and she could see even what I could not. She knew about the office politics in our literary agency, the dynamics of my family, the men I had pursued, and those who had pursued me. She was particularly helpful when it came to strategies for getting out of awkward situations, like the time when Omri and Daniel—who knew each other by sight but had never had a proper conversation—audited the same university seminar. I told Sarah about the class and asked her what to do. "Tell Daniel to be a mensch and introduce himself," Sarah advised wisely. Although Jerusalem is a big city, most of the people I know travel in similar circles, and I have Sarah to thank for setting the stage for many more amicable encounters.

The Talmud is no stranger to awkward situations. One of my favorites appears in tractate Shevuot (30b), where Rav Huna's widow is summoned to appear in court before Rav Nahman. Rav Nahman is in a bind; he can't figure out whether he should stand before the woman or not. If he stands, it may appear as if he is partial to her case. But if he doesn't stand, it will appear as if he is failing to show respect to scholars of Torah, since "the wife of a scholar is treated like a scholar." He ponders the matter and finally comes up with a creative solution. He asks his attendant to throw a duck across the courtroom so that it flies in his direction. This way, he will jump up when he sees the duck and will therefore end up standing before Rav Huna's widow without appearing to favor her. Sarah, too, came up with many such "flying ducks," saving me—and Daniel—from potentially uncomfortable encounters.

There was nothing I could not tell Sarah Ivreinu—or almost nothing. I once tried to explain (proceeding cautiously so as to test the waters) that I had "visited" a synagogue in which men and women sat side by side. Judging from her horrified reaction, it was clear that I could never tell her the truth—that I read Torah in a fully egalitarian minyan every Shabbat morning. By the same token, I sometimes had to take her advice with a grain of salt ("Clean his floor and cook him dinner every night—and don't let him touch you until he marries you!"). She encouraged me to pray, and she reminded me each week that I was in her prayers. I was reassured because I had no doubt that if anything had the power to move the heavens, it was the intensity of her fervor.

I've spent my life learning from books, but my visits with Sarah taught me how much I can learn from other people. This is a message of tractate Makkot as well. "How foolish people are," Rava exclaims. "They rise before a Torah scroll, but don't rise before a great man" (22b). There were plenty of reasons to rise before Sarah—because she was wise, and upbeat, and unflappable. Like Rabbi Akiva on the Temple Mount, she taught me to find blessing in the most unlikely situations. One day we were walking down the street and a friend stopped to greet her. Sarah turned to me and said, "Did you see that? People can walk right by me without my noticing, because I can't see them. When they stop to say hi, it's a double kindness." Another day she told me that she had to give thanks to God because her bus stop had been returned to its previous location. The stop had been just outside her home for years, and she'd taught herself to walk the twenty-one steps from her apartment to the curb so that she'd be able to catch the bus to work each morning. But when the stop was moved three blocks away, she could no longer find her way. Her neighbors rallied behind her, petitioning the municipality and carrying posters with her photograph, making her into something of a local celebrity. The stop was restored, and she was able to go back to her normal schedule. For Sarah this was nothing short of miraculous.

Sarah was with me through my divorce from Paul and my marriage to Daniel—she witnessed the devastation of Uriah's prophecy and the redemption of Zechariah's. She afforded me a hopeful perspective in the moments when I most needed it, and she taught me to appreciate and celebrate life's miracles. During our first year of marriage Daniel and I often visited her together, each of us holding on to one of her arms as we walked through the streets of Jerusalem. We watched old men and women lean on their canes, the streets crowded with boys and girls playing together as if in fulfillment of Zechariah's prophecy. Zechariah goes on to ask in the name of God, "Though it will seem impossible to the remnant of this people in those days, shall it also be impossible to Me?" (8:6). As the three of us settled outside on one of the green benches where she and I had sat so many times before, I marveled that it had not been impossible after all.

AVODAH ZARAH / HORAYOT

※

Frost at Midnight

AFTER WE GOT MARRIED, DANIEL AND I MOVED TO ABU Tor, a neighborhood not far from the walls of the Old City of Jerusalem, sacred to three faiths. We would open our windows on summer evenings to hear the chiming of the bells from the Church of the Dormition, the wail of the *muezzin* calling Muslims to prayer, and the crooning voice of a guitar-strumming Israeli pop singer setting ancient Hebrew psalms to modern tempos at a concert in the outdoor amphitheater at Sultan's Pool, just west of Mount Zion. As we sat by our window taking in this polyphonic symphony, we could not help but compare our current milieu to the American melting pot in which we were both raised. We wondered about how different our children's experiences would be from our own, a discussion informed by our study of tractates Avodah Zarah and Horayot.

Avodah Zarah means "strange worship," referring to non-Jewish practices. The tractate deals with the issues that arise when Jews live among and interact with non-Jews. Though the rabbis were writing about Jews living among Romans in the land of

Israel and among Persians in Sasanian Babylonia, the questions
they ask seemed to pertain just as well to my childhood in late-
twentieth-century America, such as: may a Jew get a haircut from
a non-Jewish barber (29a), or eat in a restaurant owned by non-
Jews (37b), or take advantage of sales during the holiday season
(13a)? I was surprised to discover how many aspects common to
the minority experience rendered this tractate relevant to the
Jewish diaspora today.

The first words of Avodah Zarah are *lifnei eideihem*, "before
their holidays," referring to the weeks leading up to the non-
Jewish holiday season, a phrase that makes me think of the candy
canes and "Jingle Bells" ubiquitous during my childhood winters.
My parents took pains to explain to me that candy corn is delicious and fir trees are pretty but Halloween and Christmas are
"not ours." Our world was starkly divided into Jews and everyone
else: the Jews were all family members and friends in school, synagogue, and summer camp; the non-Jews included the custodian
who locked the synagogue doors, the barber who cut my hair, and
the sanitation workers who cleaned the streets. Though we had
non-Jewish neighbors, we lived in sprawling suburbia and did not
know them well; most people we knew by name were Jewish.

As I got older, I became increasingly conscious of being a minority. After nine years in a Jewish day school, I attended a public
high school where I was the only observant Jew. There I was an
emissary of Jewish religion and culture to my Hispanic, African
American, Irish Catholic, and white Protestant classmates and
teachers. I could not act in any of the school plays since they were
all performed on Friday nights and Saturdays, nor could I run
in any Saturday track-and-field meets. I brought my own food for
lunch every day and ate sequestered away in a corner of the library, since I found the smell of the cafeteria so noxious. (At the
time I thought it was the odor of non-kosher meat that I couldn't
stomach, but later I realized that I simply can't abide cafeteria
food.) When I missed school for the Jewish holidays, I would ask

my friend Erin to tell the various teachers why I was out: "Ilana is absent for Shoo—I mean, Shavoo—I forget. Another holiday." My classmates learned about Judaism from me, and I benefited from my exposure to the ethos and practice of American multiculturalism, which taught me to tolerate and appreciate difference without sacrificing my own particularity.

Now that we make our home in Israel, Daniel and I think more about the questions discussed in Horayot, the Talmudic tractate that follows Avodah Zarah. Horayot is about a world in which Jews have sovereignty, taking their instructions from Jewish leaders and Jewish courts. In Horayot the sages consider issues such as: What if the rabbinic authorities permit a woman whose husband has disappeared to remarry, and then her husband is discovered to be alive after all (2a)? What happens when the rabbinic court changes its ruling on how the sabbatical year is observed (4b)? What is the protocol when the leader known as the *nasi* (the same title is used for the president of Israel today) is found to have committed a sin (10a)? These questions make sense in the modern State of Israel, where Jews are the majority culture in spite of being a minority in the broader context of the Middle East.

Abu Tor, where we still live, is technically a "mixed neighborhood," but it is in fact quite segregated—all of our immediate neighbors are Jewish, and there are no Arabs at all on our side of the hill. Daniel and I have little substantive engagement with Arabs, but as we go about our daily routine, we have much casual contact: Arabs deliver our mail, stock our food in the supermarket, fill our prescriptions at the pharmacy, and make our coffee at the local cafe. In each of these encounters, at most a few words are exchanged. Though Arabs and Jews see and affect one another regularly, the two populations lead parallel lives, and real relationships are regrettably rare. As residents of the Jewish state and as the national minority, Israeli Arabs know more about our culture than we do about theirs; certainly there are more Arabs who speak Hebrew than Jews who speak Arabic. But we lack more than just a common language. Arabs and Jews have different news media, different calendars, and different days of rest—their Friday is our Saturday. I imagine that few Arabs have any idea what the Talmud is, just as I have no real notion of what Hadith are. And if there is an equivalent of daf yomi for students of the Quran, I have never heard of it.

As residents of Abu Tor and of Jerusalem more broadly, Daniel and I wonder what sort of multicultural ethic we will bequeath to our children. Certainly they will know that we live among people of diverse faiths—they'll see Arab kids in the local park and watch Christian nuns in starched white habits file by on their way to a local monastery. Daniel attends an Arabic language class every Friday, and at some point our kids will surely sit in on a class or two. But most of their substantive interactions, too, will probably be with Jews; the local public schools where they'll study are entirely Jewish, since Jews and Arabs have separate school systems. That said, I'd like to think that my children will have a much broader concept of what it means to be Jewish than I did. As a child growing up on Long Island, my concept of a Jew was narrowly defined in terms of race and class. Most of the Jewish men I knew were doctors or lawyers, and all were white. But for our children, presumably, being Jewish will connote a much wider range of ethnic and socioeconomic possibilities: they will grow up alongside Jews who are Ethiopian, Persian, Moroccan, and French, and they will interact on a daily basis with Jews who operate cranes and sweep floors, as well as Jews who are policy makers, city officials, and soldiers. How different from my own childhood experiences.

There is so much I took for granted that my children may never enjoy. I developed from a young age a love of reading and learning that Israeli schools do not seem to inculcate. I worry that Daniel and I will have to fight an uphill battle to cultivate intellectual curiosity in this culture in which schools seem to be training grounds for the military, instilling discipline and conformity rather than creativity and passion. Even Israeli preschools seem more regimented than their American counterparts. There our children will learn to sit quietly in a classroom with thirty-five students and one teacher, and they will also be exposed to different children's classics: they will sing "Ooga Ooga" rather than "Ring around the Rosie," and they'll read the Israeli children's book about Pluto the dog from Kibbutz Megido rather than Lyle Lyle Crocodile from East 88th Street.

When they are just a few months old, we will take our children to the American consulate in Jerusalem to claim their American citizenship, but their time in America will be limited to annual summer visits with grandparents and cousins. Although we speak English at home and hope they will grow up reciting the British and American poetry we will teach them, they will likely not speak English with their own children. And so we are concerned for our children's future, but we are even more concerned for the future of their children and their children's children.

Many of my peers are also concerned for the future generations of their Israeli families, but I suspect their concerns are primarily existential: Will there still be an Israel? Will the occupation dismantle our society from within, or will our enemies destroy us from without? Having actively chosen to make my home in Israel, I share these fears, but I have philosophical concerns as well. So much of who I am and what matters to me has been informed by the education I have received—the novels I love and the poetry I memorize. This rich literary heritage is not just a conduit for deep values, but also the lens through which I view the world and the reason I write sonnets and limericks about pages of the Talmud. I wonder if the marginal notes in my volumes of Talmud will mean anything to my children and grandchildren, who will have such different literary associations.

For all that I want our children to receive the riches of our American heritage, when it comes to myself, I am forever striving to become more Israeli. I read the news in Hebrew, keep up with Israeli fiction, and am slowly developing a tougher, more assertive exterior. Still, I wonder to what extent I have succeeded in my efforts at integration. At this point I have spent twenty-six years in America and over a decade in Israel, and it is hard to know which part of my identity is more salient. I still keep up with *The New Yorker*, which my mother saves and brings each time she visits, and I am so regularly in touch with my family in Eastern Standard Time that my brain automatically calculates the seven-hour difference. I lived in Israel for three full years before I officially made aliyah, perhaps a testament to how much I still felt rooted in the diaspora.

If I have become Israeli, I am an Israeli with full consciousness of the diasporic road not taken. The Talmud in Horayot (11b) teaches that a ruler who sins must bring a he-goat sacrifice as atonement. Rebbi, the leader of the Jewish people in the land of Israel, asks if he himself must bring a he-goat—that is, he asks if he is considered the ruler of the Jews. Rav Hisda responds by putting him in his place: "Your rival is in Babylonia." That is, although Rebbi is the leader of the Jewish community in Israel, there is a competing community in Babylonia with a leader of its own. For me, too, living in Israel has meant that I have a heightened consciousness of Jewish life in the diaspora and of all the cultural riches that I will have to make a conscious and deliberate effort to pass on.

Tractate Horayot (13b) recounts a struggle for power that takes place in the study house. Rabbi Meir and Rabbi Natan seek to oust Rabban Shimon ben Gamliel, whom they regard as unfit to serve as patriarch, a title used for the leader of the Jewish community in the land of Israel. Plotting against him, they decide that they will catch him unprepared and quiz him on the obscure tractate Uktzin, which they are sure he does not know well. They explain that if there is any part of Torah that the patriarch does not know, then he is not worthy of his title. Rabbi Meir explains his reasoning by quoting from Psalms (106:2): "Who shall utter the mighty acts of God? Who can declare all his praises?" They read this verse as meaning that the only person fit to utter the mighty acts of God and serve as the leader of the Jewish community is someone who knows how to utter *all* His praises, that is, someone who knows all of God's Torah—even Uktzin. Many Israeli students probably relate to Wordsworth as students of Talmud relate to Uktzin—something within the known universe but remote and recondite. I wonder what my children and grandchildren will know of my beloved Romantics. Will they be able to write an essay about memory and loss in "Tintern Abbey," a poem that captures these experiences so deeply? And if not, what will be the "abundant recompense"?

Living in Israel means that Torah is a fundamental part of our identities and of our relationship with one another. And it is this legacy, above all, that we wish to bequeath to our children: Zion not as an experiment in Jewish self-government but as a rich and vibrant hub of Jewish learning. I would like our children to grow up in Jerusalem, where the billboards are plastered not only with movie and theater advertisements but also with announcements about rabbis teaching classes at various synagogues around town. The Talmud in Avodah Zarah contrasts theaters and circuses with Torah learning (18b), and I can only wish that our children, like their parents, will want to spend their leisure time engaged in study. I hope that living in the promised land and in the land where the Mishnaic sages established their study houses will deepen their encounters with Torah and Talmud. "A person does not learn Torah except from a place where his heart desires it," the rabbis teach in Avodah Zarah (19a), and for both Daniel and me, Israel has been that place.

Israel—and Jerusalem in particular—enables us to remain true to the Jewish religious milieus in which we feel most

comfortable. Daniel grew up attending an Orthodox synagogue where men and women sit separately and where certain
ritual roles are limited only to men. In my father's Conservative synagogue, in contrast, men and women sit side by side and
participate equally in all parts of the service. If Daniel and I
lived in suburban America, where there are rarely two synagogues within walking distance of each other, we probably
would have had to choose one affiliation or the other. But here
in Jerusalem, where Jewish life is so rich, the synagogue is really
just a place to pray and not a Jewish center. Like several couples
we know, we have each been able to remain active members of
our own synagogues while still being part of the same social
circle.

During the first year of our marriage we spoke about what
our children's Judaism would look like—would their concept of
synagogue be one in which men and women sit separately or together? Would they grow up with images of women wrapped in
prayer shawls, or would this ritual garment be coded male for
them? As a feminist, I considered it important that both my sons
and my daughters be exposed to egalitarian prayer; I was as concerned about my daughters being excluded as I was about my sons
taking part in that exclusion. And so we decided that we would
take turns bringing our children to synagogue with us. The Talmud in Avodah Zarah (19a) cautions that "anyone who learns
Torah from only one teacher will never see blessing." We like the
notion that our children will have multiple models of how to live
a meaningful and committed Jewish spiritual life, and we feel
fortunate that we live in a city that has made this possible.

By raising our children in Israel we hope that they will internalize the rhythm of Jewish life—that they will watch the city
slow each week to the pace of Shabbat and that they will know
which holiday is approaching based on the storefront displays:
jelly donuts in the bakeries before Chanukah; costumes in the
toy stores during the month before Purim; matzah and hard,

stale Pesach cookies lining the supermarket aisles as spring sets in. Even if they do not go to a religious preschool, they will mold candelabras out of clay for Chanukah; they will reenact the story of the ten plagues before Pesach; and they will roast potatoes over bonfires for Lag Ba'Omer, a day celebrating the spiritual light of the Talmudic sage Rabbi Shimon bar Yohai. In Israel these are not just Jewish holidays but also part of the national culture. I am grateful that for our children, living Jewishly will be as natural as the air they breathe (including those smoky Lag Ba'Omer bonfires), permeating every fiber of their being.

We hope, too, that by growing up in Israel, our children will develop a sense of collective responsibility for the Jewish people at large and for Israeli society in particular. The Talmud in Horayot (12b) mentions the anointed priest in charge of encouraging the Jewish soldiers on the eve of battle. Our children, if they are of sound body and mind, will be expected to join the army or take part in the national service corps. If nothing else, these experiences should give them a strong stake in the welfare of the State of Israel. We hope our children will discover the social and political issues about which they are passionate and will take part in the relevant public discourse—each in their own way working to create a more just and ethical Jewish society.

In "Frost at Midnight," Coleridge addresses his infant son slumbering at his side, telling him that he will grow up in a very different environment from his father's: "Thou shalt learn far other lore / And in far other scenes!" Whereas Coleridge grew up "in the great city . . . and saw naught lovely but the sky and stars," he rears his son in the countryside, "by lakes and sandy shores, beneath the crags of ancient mountain, and beneath the clouds."[27] The poet celebrates his ability to bequeath a utopian childhood to his son, who will never know the drudgery of dark city schoolrooms with their stern preceptors. Our children, too, will grow up in a very different environment from the one in which their American-born parents were reared. But perhaps one day it will be not we who feel the need to bequeath so much of our literary and cultural heritage to our children, but our children who will teach us about the "far other lore" of the society in which they were born and raised. Most of our closest friends here in Israel are American immigrants like ourselves, and there are many aspects of the local culture that remain a mystery to us. Perhaps through our children we will learn the latest Hebrew slang popular among their peers or finally understand the various units of the Israeli army and what they do.

Of course, I cannot know where our children will ultimately choose to build their own lives and whether it is the questions of Avodah Zarah or Horayot—of diaspora or national sovereignty—that will speak to them more deeply. At the end of "Frost at Midnight," Coleridge blesses his son: "Therefore all seasons shall be sweet to thee, whether the summer clothe the general earth with greenness, or the redbreast sit and sing. . . ." I hope that Daniel and I will merit to raise children who experience both the richness of Judaism and the value of living in a multiethnic society regardless of where they make their homes. Whether it is the hot Jerusalem sun that beats down on them or the New England redbreast that sings in their backyard, may the seasons of their lives always be full of sweetness.

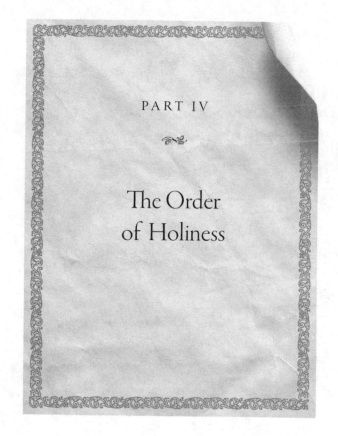

PART IV

The Order
of Holiness

ZEVAHIM / MENAHOT / HULLIN

❧

Holy Eating

IF THERE WAS ANY QUALITY THAT DANIEL AND I WERE certain we did not want to pass on to our children, it was my vegetarianism. I did not think of myself as a vegetarian until I met Daniel and joined his family at a Shabbat table laden with roast beef, rack of lamb, and sautéed duck, none of which I could identify. His mother noticed that I filled my plate with rice and broccoli and asked if I was vegetarian. "I guess so," I told her, wondering about it myself. I did not avoid meat as a matter of identity or principle, but as a general aesthetic preference: why pick the flesh off the wing of a dead bird when there was fresh quinoa salad on the table? I became a full-fledged vegetarian only a year later, after learning Seder Kodshim, the order of the Talmud that deals primarily with sacrifice and ritual slaughter.

Sacrificial worship ceased to be an element of Jewish religious life following the destruction of the Second Temple in the first century, but this did not prevent the rabbis of the Talmud from expounding at great length on the details of the sacrificial rites—both as a way of commemorating the practice and as an expression of longing for a redeemed world in which sacrifice would be restored to Zion. The first tractate of Seder Kodshim, Zevahim, is essentially a giant barbecue. We learn about which animals may be burnt on the altar and what happens if they are left to burn for too long or sacrificed with improper intentions or accidentally mixed with other sacrificial offerings. The Talmud enumerates four primary sacrificial rites: slaughtering the animal, receiving its blood in a basin, carrying the animal to the altar, and sprinkling the blood on the cover of the ark. Sacrifice was such a bloody business that there were holes in the floor of the Temple intended for draining the excess blood, which would flow into the Kidron river valley (Zevahim 35a). And the pile of ashes from a day's worth of sacrifices grew so high that it had to be cleared off first thing every morning.

I learned about how the priest would kill sacrificial birds by a process known as *melika,* slicing the neck with his nail while taking care not to sever it completely (Zevahim 64b). That was when I decided that I could no longer eat my mother's chicken soup, my last carnivorous vestige, which I'd previously permitted myself because it didn't look anything like flesh and—well—because it was delicious, and it made my mother happy. I realized that chicken soup, too, was once a thing with feathers. In consciously renouncing flesh-eating I was perhaps bringing myself back to that antediluvian stage before God permitted Noah to eat meat (Genesis 9:3), that idyllic era in which the trees of the garden provided for all of humanity's needs. At the very least I was returning to the period of the Israelites' desert wanderings, when, according to Rabbi Yishmael, they were forbidden to slaughter "lustful meat," that is, meat that they desired to eat for their own nourishment and pleasure, without any sacrificial component. Rabbi Akiva disagrees, arguing that although the Israelites had not yet been given the laws of ritual slaughter, they were permitted to stab animals with a knife—a process known as *nehira*—and consume the flesh (Hullin 17a). I was prepared to engage neither in slaughtering nor in stabbing, and I decided that I would simply abstain from meat altogether.

My aversion to meat-eating has nothing to do with any affinity for animals. I live in fear of the cats that leap from the municipal garbage bins (known as "frogs" in Hebrew because they are big and green) when I try to throw out the trash. But as I made my way through Seder Kodshim, I was struck that alongside countless passages about bloody dead animals and their entrails, the Talmud also contains several stories and legends about animals who are very much alive, many of them so outlandish that later generations of scholars struggled with whether to dismiss these tales as fanciful or to regard them as philosophical allegory, since they could not possibly be taken at face value. There is the discussion at the end of tractate Zevahim (113b) about how the mythical *re'em*—a kind of unicorn—survived the flood; surely it could not fit in Noah's ark, since, as Rabba bar bar Hana testified, "I once saw a young unicorn and it was as big as Mount Tabor!" The rabbis suggest that perhaps Noah inserted the tip of its nose into the ark. But then wouldn't the waters of the flood plunge the unicorn up and down, another rabbi asks? No, reassures Reish Lakish, they tied its horn to the ark and thus it was spared from drowning. But weren't the waters of the flood boiling as punishment for the hot passion with which people sinned? Yes, but the waters adjacent to the ark were cooled so that the unicorn could survive, just as the waters of the ocean depths remained cool for the fish. And thus the rabbis manage to spare the unicorn not just from the flood but also from their own barrage of Talmudic questioning.

Another richly imagined animal tale is that of the emperor and the lion (Hullin 59b). The Talmud contains several stories in which the Roman emperor challenges one of the sages with a theological question, presumably playing out a rabbinic fantasy about being on intimate terms with the highest echelons of power. In this case, the emperor asks Rabbi Yehoshua ben Hanania about a biblical verse (Amos 3:8) that compares God to a roaring lion. The emperor asks how God can be so great if He is likened to a lion; after all, any good horseman can kill a lion. Rabbi Yehoshua responds that God is not likened to an ordinary lion, but to a special kind of lion from Bei Ilai. "Show him to me," demands the emperor, and Rabbi Yehoshua warns him that he will not be able to behold this creature. But the emperor insists, and so Rabbi Yehoshua appeals to God in prayer and the lion sets out. When it is still quite a distance away, it roars. Immediately all the pregnant women miscarry and the walls of Rome collapse. When it comes a little closer, it roars again and the teeth fall out of the mouth of every man, including the emperor himself. Like Pharaoh begging Moses to stop the plagues, or like the Israelites beseeching Moses to shield them from God's voice at Sinai, the emperor pleads with Rabbi Yehoshua to pray that the lion return to its place. And so it does.

The lions and unicorns of Kodshim were far more appealing to me than the detailed anatomical diagrams of gullets and gizzards that filled the back pages of the illustrated edition of Hullin that I'd purchased to help me make sense of the rabbinic conversation. Hullin deals with *kashrut*, the Jewish dietary laws stipulated in the Bible. Jews are permitted to eat many kinds of animals, so long as they are properly slaughtered in accordance with Jewish ritual law. It is not kashrut that dictates my vegetarianism, but rather a general minimalist tendency. I like to get by on less, and this has become not just a principle of economy but of aesthetics too. The laws of kashrut appeal to me because they limit what we can and cannot eat, reducing the overwhelming number of choices out there. Vegetarianism takes this one step further. The world is enough with beans and grains and chocolate; I do not need hamburgers too. Besides, at least according to Rav Nahman's wife, Yalta, everything that is forbidden has a kosher counterpart that tastes just as good (Hullin 109b)—for every bacon there are bacon bits. Yalta gives several examples: it is forbidden to eat pig, but we can eat the *shibbuta* fish, which tastes similar (though one has to wonder how she knew what pig tastes like); it is forbidden to eat the blood of animals, but we can eat liver. The story ends when the ever-truculent Yalta insists that she wants to taste meat and milk together but can find no kosher equivalent. Thereupon her husband instructs the butchers, "Give her roasted udders."

Vegetarianism is not kashrut, though many people confuse the two. "Oh, I'm so sorry, I should have cooked the potatoes separately from the meat," our Shabbat host will apologize. But I have no problem eating potatoes that were cooked with meat; there is no issue of *noten ta'am*—of a forbidden substance lending its taste to a permitted substance—when it comes to vegetarianism. And I am far more flexible with my vegetarianism than with my kashrut. When it comes to vegetarianism, I have my own mental hierarchy of the increasingly permissible—from fish to chicken to beef. I try to eat the "most vegetarian" option available without inconveniencing myself or my hosts.

My notion of hierarchy is not entirely foreign to the Talmudic sages, who discuss how many "signs" various kinds of living things must have in order to be considered kosher. These signs are essentially anatomical elements that must be severed (Hullin 27b). The hierarchy reflects a primitive evolutionary theory: Animals, which the sages say were created from land, need two signs—both the trachea and the esophagus must be incised. Birds, which were created from swamps (and which the rabbis claim have scales on their feet like fish), need only one sign—either the esophagus or the trachea must be cut. But fish, which were created from water, need no signs; fish may be eaten even without ritual slaughter. My preference is always to eat the food with the fewest signs.

For me, there are so many gustatory pleasures that are not meat—or wine, for that matter, which I eschew for similar reasons. A dark chocolate bar or a steaming cup of coffee are infinitely more appealing than the most expensive cut of lamb. These are simple pleasures, I know. But the Talmud advises that a person should always spend less on food and drink than his means allow and honor his wife and children more than his means allow (Hullin 84b). And so perhaps the rabbis would be sympathetic to my restraint.

As for my children, I prefer to give them the freedom to elect to become vegetarian of their own accord, or not. When they are young, I care most that they see me modeling healthy and respectful eating. In tractate Menahot, which deals with grain offerings, the Talmud references Ben Drosai (Menahot 57a), a highway robber contemporaneous with the early Talmudic sages who was so impulsive that he would grab his meat off the fire before it was fully cooked. When I come home ravenous and I'm inclined to devour all the dried fruit and nuts readily accessible in the cupboard, I remind myself not to eat like Ben Drosai but to stop and sit down like a civilized human being and take pleasure in my food. "Food is *kadosh* [holy]," I will later tell my son when he tries to throw his supper or leave too much on his plate. I'll repeat this so many times that when I then take him to synagogue and point to the Torah and tell him it's kadosh, he'll look at me earnestly and ask, "Can we eat it?" Still, I find it appropriate that the order of the Talmud that includes the laws of kashrut is known as Kodshim, holy things. The rabbis teach that following the destruction of the Temple, a man's table resembles the altar (Menahot 97a)—a reminder that in a world without sacrifices, the food that we eat has the potential to bring us close to the sacred.

BECHOROT / ERCHIN / TEMURAH / KERITOT / MEILAH / TAMID / MIDDOT / KINNIM

❦

Poets & Gatekeepers

By THE TIME OF OUR FIRST ANNIVERSARY, I'D BEEN working at the literary agency for nearly five years, and I was ready for a change. But it was only when I came to a passage in one of the many short tractates at the end of Seder Kodshim that I realized just what that change should be. Amidst a discussion of the roles performed by the various Levites who worked in the Temple, the Talmud (Erchin 11b) distinguishes between the *m'shoarin* (gatekeepers) and *m'shorerin* (poets). The gatekeepers were responsible for locking the gates of the Temple and, presumably, for other administrative tasks. The poets were responsible for the vocal music in the Temple: whenever the daily sacrifice was offered, they would provide musical accompaniment. The Bible describes the two as inherited roles that had to be kept distinct. A poet could not perform the duties of a gatekeeper, nor vice versa, as cautioned by the following tale:

> A story is told of Rabbi Yehoshua ben Hanania who went to help Rabbi Yohanan ben Gudgada with the closing of the

gates. Rabbi Yohanan ben Gudgada said to him: My son, turn back! For you are one of the poets and not one of the gate-keepers! (Erchin 11b)

Both of the sages who figure in this story were Levites, members of the tribe of Israel biblically designated to serve in the Temple. Rabbi Yehoshua ben Hanania was one of the poets, though in the Talmud he is better known for helping to smuggle his teacher Rabbi Yohanan ben Zakkai out of Jerusalem in a coffin on the eve of the Temple's destruction (Gittin 56a). He then became the rabbinic leader of the academy at Yavneh, the site of the Jewish court in the immediate aftermath of the Temple's destruction. It was he who asserted, "There can be no study house without novel teaching" (Hagigah 3b), perhaps a sign of his own creative bent. Rabbi Yohanan ben Gudgada was a gatekeeper who was known for his strictness about purity matters. Like any good administrator, he liked rules. He was responsible for keeping everyone locked into their particular roles, which explains his rebuke of Rabbi Yehoshua.

This story inspires a rather stern Talmudic injunction about the division of labor in the Temple, warning about *m'shorer she-shier u'mshoar she-shorar*, a poet who guards and a gatekeeper who composes. This brilliant conjoining of sound and sense—itself a poetic injunction about gatekeeping (or policing) who may do what—refers to someone who fulfills a role that is not his own and is consequently sentenced to death. The rabbis invoke a biblical verse in which the term "stranger" is used to refer to any non-Levite who encroached on the sanctuary. According to the rabbis' creative interpretation, the term "stranger" may refer more broadly to anyone who is estranged from the labor that he is meant to perform. Someone like Rabbi Yehoshua, who was meant to be a poet, must compose and sing rather than engage in administrative affairs, which are the domain of Rabbi Yohanan and his fellow gatekeepers. The Talmud seems to be arguing for a clear division of labor, in which we all do what we were destined for. Otherwise we risk becoming estranged—from our destinies and from our true selves.

After I learned this passage about poetry and gatekeeping, I began to think more about these categories. A poet is preoccupied with content, whereas a gatekeeper is preoccupied with flow. A poet determines the quality of the material, while a gatekeeper determines who has access to it. While both roles are essential, I could not help but privilege the former over the latter. The poet is creative and original, and his work is one of a kind; no two Levites sang exactly the same way because no two human voices are identical. In contrast, the gatekeeper's work is important because of its precision, its replicability, and its reliability—anyone else would have to do that work in exactly the same way.

The Mishnah (Middot 36b) details exactly how the gates of the Temple had to be locked and unlocked, leaving no room for creativity. The main gate to the sanctuary had two smaller gateways, one to the north and one to the south. No one ever entered the southern gateway, per a pronouncement in the book of Ezekiel (though it sounds more like J. R. R. Tolkien): "This gate shall be shut; it shall not be opened, neither shall any man enter in by it" (Ezekiel 44:2). The gatekeeping priest would turn a key in the northern gateway and enter into a small chamber, which in turn led into the sanctuary, whose doors he would then unlock, in exactly that order.

As a literary agent, my job was to be a gatekeeper for literature, responsible for what would be translated into Hebrew and by whom. Each day I received dozens of books and manuscripts, which I submitted to the appropriate Israeli editors. When multiple editors competed for the rights to translate a single work, I conducted an auction to determine who won the right to publish that book. I loved reading the books our agency represented, but editors rarely called to ask my opinion about literature; they turned to me because I controlled access to the books, and they wanted me to unlock the gates.

Unlike my own gatekeeping existence, most of my friends, it seemed, were poets. They were writing PhD dissertations, or sitting in cafes drafting short stories, or reporting for the local newspapers, or even (literally!) writing poetry. At the end of the day, they could point proudly to their own creative work with the confidence that no one else in the world would ever produce a final product identical to theirs. Whereas I, at best, could walk into a bookstore and point to a book I had edited or translated—both tasks that I'm sure many other competent people could have accomplished in my stead. *Thrice an editor, never an author*, I chided myself—though in my case it was more like five hundred times an editor. I did not feel proud or proprietary about my editorial work. Certainly I could not imagine ever reacting like Rav Sheshet, who grew furious when his student quoted one of his teachings without attribution and hissed, "Whoever stung me in this way— may he be stung by a scorpion!" (Bechorot 31b).

My attitude toward my work bothered me, and I wondered if my anxieties were the first signs of a midlife crisis. Maybe this happens to everyone in their thirties; suddenly they realize that their lives are no longer completely ahead of them. When we are young, the world seems open with possibility; but as we approach thirty-five—the age I was scheduled to finish daf yomi—we realize that the choices we have made have opened some gates but closed others. What was I doing with my "one wild and precious life," to invoke the words of Mary Oliver[28]—since it is always the poets and not the gatekeepers whom we quote?

Perhaps not coincidentally, the passage about poets and gatekeepers appears in the tractate of the Talmud that deals with questions of self-worth. The name of the tractate, Erchin, comes from the Hebrew word for "value" and refers to individuals who consecrate their value to the Temple. As the Torah teaches, people as well as property could be devoted to God, and a person might elect to donate the monetary equivalent of his worth to the Temple as a show of thanksgiving. But it is impossible to evaluate the worth of a human life, so the Torah establishes set values for these vows that depend on the age and gender of the person: "If it is a male from twenty to sixty years of age, the equivalent is fifty shekels of silver by the sanctuary weight" (Leviticus 27:3). I wondered how much my own life would be worth and how I could make my time more valuable. Was I not destined for a more poetic vocation?

Until that point, I moonlighted as a translator. When I got home from the literary agency office I worked on translating a series of books about the rabbis of the Talmud. I spent my evenings traveling to Rome with Rabbi Yose to view the blood-stained ark cover held captive in the Caesar's palace (Meilah 17b), or asking halachic questions in the meat market in Emmaus about men who have sexual relations with five menstruating wives (Keritot 15a), or enumerating the various musical instruments that can be made out of a dead sheep (Kinnim 25a). Absorbed in these musings, sometimes I would look at the clock and discover it was past midnight, and I'd have to force myself to take leave of the sages and go to bed.

The rabbis in tractate Tamid (32b) extol the virtues of learning Torah at night, claiming that the divine presence accompanies anyone who does so. I was lucky to be engaged in work that brought me closer to the divine, even if it did not necessarily draw on the divine spark within me. I learned so much from translating the rabbinic biographies that I often quipped that I was being paid to study and to spread Torah, a practice explicitly forbidden in the Talmud (Bechorot 29a): Since God taught Torah to Moses for free, teachers of Torah are forbidden to accept a fee for their work. Fortunately this statement is then qualified by later rabbinic authorities, who provide a convenient loophole: a person can accept payment for all the other gainful work he is unable to do because he is instead teaching Torah. In any case it was good to be remunerated, and I began to set my sights on other books about Talmud and rabbinic literature that seemed like potential translation projects. Soon I had enough work that I could support myself with my translations alone. So I stopped moonlighting as a translator and made it my full-time job, in fulfillment of the verse from Joshua (1:8), "And you shall contemplate it [Torah] day and night."

I have come to see that translation can also be a sacred calling, not unlike gatekeeping in the Temple. When I translate Jewish books, my job is to enable words of Torah to reach a wider audience. I must remain faithful to the original text, especially in the age of mass production, when any error I introduce would be reproduced countless times in every copy of the English edition. In tractate Temurah (14b) Rabbi Yohanan declares that anyone who writes down Jewish laws is like someone who burns the Torah, and anyone who learns from written texts will receive no merit—perhaps to safeguard against error, or to maintain rabbinic authority, or to prevent these texts from falling into the hands of heretics. He then concedes that the Oral Torah may be written down if doing so will prevent Torah from being forgotten by the people of Israel. In translating books about the Oral Torah—as the Mishnah and Talmud are commonly known—I am doing my own small part to ensure that passages of Torah will not be forgotten, at least not by English-speaking Jews. Often I am filled with trepidation when tempted to exercise undue creative license as a translator. "Turn back," I imagine Rabbi Yohanan ben Gudgada staying my hand, "for you are one of the gatekeepers, and not one of the poets."

Much as I enjoy translating, it does not allay all my anxieties about creative labor. These anxieties come to the fore when I frequent the National Library of Israel, with its austere, stately Judaica reading room, where many of the greatest scholarly minds of our generation sit at the long rows of tables poring over ancient tomes. Some are rabbis who teach religious wisdom, but most are professors who employ critical methods to study Talmud academically in university departments. The Talmudic rabbis teach (Keritot 6a) that a student learning Torah should look upon the mouth of his teacher, in fulfillment of the verse, "Your eyes will behold your teacher" (Isaiah 30:20). But looking up from my laptop screen at so many Talmudic luminaries seems more intimidating than inspiring.

Whenever I enter the reading room I think of a passage from tractate Middot, which deals with the dimensions of the Temple. The rabbis consider the question of how it was possible to clean the Holy of Holies, a space so sacred that only the high priest could enter it, and only on Yom Kippur, the holiest day of the year. They explain that there were trapdoors in the upper chamber opening into the Holy of Holies through which workmen were let down in baskets "so that they would not feast their gaze on the Holy of Holies" (37a). I sometimes think about getting a part-time job in the library once again—perhaps shelving books, or sitting behind the reference desk—so that I can have an excuse to feast my eyes on its sights, without feeling so presumptuous as to think that I, like the high priesthood of academic scholarship, have a right to be there.

In these moments of self-doubt I identify with the figure of Bava ben Buta in tractate Keritot (25a), whose name incidentally means "gate." Ben Buta used to bring a guilt offering to the Temple every day, convinced that he had done something wrong. I live my life much like Bava ben Buta, ever anxious about how I spend my time. And yet in the next tractate of Kodshim we are reminded that "the Torah was not given to the ministering angels" (Meilah 14b) but to fallible human beings who can only try their best. The phrase appears in the context of a discussion about whether the wood for the Temple is pre-sanctified, or built with and then sanctified. The sages rule that the wood should not be sanctified first because perhaps one of the workers will get tired and will want to sit down and rest on one of the planks. Were it already sanctified, he would be guilty of *meilah*, that is, of "stealing" benefit from the Temple, which is the subject of the eponymous tractate. The Torah was given to flesh-and-blood humans who sometimes need to sit down and rest. It is a message I wish I had internalized when I started out as a translator. In the next two years, I would give birth to three children. If only I could turn back the clock, I would encourage my insecure self to sit down, relax, and enjoy the quiet of the library while I still could.

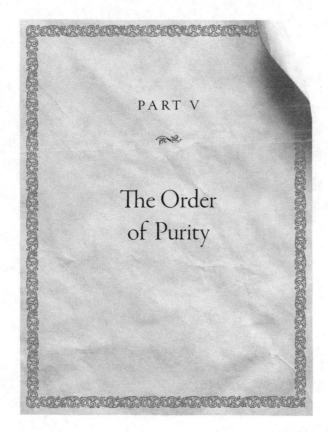

PART V

The Order
of Purity

NIDDAH

❧

A Folded Notebook

As a child I dreamed of having twelve children.
I filled pocket-sized spiral notebooks with lists of names and ages
of the kids in my imaginary family, as if their ages would be fixed
and unchanging. At night I lay in bed thinking about alliterative
names for my ten-year-old twins and eight-year-old triplets, privi-
leging sound over sense and often drawing inspiration from my
school vocabulary lists: Chevrolet and Chevron, or Parsimonious,
Avarice, and Evanescent. I had little idea what having children
might actually entail—that it would be necessary to have a partner, that there was a certain window of time in which a woman
was fertile, that conception was not automatic but involved
chance, luck, divine intervention, or all of the above. Two decades
later, when I'd long ago abandoned the dream of *Cheaper by the
Dozen* and finally became pregnant with my first at age thirty-
two, it was with full awareness of just how many stars had aligned
to allow for this miracle to transpire.

My appreciation for the miracles of conception and pregnancy were deepened by my study of tractate Niddah, which

deals with menstrual purity and childbirth. I thought about this tractate while sitting in the waiting room of the health clinic in Ramot, a suburb of Jerusalem. I'd traveled all the way there—over an hour by bus—because there were no ultrasound appointments available anywhere closer that week, and I was too excited to wait. Just a few days earlier I took a home pregnancy test which seemed to indicate that I was in fact pregnant. I could not quite fathom my good fortune, and I was afraid of being disappointed until I knew anything for certain. I even repeated the pregnancy test just to be sure that my eyes weren't deceiving me—I had one kit that I'd bought at Super-Pharm in Jerusalem, which had instructions in Hebrew, Russian, and Arabic; I had another kit from CVS with English and Spanish guidelines. But both times two pink lines appeared in the window of the plastic stick, suggesting that in at least five languages, you would have to say it was so.

And so I sat in the waiting room anxiously anticipating my turn for an ultrasound that would confirm what I dared not yet allow myself to believe was true. All around me were women with far more visible baby bumps, and I wondered if that would be me in a few months. The Talmud in Niddah speaks of Layla, the angel responsible for pregnancy, who brings a tiny seed to God and says, "Master of the Universe, what will become of this droplet? Will it be brave or weak, wise or foolish, wealthy or poor?" (16b). I wondered about these questions too, but my reverie was interrupted when a woman in a white coat called out my name and ushered me into a cubicle-sized room. There I was instructed to lie on the chair and lower my pants. I shivered as the technician spread cold jelly on my lower belly and turned on the machine. I heard a sound that resembled the trotting of horses, but turned out to be the beating heart of the new life growing inside me. "Please God, may everything be normal," I prayed as the technician examined the screen and printed out what looked like a photo of intergalactic space. Even after she assured me several times over that the baby looked fine, I could not stop my lips from mouthing their silent prayer.

In general I tend not to invoke God in my daily speech. I do not say "please God" or "with God's help" or any of the other phrases I associate with those more devout than I. Yet all this changed when I learned I was pregnant. Suddenly I was overwhelmed by the sense of how much was beyond my purview even though it was taking place just millimeters beneath the surface of my skin. The Talmud in Niddah (16b) teaches that "all is in the hands of heaven except the fear of heaven." It is a famous and oft-quoted line, though few people know that it appears in the context of fetal development. To me this makes perfect sense. There is nothing like pregnancy to remind us how little is in our control. In a related teaching, the rabbis assert that there are three keys that are in the hands of God, which God does not entrust to any messenger (Taanit 2a). These are the key to rain, the key to childbirth, and the key to the revival of the dead. We pray for two of these keys during the second blessing of the Amidah, the central Jewish prayer, where we ask God to cause the rain to fall and to revive the dead. Why not pray for childbirth as well? I resolved that I would pray for the health and welfare of the unborn child inside me each time I came to this blessing.

When I didn't have time for formal prayer, I simply placed my hand on my stomach and recited a version of the prayer that Rabbi Yehoshua's mother used to recite. The Mishnah teaches that Rabbi Yehoshua's teacher praised him by saying, "Blessed is the one who gave birth to him" (Avot 2:8). Rashi explains that Rabbi Yehoshua's mother used to pass by the study houses of her town and ask the sages, "Please pray for this unborn child in me that he should become a Torah scholar." I modified her prayer only slightly: "Please pray for the unborn child in me that he or she should be healthy, with a good head and a good heart, and a love for Torah."

It was always "he or she" because Daniel and I decided not to find out whether we were having a boy or a girl, though the information was readily available to us. We asked the doctor to jot down the sex in the back of a notebook whose last page we never turned. I suppose that on some level, I wanted to retain my sense that "everything is in the hands of heaven." Amidst the harsh fluorescent lighting of medical examination rooms and the lurid glow of X-rays, that dark realm of the unknown seemed ever more elusive. Even if the unknown was not unknowable, I wanted to hold on to as much mystery and wonder as possible. And so I left the key to the sex of the child in God's hands, feeling no need to unlock that door just yet.

We waited, too, before sharing the news of the pregnancy with others. The Talmud states in tractate Niddah that there are three partners in the creation of every human being: the Holy One Blessed Be He, the father, and the mother (Niddah 31a). For a little while at least, we wanted to keep it among ourselves. In any case this tractate also teaches that a pregnancy is not visible for three months, based on the story of Judah and Tamar in Genesis in which Judah finds out that Tamar is pregnant after three months have elapsed (Genesis 38:24; Niddah 8b). It was only when the bump became too big to hide that we shared what most of our family and friends were already suspecting. And so the circle widened like ripples on the surface of a pond created when a pebble is cast into the water.

That pebble grew until it was the size of a pea, then a blueberry, then a lime. I tracked the baby's development on an American pregnancy website that featured a different fruit for each week of gestation: "You are nine weeks pregnant. Your baby is now the size of a grape." Sometimes these weekly produce updates were confusing: How could the baby already be the size of a banana when last week it was an heirloom tomato? And what size is an heirloom tomato anyway? Instead I decided to use the Talmud's measurements, which were more familiar. At first the baby was a *k'zayit*, the size of an olive, which is the minimal volume of food for which one must make a blessing after eating. A month later it was *k'kotevet hagasa*, the size of a large date, the amount of food that the rabbis thought would satisfy one's appetite and therefore render an individual liable for violating the commandment to afflict oneself by fasting on Yom Kippur. Just a few weeks later it was *k'beitzah*, the size of an egg, which is the amount of leftover sacrificial meat that would render the individual who came into contact with it impure. I hoped that it would take me less time to give birth than *k'dei achilat pras*, the time it takes to eat half a loaf of bread, which the sages ruled was the amount of time within which a person must consume the requisite amount of matzah at the Passover seder.

Pregnancy has a timeline of its own, but mine seemed to follow a sacred rhythm. The very same week that I first felt the baby kick in the womb, we began reading the book of Exodus in the weekly Torah portions. Exodus describes the enslavement and liberation of the Jewish people from their Egyptian taskmasters. But the Bible also tells us that while the Israelite men were laboring to build the pyramids of Pithom and Raamses, their wives were laboring to bring forth children in astounding multiplicity: "The Israelites were fertile and prolific; they multiplied and increased and reproduced and grew mightier very very much, and the land became filled with them" (Exodus 1:7). The language of the text, with its rapid succession of synonyms and its doubled "very very," reproduces itself, replicating the embodied experience on the semantic plane. And so Exodus starts off as a book about pregnancy.

Early in the book of Exodus, during their encounter at the burning bush, God tells Moses that he has "taken note" of the people's suffering. The Bible's word for "taken note" is *pakad*, which is the same word used to describe how Sarah became pregnant: "And the Lord took note of Sarah as He had promised, and Sarah conceived and bore a son" (Genesis 21:1). God takes note of the Israelites, causing them to reproduce en masse. But amidst all their laboring in Egypt, God reassures the Israelites that they are not alone. "I will deliver you," God promises through Moses. In the Bible Egypt is known as *Mitzrayim*, which comes from the Hebrew word for "narrow." God pledges to deliver the Israelites from the narrow birth canal of Egypt, parting the sea to allow for the deliverance of His firstborn Israel.

As Passover approached and my pregnancy progressed, I wondered whether the convulsions of childbirth would be as cataclysmic as the splitting of the sea and whether I would feel the divine hand that guides each firstborn through the narrow womb never before stretched by a child. I imagined my moans and groans and cries and shrieks reaching to the throne of the One who is responsible for the creation of all new life, the One who takes note and delivers. A couple of months before my due date, Daniel and I enrolled in a natural childbirth class, where we filled an entire notebook with strategies and tips for a smooth and successful childbirth. But when I thought about tractate Niddah's discussion of women who have extraordinary difficulty giving birth and go into labor for three days (36b), I put my notebook aside and, like the Israelites, addressed my pleas directly to Heaven.

In the end I carried all the way to term and went into labor a few weeks after Passover, on the morning of Yom HaZikaron, Israel's national memorial day. Daniel and I adopted a friend's annual tradition of visiting the military cemetery at Mt. Herzl to speak with bereaved families at the gravesides. It is a way for us, new immigrants who do not have anyone to mourn, to take part in the national mood and to try to offer comfort. We took a bus to the cemetery, but instead we walked the whole way home in the hope of speeding up my labor. The walk was over an hour downhill, and I was sure I felt the baby moving down the birth canal with each step I took. The Talmud teaches in tractate Niddah that "in the first three months of pregnancy, the baby is in the lower region. In the next three months, it is in the middle region. In the last three months, it is in the upper region. And when it is time for it to emerge, it flips over and comes out. And this is the pain of childbirth" (Niddah 31a). My baby seemed to be flipping countless times over, and there was no mistaking the pain.

Yom HaZikaron leads directly into Yom Haatzmaut, Israel's independence day, with the mood flipping 180 degrees from sorrow to joy. By Yom Haatzmaut morning, my contractions were still a half hour apart, and I realized that the situation called for more drastic measures. So I decided to attend Hidon HaTanach, the national Bible quiz show which takes place every year on Independence Day. I thought that perhaps my baby was waiting for the chance to review all the Torah learned in the womb, as the rabbis teach: "What does the fetus resemble in its mother's womb? A folded notebook. . . . And a candle burns for him above his head . . . and they teach him the entire Torah. . . . And when he comes out to the air of the world, an angel comes and slaps him on the mouth and causes him to forget the entire Torah" (Niddah 30b). I was confident that my baby, who had learned nearly three hundred pages of daf yomi—spanning several tractates—during the nine months of my pregnancy, knew all the answers to the questions being asked on the stage of the Jerusalem Theater where I sat between my husband and mother, who was visiting in anticipation of the birth. Conscious that they were both watching me, I tried not to grimace too visibly each time another contraction came on.

Thankfully the Hidon did the trick, because by the time we got home that afternoon, I was already counting the minutes between contractions and recording them in the notebook I'd used throughout our childbirth class, that very same notebook in which the sex of the baby had been jotted down—so I trusted—on the final page.

I stayed up all night that night, with my mother and husband taking turns rubbing my back and guiding me through each of the contractions. It was a *leyl shimurim*, "a night of vigil," as the Bible describes the night before the Israelites left Egypt. The pain wracked my body like the plagues that devastated Egypt, and I fought through the pain with my howls. "Thus said the Lord: At midnight I will go forth among the Egyptians. . . . And there shall be a loud cry in all the land of Egypt, such as has never been nor will ever be again" (Exodus 11:4–6). They say it is always darkest before dawn, and indeed it was just before the sun began to rise that I felt myself trembling and shivering, as if enveloped in darkness and cold. How crazy was I to have thought I once wanted twelve children! I was never going through this again, I swore, like the woman in tractate Niddah who "at the hour she bends down to give birth, jumps up and swears that she will never sleep with her husband again" (31b). As I hobbled to the car supported by Daniel on one side and my mother on the other, I knew just how she felt.

We drove to the hospital as quickly as possible. The rising sun was painting the sky in streaks of pink and red as we headed toward the hills of Ein Karem, but I was oblivious to the world around me because I felt something as heavy as a bowling ball trying to push its way out of my bottom. Convinced that the baby was going to fall out of me then and there, I crouched on all fours in the backseat, trying to hold it in for dear life. When we arrived I refused to be placed in a wheelchair, unable to sit down because of the immense pressure on my posterior. The nurses laid me on a gurney and determined that the time had come. There was no time to take my vitals, no time to administer any drugs, no time to let the bread rise. Within twenty minutes of our arrival at the hospital, our son had made his way out from my very narrow womb into the air of the world, where he was slapped by the angel and delivered into my waiting arms. The candle was no longer burning on his head but his eyes were bright as he looked up at me, blinking and bewildered. Who would this child become? I wondered. Would he be brave or weak, wise or foolish, wealthy or poor? In the notebook folds of his ruddy skin, the story of his life began to be written.

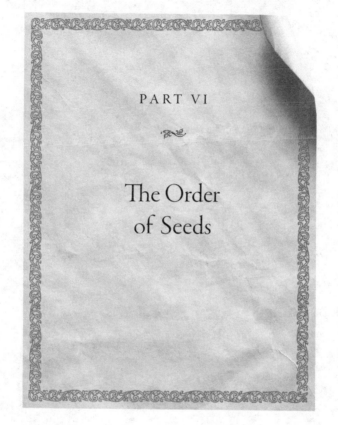

PART VI

The Order
of Seeds

BERACHOT

❧

Writing About Prayer
Is Easier Than Praying

I DISCOVERED THAT I WAS PREGNANT WITH MY FIRST-born while leading the congregation in Yom Kippur services. All of a sudden, in the middle of my recitation of the Avodah—the part of the liturgy that describes the high priest's terrifying entrance into the Holy of Holies on the most awe-inspiring day of the Jewish calendar—I grew weak, saw stars, and collapsed. That evening, after breaking my fast, I took a home pregnancy test and understood why I had been unable to make it through the Avodah. But even before I became pregnant, my relationship with prayer was complicated and contentious. Having children only enlivened that struggle, and gave it new shape.

As I sit down to write these words today, I find myself experiencing this struggle yet again, in real time. I thought that before I wrote about Berachot—which deals with prayers and blessings—I would first open my siddur (prayer book) and recite *shacharit*, the morning service. But that was at 6:00 a.m., when I woke up to the cries of my hungry twin daughters. Three hours later, with the kids all fed, clothed, and deposited in their respective preschool programs, I am anxious to start writing. Once again, my compulsiveness has gotten the better of me, and I sit before the computer with the blinking cursor beckoning me more urgently than the siddur lying unopened on my desk.

℘

And so the history of my prayer life is less a history of praying than of trying—and generally failing—to carve out the time and mental space to pray. When I first came to Israel and studied at a yeshiva, an institution for the religious study of Jewish texts, we prayed in the *beit midrash*, the study house. The walls were lined with Jewish religious texts, and I stood in a corner surrounded by bookshelves and learned Talmud during *davening*, the Yiddish term for praying and the term commonly used in religious circles. Apparently I was in good company. The Talmud (Berachot 30b) relates that Rabbi Ami and Rabbi Assi lived in a town with thirteen synagogues, but they would pray only in the study house where they learned Torah. But I suspect this practice is not ideal. One day my teacher came up to me after services and spoke harsh words, though he had a twinkle in his eye: "Wow, you must be quite a Torah scholar given all the Talmud you learn during davening. But tell me—if you're such a Torah scholar, shouldn't you know better than to learn Talmud during davening?"

The question continues to haunt me. Any time I have to choose between praying and learning, inevitably I choose the latter. Studying Torah is about novelty. It is about conquering new territory, synthesizing more and more information, and coming up with insights that cast everything that came before in a whole new light. Prayer, on the other hand, is about repetition and return. The rabbis caution that one should not make one's prayer into a "fixed task" (Berachot 28b), but this injunction only reflects how difficult it is to do anything but. Each day and each week and each year, we recite exactly the same liturgy as the days and weeks and years that came before. The Shema—a prayer consisting of biblical verses that constitutes the credo of Jewish faith—is the same when we recite it this evening as yesterday evening; the Shabbat afternoon service this week is identical to the Shabbat afternoon service last week; and we will say the prayer for dew this Pesach as we said it last Pesach. Whereas Torah study is about taking the unfamiliar—the next page of Talmud, a new midrash, a new interpretation—and internalizing it until it becomes familiar, prayer is about taking the familiar—the same words we say day after day—and saying them with such concentration and fervor that it is as if we are renewing each day the miracle of their creation.

People who love the study of Torah are those who are never content to stay in one place, for it is for this purpose that they were created. They know that Torah demands that we keep moving, that we keep turning it over and over, and that we do not stop even for a moment to notice, say, a beautiful tree by the roadside. Prayer, in contrast, is about standing still and looking inward. The central prayer—the one that the rabbis refer to as HaTefilla (the prayer)—is commonly called the Amidah (the "standing prayer") because it must be recited while standing in place, our feet pressed together in imitation of Ezekiel's vision of the angels (10b). If I want to daven, I have to wholly inhabit myself and my space. I have to be comfortable enough in my body to sit and stand and bow freely, all without ever stepping out of a very small imaginary circle drawn around my feet. I have to be focused and present and at peace. It reminds me of the way friends describe how they feel when they do yoga, and so a few years ago I signed up for a yoga class in the hope that it might furnish me with the skills to become a better davener.

In my two-month stint as a yogi—alas, that was all it lasted—I came to appreciate the similarities between prayer and yoga, even if I remained hopeless at both. First, prayer, like yoga, is an embodied practice. The prayer service is choreographed: there are times to stand and times to sit, and like the synchronized movements of a yoga class, everyone gets up and down at more or less the same times. While davening is not quite as physically taxing as yoga, it too is a spiritual discipline achieved through physical movement. As such, it requires specific poses and positions—bowing, taking three steps back, lifting our bodies up on our tiptoes three times, resting our head in our hands. The Talmud relates that Rav Sheshet would bend to bow like a reed and then raise himself up like a serpent (Berachot 12b). I don't think my prayer posture is as dramatic, but I am certainly very aware of my body when I pray. If I feel uncomfortable in my own skin, I find it difficult to sit through services. For many years, I davened in a minyan with hard plastic chairs lined up in rows. Occasionally I would visit a more established synagogue—one that had cushioned seats and a place to rest my siddur in front of me, so I could sit comfortably with my hands at my sides and my siddur at eye level before me. This, I thought, is the right position for prayer.

But even the most comfortable chairs are worthless unless there is a commitment to sit in them regularly, because prayer, like yoga, is a discipline. It wasn't easy to attend a yoga class several times a week; nor is it easy for anyone to wake up for minyan every morning. The rabbis teach (Berachot 32b) that prayer is one of four activities that require vigorous strength (the others are Torah study, good deeds, and the pursuit of a trade). But regardless of what it takes, there is no substitute for regular practice. I don't think it is possible to come to synagogue once a year and have an all-time spiritual high. Rather, it is the accumulation of many early mornings, afternoons, and evenings spent in prayer that ultimately results in a moment of transcendence. The eleventh-century poet and philosopher Yehuda HaLevi wrote that "prayer is to the soul what food is to the body." Just as we are supposed to eat three times a day, so too must we pray three times a day. While I've been tempted at times in my life to pray just when the spirit moves me, the effect was something akin to all-day snacking, with nothing filling or fulfilling.

Praying regularly is difficult, in large part because it requires a significant sacrifice of time. If I wanted to pray before writing this chapter today, I would have had to give up twenty minutes of writing. This relationship between prayer and sacrifice as acts of "giving up" dates back at least to the destruction of the Second Temple, when prayer became a substitute for sacrifice, as the Talmud teaches in Berachot (26b). The rabbis insist that regardless of the competing demands on our time, prayer comes first: we learn in Berachot that we should daven before we eat breakfast (10b) and that anyone who takes care of his own needs before praying is regarded as if he has built an idolatrous shrine (14a). Nonetheless, it's reassuring to me to know that it was not easy for the rabbis either, as reflected by the license they grant to study Torah before praying (Berachot 11b).

When it comes to prioritizing prayer, Daniel is my model. Each morning when he wakes up, he wraps himself in a prayer shawl, puts on tefillin, and stands in prayer—no matter what else he has to do. To some extent this is emblematic of who he is: in all aspects of his life, he puts others first. When he calls his mother, he first wants to hear all about how she is doing, and only then does he tell her anything about our lives. When he walks in the house at the end of the day, he runs over to give each child a hug, and only then takes off his heavy backpack. But I suspect that this is not just about Daniel, and that anyone who follows the Talmud's injunction to pray before attending to his own needs is more likely to internalize the value of prioritizing the needs of others.

Unlike Daniel, for whom prayer is a regular discipline, I tend to daven most when my days have the least shape because I look to prayer as an organizing principle. When I was in the hospital after giving birth to my children, the days seemed to drag on in an endless cycle of baby feedings and vital sign measurements, so I davened three times a day as a way of remaining cognizant of the passage of time. It was helpful that each service has to be recited at a set time of day, as we know from the first chapter of Berachot, which begins with a discussion about how early one can recite the evening Shema (2a). By davening regularly I remained attuned to the passage of the sun across the sky, even in my windowless hospital room.

I once met a religious family who homeschooled their children. I found the idea fascinating and bombarded them with questions: "How do you decide when the school day begins, given that the kids don't have to show up at any specific time?" The father looked at me as if the answer were obvious. "We wake up when it is time to say shacharit, and then eat breakfast and start studying." His response reminded me that prayer can provide the rhythm to our days, punctuating the hours we rise and the hours we lie down and preventing the days from flowing meaninglessly into one another—which is perhaps what the Hebrew poet Leah Goldberg meant when she wrote, "Teach me, my God, to bless and to pray . . . Lest my day be today like yesterday before / Lest my day be like one unthinking haze."[29]

Prayer is an escape from this unthinking haze. If today's prayer is to be different from yesterday's, it must be suffused by an intentional awareness of what it is that I am praying for at this particular moment. To pray meaningfully I must be able to identify what is most urgent and important to me and articulate those wishes in the context of the liturgy. For years I prayed that I would marry the right man. I included this prayer in the fourth blessing of the Amidah: "Grace us with knowledge, understanding, and discernment." I was praying not for this man to land in my life miraculously but for the wisdom to recognize who he was, and who he was not.

I know people who swear by prayer's efficacy, confident that their prayers have been heard and answered. My friend Rimona resolved on her thirty-fourth birthday that she was going to get married before she turned thirty-five. Each morning she walked to the Kotel and prayed to God that she would meet the man of her dreams. Sure enough, by her thirty-fifth birthday, she was wed. For Rimona, this was proof that prayer "works." But I suspect it's more complicated than that. After identifying her deepest aspiration, Rimona was motivated to concentrate all her energies on making that dream come true. Prayer, then, is the language for articulating our dreams—which may explain why the Talmud's long and fascinating excursus on dream interpretation appears in tractate Berachot. Here the rabbis anticipate Freud in their assertion that "a person is shown in a dream only that which troubles his own heart" (55b), and they go on to give various examples: a person who dreams of a camel has been spared the fate of an early death; one who dreams that his front and back teeth fell out is at risk of losing his sons and daughters; and one who dreams of reciting the Shema will be guaranteed a place in the world to come.

Prayer challenges me to think about what I dream for the world and what I dream for myself. It is a regular reminder of the kind of person I want to be, which in turn inspires me to grow and change. The transformative power of prayer is reflected in the Hebrew word *l'hitpalel*—to pray—which is in the reflexive form. And yet all too often, transformative prayer seems remote and inaccessible. On trapdoor days, when I wake up sad and despondent and ill-equipped to face the day, I am overcome by how much I need to pray for, yet I'm unable to pull myself together to speak to God. And when life seems rich and full and there is little that feels wanting and even less time to ask for it, I rarely feel inspired to pray, even if I am stable and centered enough to do it. I tell myself that prayer is an insurance policy because you need to pray on the good days, when prayer feels least urgent, so that the channels of communication remain open on the bad days, when prayer is most vital.

The Talmud teaches that "a person is obligated to bless God for the bad just as he blesses God for the good" (54a). And yet it seems clear that we need to invoke God when times are bad; often we cry out instinctively to God in such moments. It is when the going is good, too, that we must remember to cultivate gratitude lest we come to think of our blessings as our rightful due, or as the work of our hands alone. In the poem "Sunday Morning," Wallace Stevens writes about the "complacencies" of a woman who chooses to stay home in her nightgown rather than go to church and pray. She views the world as "unsponsored," disconnected from the divine source of blessing.[30] But the rabbis maintain that everything in our lives is sponsored by God, as if an infinite number of invisible kite strings connect all that we hold most dear to the One who is on high.

☙

I felt most aware of divine sponsorship in the early years of my marriage to Daniel, when I could hardly get over my joyous surprise that such a man had landed in my life, and had stayed. I identified with Isabel Dalhousie in Alexander McCall Smith's novel *The Careful Use of Compliments,* who also got married against all odds. Isabel would look at her beloved Jamie and wonder if he were really truly hers. So too I would look at Daniel as he got out of the shower at night, a towel wrapped around his waist and drops of water glistening on his shoulders, and wonder: *Are you really mine? Is it really my good fortune to be with you? Can there really be someone who loves me, with all my foibles and with all my flights of fancy?* It did not seem possible that such supreme joy could be my rightful lot. I found myself becoming nostalgic for the present, which seemed already fleeting at the very moment it alighted on my shoulder. I worried that Daniel— the present of his presence—could not possibly be real, and that I would wake up one day and discover it had all fled like a fanciful dream, flapping its dazzling wings and taking off, never to return again.

Isabel Dalhousie ultimately tells herself that no, Jamie is not hers: "She realized that Jamie was on loan to her, as we are all to one another, perhaps."[31] Her conclusion reminds me of a story about the Talmudic sage Rabbi Meir and his wife Beruriah. The Midrash on Proverbs (31) tells of how Beruriah discovered that their beloved sons died suddenly on the Sabbath, but she hid them from her husband so as not to cause him distress on Shabbat. She laid their bodies on the bed, spread a sheet over them, and told her husband that they had gone to the study house. After he made the Havdalah prayer, she posed this question to him: if someone were to lend her a pledge and later come back to claim it, should she return it? Rabbi Meir responded that of course she should return it. Beruriah then took her husband by the hand and led him to their bedroom, where she removed the sheet covering the bodies of their sons. When Rabbi Meir began to wail, Beruriah reminded him of his own assertion that one must return a pledge to its rightful owner. Her husband replied, "God has given, and God has taken away. Blessed be the name of the Lord."

Rabbi Meir and Beruriah realize that everything in the world belongs to God, and we can at best merit to be custodians. This is a mentality that underlies all of tractate Berachot, since it is only when we realize that everything comes from God that we feel the impulse to bless. In the sixth chapter of the tractate, which deals with the blessings over various foods, Rabbi Hanina bar Papa asserts, "All who benefit from this world without first saying a blessing are as if they are stealing from the Holy One Blessed Be He" (35b). Just a few lines earlier, the Talmud tries to reconcile two conflicting biblical verses: How can it be that "the heavens are the Lord's and the fullness thereof, the earth and its inhabitants" (Psalms 24:1) and yet "the heavens belong to God and the earth was given to men" (Psalms 115:16)? Does the earth belong to man or God? Rabbi Levi explains that everything in the world belongs to God until we make a blessing, but that once we bless something, it is on loan to us.

Paradoxically, it was only when I adopted the notion of love on loan that I could allow myself to trust enough to be able to love Daniel without being tortured by the fear of losing him. Only when I realized that he was not mine forever could I revel in the fact that he was mine for now. During our first year of marriage I woke up before him each morning and watched the sun stream in through the windows and dance across his still-shut eyelids, pinching myself to make sure he was real. I thanked God not just for restoring my soul to my body, as the Talmud mandates (Berachot 60b), but for restoring Daniel to me. For there he was, here with me on yet another blessed day!

Grateful for each day, I came to appreciate that nothing beautiful lasts forever. An inherent characteristic of beauty is that it unfolds in time: a real flower is more beautiful than a plastic one in part because the real flower will ultimately wither. This is the meaning behind a story about Rabbi Elazar and Rabbi Yohanan in tractate Berachot (5b). The Talmud relates that when Rabbi Yohanan came to visit Rabbi Elazar on his deathbed, the former pulled up his sleeve and a brilliant light fell from his arm. Rabbi Elazar was moved to tears by his visitor's beauty, which is elsewhere compared to a glass of pomegranate seeds in the sunlight; this is one of several occasions in which the Talmud describes and remarks upon male beauty. Rabbi Yohanan then asked: Why are you crying? Rabbi Elazar answered: I am crying for this beauty that will be ravaged by dust.

As this story teaches, evanescence is beauty's hallmark. Or, in the words of Wallace Stevens in "Sunday Morning," "Death is the mother of beauty."[32] A thing of beauty is not, in fact, a joy forever. It is the knowledge that the object of our love, in all its beauty, is not guaranteed to be ours forever that renders our love so precious and so prized. We are on loan to one another, which means that sometimes we must acknowledge that "God has given, and God has taken away." We live in spite of those moments. But there are also the moments we live for, when the impulse for blessing comes from another acknowledgment, uttered in wonder and incredulity: God has taken away, but God has also given.

It is this wondrous acknowledgment of blessing that inspires the prayer of the biblical figure of Hannah, whom the rabbis frequently invoke in the fifth chapter of Berachot. In the book of Judges, Hannah offers two very different kinds of prayer. First, she prays tearfully for a child of her own each year when she comes to bring sacrifices at the altar in Shiloh with her husband, her husband's other wife, Peninah, and Peninah's children. Her distress is so great that the high priest Eli mistakes her for a drunkard, and she must rally to her own defense: "I am not drunk, but I have been pouring out my heart to God. Do not mistake me for someone worthless. I am praying out of my great anguish and distress" (I Samuel 1:15–16). Later, when her son Samuel is born, Hannah finds herself at the opposite end of the emotional spectrum, praying out of joy and gratitude.

For the rabbis, Hannah is invoked as a model of how to pray. Yet this invocation is surprising because it follows on the heels of the Mishnah's injunction that a person must pray in a "reverent frame of mind" and must countenance no interruption. Hannah meets neither of these criteria. She does not seem particularly reverent. On the contrary, the Talmud relates that she speaks to God with the utmost chutzpah: "Master of the Universe, nothing that you have created in a woman is for naught: Eyes to see, ears to hear, a nose to smell, a mouth to speak, hands to work, legs to walk, breasts to nurse. But these breasts that you placed on my heart— what use are they? Give me a son that I may nurse him!" (31b). Nor does she pray without interruption. When Eli asks if she is drunk, she stops praying to defend herself, once again contravening the rabbinic injunction.

Perhaps the rabbis nonetheless invoke Hannah as a role model because of her ability to pray through both her pain and her joy. When she speaks to Eli, Hannah describes herself as a "woman of hardened spirit" (I Samuel 1:15). She has been hardened by the agony of her years of childlessness as year after year she has endured both the taunts of her rival Peninah and her husband's inability to comfort her. Yet the very same biblical verse that describes her bitterness also tells of how she cried to God: "Hannah was bitter of heart, and she prayed to God, weeping all the while" (I Samuel 1:10). In spite of her bitterness, Hannah does not become hardened past the point of tears, nor does she renounce all relationship with a God who created a world with so much suffering. Though all she can do is rage at God, she continues to engage Him. Perhaps she knew, as the rabbis go on to say later in this same chapter in Berachot (32b), that even when the gates of prayer are locked, the gates of tears remain open, as if tears oil the hinges. And while the gates may open just a very tiny bit, miraculously that proves to be enough: God opens Hannah's womb and she conceives and bears a son, who inspires her prayers of thanksgiving.

And so Hannah prays both out of need and out of gratitude. From a literary perspective, her petitionary prayer is far outmatched by her prayer of thanksgiving, which takes the form of ten jubilant poetic verses: "My heart exults in the Lord / I have triumphed through the Lord. . . ." (I Samuel 2:1). Perhaps Hannah can wax more poetic once her heart is no longer hardened. Once she is no longer overflowing with tears, she can compose herself and compose her thoughts in more measured form. She can hold herself back, which is what the line breaks of poetry demand. In prose, one line spills into the next, like a woman crying out in uncontrollable tears; in poetry, each line ends in a finely modulated caesura, like a graceful dancer holding herself momentarily still before the music starts up again. By the time Hannah offers her poetic prayer of thanksgiving, she has learned the eloquent rhythm of expressiveness and restraint. No wonder the rabbis turn to her as a model of how to pray.

I am inspired by the rabbis' invocation of Hannah's prayer not just because it is so lyrical, but also because Hannah is a mother, and praying as a mother poses its own host of challenges. Not long ago, I was walking along the park that lines the old railway tracks linking our home with my daughters' *gan*, a term used for the various daycares and preschools that Israeli children attend from infancy until the start of first grade. I ran into a man who looked vaguely familiar, and he smiled at me as if he knew me well. "I know you! You're the *tehillim* lady," he told me. When I looked back at him quizzically, he continued, "I hear you singing tehillim every morning. You're so devout!" I tried to make sense of his words. Tehillim are psalms, which as far as I know, I never chant. But then suddenly I understood.

Every weekday morning, as I push the girls' double stroller on our way to gan, I "daven" aloud with them. I put the word "daven" in quotes because it's a far cry from serious prayer. I do not have a siddur open before me, and I do not recite the full liturgy, nor do I stand and sit at the appropriate points since I am pushing a stroller all the while. Rather, I sing my favorite melodies from the morning service as we walk: I recite the Modeh Ani and Mah Tovu prayers as we head down the hill to Hebron Road, the four-lane highway that marks the border of our neighborhood; I chant Ashrei and other psalms as we cross at the light; and then I belt out a few "hallelujahs" as we make our way through the parking lot toward the park. Many of these prayers are indeed psalms, which explains the misperception. By the time we get to the gan, I am usually up to the blessings before the Shema. But at that point I stop to take the girls out of their stroller, deposit them on the floor surrounded by toys, and bend over to kiss them goodbye on the tops of their heads.

I did not realize until now that anyone overheard my morning davening, and I'm a little embarrassed by it all. After all, the proper way to daven is in synagogue with a minyan, while holding a siddur and bending and bowing at the appropriate moments. And yet my approach to prayer is not without precedent. In the third mishnah of Berachot (10b) we are told of a famous debate between the schools of Hillel and Shammai about how to recite the Shema. Shammai says that at night one should recite the Shema while lying down, and in the morning one should recite it while standing, to fulfill the verse, "When you lie down and when you rise up" (Deuteronomy 6:7). Hillel, who is generally more lenient, says that any position is acceptable, in fulfillment of the previous part of the verse, "When you go along your way." That is, Shammai would never approve of the way I daven on the walk to gan, but Hillel would have no problem with my ambulatory shacharit.

Praying "along the way" has become habitual at this stage of life, and I do it even at home. When I wake up in the morning it is usually to the sound of someone calling out from the next room, and I rarely have time in bed to recite Modeh Ani. But I sing it aloud as I rush into the twins' room to find them jumping up and down while clutching the crib railing, excited to see me. Then I walk to the window and open the shades to let the light pour in as I say, "Blessed are You . . . Who gives the heart understanding to distinguish day from night."

The Talmud in the ninth chapter of Berachot (60b) lists the various blessings that Jews are supposed to recite in the morning: "When he gets dressed he should say, 'Who clothes the naked.' When he stands up he should say, 'Who uprights the bent.' When he puts his feet on the ground, he should say, 'Who spreads the earth above the waters.'" Though today these blessings are generally recited in the synagogue rather than the home, we learn from the Talmud that they were originally recited to accompany the various stages of waking. And so this is what I do as well. I wipe the green crusts from my girls' eyelashes and recite, "Blessed are You, Lord our God . . . Who removes sleep from my eyes, and slumber from my eyelids." And I rub my own sleepy eyes and recite, "Who gives strength to the weary."

Daniel, too, has a hard time finding time for prayer during our rushed and busy mornings, so he has come up with his own creative solution. He places our kids in their booster seats and high chairs with breakfast in front of them and then brings his siddur and tefillin to the table, where he davens. Matan enjoys singing along, though he knows that he is not allowed to touch the "feeleen" boxes until he finishes eating and washes his hands, after he and Daniel have sung Adon Olam, the closing hymn. And Daniel is grateful for the opportunity to daven, though he looks forward to the day when he can return to minyan and not have to worry about picking Cheerios off the floor in between the Shema and the Amidah.

When I consider where we are in our prayer lives, I think of the Mishnah's injunction to pray in a reverent frame of mind. The phrase used in the Mishnah is *koved rosh*, which literally means "heavy-headedness." If Daniel and I feel any heavy-headedness, it is not from our tremendous powers of concentration but rather from the chronic sleep deprivation that is the inevitable lot of parents of young children. The Mishnah goes on to state that the early pious ones used to wait an hour before praying in order to get into the proper frame of mind for speaking with God. And so I like to think of our prayer these days as analogous to that preparatory hour of the early pious ones. It is not really prayer, but a preparation for the rest of our prayer lives. If we were to stop praying altogether, it would be much harder to return to the discipline of daily worship. And so instead we pray "along the way" or at the breakfast table. It is just enough to stay in shape so that when we do indeed have time to recite the full service properly, our souls will not have forgotten how.

For my own part, I am grateful that I've found a solution to my difficulty with stopping to make time for prayer. Instead of stopping, I pray along the way, like Hillel. And I do not feel idle and impatient while davening because, like Hannah, I am praying as a mother—sometimes while worrying about the toddler who is out of my sight, and sometimes while observing my new crawlers as they clamber underfoot. I rarely have to fight the impulse to pick up a volume of Talmud in synagogue anymore because I don't usually have a free hand. This is not an ideal situation. But as I set off in the mornings with the wind blowing through my hair and my gorgeous children sitting in the stroller before me, it feels like enough. My heart exults in the Lord, and I feel so full of gratitude that I cannot help but pray.

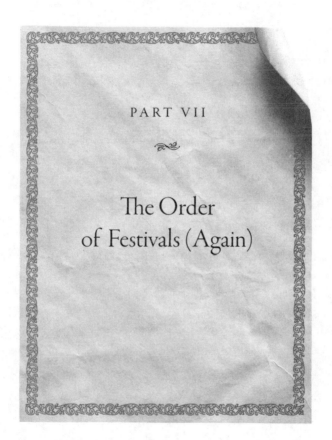

PART VII

The Order
of Festivals (Again)

SHABBAT / ERUVIN

※

A Pregnant Pause

Shabbat is meant to be a day of rest, and tractate Shabbat enumerates the thirty-nine categories of work that are prohibited on this day—including cooking, weaving, building, and hunting. But for Daniel and me, Shabbat ceased to be restful when our twins were born on the cusp of tractates Shabbat and Eruvin, in February 2013. Our family grew quite dramatically from three to five, and our notion of Shabbat—and of what it means to rest—was never quite the same.

Early in my study of tractate Shabbat, when I was just starting my second trimester, I was placed on bedrest. The doctor was concerned that my amniotic fluid was leaking and ordered that I remain as horizontal as possible for at least two weeks. I lay there on the couch, legs propped up on three pillows, holding up my heavy volume of Talmud over my head (Shabbat is one of the longest tractates) as I learned the opening pages about transferring objects in and out of houses on Shabbat. This prohibition, which is the basis of several chapters in tractate Shabbat and all of tractate Eruvin, derives from the biblical commandment to "let everyone remain where he is: let no one leave his place on the seventh day" (Exodus 16:29). By lying low and resting, we affirm that God created the world in six days and rested on the seventh. But for me, stuck there with no possibility of leaving the couch, let alone the private domain of our apartment building, every day felt like Shabbat.

Ever bent on productivity, I tried to set goals for myself that I could accomplish without getting up, including reading all nine hundred pages of Hilary Mantel's first novel about Oliver Cromwell, *Wolf Hall*, and writing every day in my journal. But my frustration with bedrest was the same as my ongoing frustration with Shabbat—there is always so much I want to accomplish, and nothing gives me more pleasure than checking things off my list, so enforced stasis is torturous. Breakfast in bed is my worst nightmare—second only to a beach vacation. "How dull it is to pause," Tennyson's Ulysses declares in a line I often quote to myself.[33] This time, though, I had no choice. And so the laundry piled up, the e-mail went unanswered, and for two weeks I did little but pause.

During my fortnight on bedrest I tried to reconceive my notions of pregnancy and productivity. I told myself that pregnancy was in fact a period of maximal productivity: even when my mind was idle, my body was hard at work creating new life. Two new lives! I vowed that I would use bedrest as an opportunity to cultivate patience, and to appreciate the value of sitting still. It is a skill I've long wanted to acquire. I'm not a good researcher because I am so eager to start writing immediately that I rarely give ideas the time they need to gestate. I also can't write fiction because I am afraid to let my characters take me along for the ride; I want to have it all planned out in my head before I even sit down at the computer. While this compulsiveness has made me very productive, it has also made me less creative. So long as I am single-mindedly focused on getting things done, I do not allow myself to be receptive to the manifold possibilities of distraction. But I was determined to comply with bedrest and give things—the babies, and also my thoughts—the time they needed to take shape.

In spite of this noble resolve, in actuality I spent most of my bedrest gritting my teeth and trying to bear it as Daniel managed all the household chores, cared for Matan, and kept me supplied with steaming cups of tea and long novels. The experience left me with a deeper appreciation for what Shabbat is supposed to be— not a time to stay up all Friday night reading by the bathroom lights (the only lights still on once the Shabbat timers have turned the others off), and not a time to embark on hour-long afternoon walks (though I often do). Presumably what the rabbis had in mind was more in line with bedrest—a period of calm and contemplation, of sitting and studying.

In my case bedrest was complicated by an increasingly rambunctious Matan, now toddling around the apartment and getting himself into all sorts of trouble. Matan, too, did not know how to sit still. He was fascinated with wires and switches and ran all around our apartment turning our various lamps on and off. At eighteen months his vocabulary included the words "light" and "on," and he screamed "On, light! On, light!" each time he successfully flicked the switch. He grew frustrated when we walked in the house in the evening and the lights were off. "Off? Off?" He'd look at me imploringly, and I'd try to explain that yes, the lights were off now, but they could be turned on later; even when they were switched off, they bore within them the latent potential to be on. "It's like God," I tried to explain. "We can't always see and feel God, but even when God seems to be turned off, He is still there, waiting for us to be able to see Him again." No one provides better fodder for theological musings than a relentlessly inquisitive toddler.

In his fascination with electricity, Matan made no distinction between Shabbat and weekdays. So we tried to teach him about *muktzeh*, which is the subject of the seventeenth chapter of tractate Shabbat. Muktzeh means "set aside," and refers to the rabbis' injunction that anything that is not prepared in advance for use on Shabbat is considered out of bounds for use on the day. One category of muktzeh includes items that are prohibited because their primary purpose is forbidden on Shabbat, such as electrical appliances. Unfortunately, most of Matan's favorite toys were muktzeh: the blue desk lamp he'd ask us to put on the floor so he could crouch down and talk to it, the electric mixer known as the "jigger" which he clutched to his chest and toted around the house, and the light switches on the stairwell that he turned on at will as I carried him past. "Muktzeh, muktzeh," I told him on our way out to synagogue, hurrying down the stairs and trying to distract him. But to my consternation, the next morning he started pointing to the light switch and saying "muktzeh," as if this were a new word for light. And so with the day of rest behind us, creation had to begin all over again on Sunday, as Matan and I spoke light into being.

⟨⟩

The second chapter of tractate Shabbat deals with the commandment to light Shabbat candles as the sun sets on Friday evening. The candles must remain lit until they burn down, unless there are extenuating circumstances, such as a sick person who cannot sleep because of the light. For most of my adult life, I found this a difficult religious obligation to fulfill. I wanted to go to synagogue every Friday night, but it did not seem safe to leave the candles burning unattended at home. If a woman lives alone, or if she wants to go to synagogue with her husband, then who is left to keep watch over the flickering flames? Ironically, although so much else in my spiritual life fell by the wayside after I became a parent, it was then that I began lighting candles regularly. It was impossible for both Daniel and me to go out on Friday night because someone had to stay home with Matan, and so we could leave the candles burning while one parent—not necessarily Daniel—went to synagogue to welcome Shabbat.

As I lit candles each week, I was increasingly troubled by the way this commandment is treated in the Talmud. The rabbis teach that every Friday evening a man must ask his wife if she has lit candles (Shabbat 34a), as if she could not possibly be relied upon to observe the law. Even worse, the sages enjoin that there are three sins for which women die in childbirth, namely for not being careful with the commandments regarding menstrual purity (*niddah*), the separation of a portion of dough (*challah*), and Shabbat candle lighting. All of these commandments are gendered: Niddah relates to a woman as a reproductive vessel, challah assumes that the woman's place is in the kitchen, and candle lighting keeps her stuck at home. I did not wish to see myself in any of these lights. Even so, I was haunted by the Talmud's cautionary words, especially because I was pregnant with twins.

The Talmud goes on to question why a woman is punished specifically during childbirth, and Rabbah responds, "When the ox is fallen, sharpen the knife." That is, when a person is at her most vulnerable, her life is most likely to be endangered. The Talmud then asks when a man's life is most at risk, concluding that it is when he crosses a bridge. (Apparently the bridges of the early centuries of the Common Era were less structurally sound.) The passage concludes with the warning that "a person should never stand in a place of danger and assume that a miracle will be performed for him, lest it will not." Such miracles are indeed performed—the Talmud later tells of a man whose wife died in childbirth but who could not afford a nursemaid; this man miraculously sprouted breasts and was able to nurse his son (Shabbat 53b). But I certainly wasn't going to count on it. And so at a time when my physical body included more than half the family we were creating, I made sure to light candles on time—with considerable trepidation.

Even so, I was not content with the rabbinic understanding of childbirth as a time of vulnerability and danger. That may be true, but childbirth is about something much more profound as well. It is while birthing a child that a woman most resembles the divine Creator, the One who created the first human beings on the day preceding the world's first Shabbat. The rhythm of Shabbat, of course, is about imitating the Creator, creating for six days a week and then resting on the seventh. On Friday evenings a person is obligated to recite the verses from Genesis (2:1–3) that describe the Sabbath, beginning with, "And the heaven and earth were finished." The Talmud (Shabbat 119b) teaches that since the Bible is not vocalized, the word for "finished," *vayehulu*, may also be read as *vayehalu*, meaning "and they finished," suggesting that God and humanity are partners in creation. And so it seems reasonable that if a woman is not careful about her Shabbat observance, then she will not merit to emulate the Creator by bringing life into the world.

And yet I preferred to look at it in a more positive light. The Talmud teaches that the reward for lighting candles is the promise of scholarly children (Shabbat 23b). I hoped that our children would watch both their parents light candles, attend synagogue, and study Talmud, and grow up to do the same.

ॐ

My pregnancy lasted through the fall and into the winter, the period of time in which we read the book of Genesis in synagogue each Shabbat. In Genesis, conception is a sign of divine favor. One of the primary ways that God intervenes in the world is by enabling the barren to bear children, as with the matriarchs Sarah and Rachel, who undergo long periods of waiting before they become mothers. Rebecca, in contrast, is spared the pain of barrenness and is blessed from the outset with twins.

Avivah Zornberg points out that in Hebrew, Rebecca's name, Rivkah, is an anagram of *kirbah*, that interior space where the babies struggled. "And the babies struggled inside her [*b'kirbah*]." While pregnant with twins, Rebecca's very identity was jumbled inside her, to the extent that she could no longer recognize her-self: "If so, why do I exist?" (Genesis 25:22), she asks in a moment of existential doubt. Rebecca did not have the advantage of mod-ern ultrasound technology, nor did she have an entire shelf of books to tell her what to expect when she was expecting. Instead, God had to serve as her ultrasound and her sounding board, illuminating the reason for her distress and discomfort: "Two nations are in your womb. Two separate people shall issue from your body."

Like Rebecca, I also had two babies struggling within me, though I identified more with Sarah's delight at the news of her annunciation than with Rebecca's dismay. When the ultrasound technician first informed me that I was having twins, I burst out in joyous and incredulous laughter. It seemed so wildly wonder-ful and impossible—I was hoping for a baby to grow inside me, and lo and behold there were two! Of course it was too early to tell anyone, and I wanted to wait a few hours even before telling Daniel, lest I disrupt his concentration at the library. But my excitement was so great that it was uncontainable. So I left the health clinic, boarded the bus, and announced to the bus driver that I was pregnant with twins. He looked at me as if I were crazy, and asked if I wanted to pay three fares.

༄

The babies inside me soon made their presence known. From very early on I was able to detect two distinct patterns of fetal move-ment. The one on top gave sudden, jolting kicks, as if leveling a blow at an imaginary opponent; when this baby moved, my whole stomach protruded and the motion was visible even through my shirt. The baby on the bottom didn't so much kick as undulate, fluttering around just above my pelvic bone in a gentle, rhythmic dance. I couldn't help but ascribe personalities to them: The one on the bottom would be sedentary like Jacob, whom the Bible de-scribes as a "simple man, dwelling in tents" (Genesis 25:27). The other would always be on the prowl, like Esau the hunter. And so I referred to the two fetuses as Jacob and Esau, addressing various passages from my learning to them.

As I paged my way through tractate Shabbat I noticed the babies kicking along as if wanting to participate in the Talmudic discussion, which was surprisingly relevant. The eighteenth chapter of tractate Shabbat deals with births that take place on Shabbat (is this kind of labor permissable?), and the nineteenth chapter extends this discussion to the question of circumcision on Shabbat (is it permissible to carry the knife to the ceremony?). The answer, in both cases, is yes. It is permissible, too, to violate Shabbat to satisfy any of the demands of a laboring woman, no matter how irrational they may be (128b). Even if she is blind but insists that someone light a candle for her, one should go ahead and do so. I was sure Matan would love that one.

I did not have many irrational demands during my pregnancy. I didn't crave pickles or ice cream at midnight but continued to eat my regular vegetarian diet of bean and lentil soups, quinoa, bread, and outrageous quantities of dark chocolate—plus a few dates and nuts for extra calories. Nor was I plagued by varicose veins or stretch marks; my body continued to serve me well. I jogged into my sixth month and swam once I became too heavy to jog. In those last few months, people sometimes asked me why I didn't take it easy and give my body a rest. "For me, resting is running," I responded, hurrying along on my way. As my due date approached I felt productive, alive, and teeming with excited anticipation.

Like Matan, the twins arrived late. I carried to full term, determined not to let the doctors induce me. I was confident that the babies would come when they were ready, and hopefully when I was ready too—that is, once I had finished tractate Shabbat. I had five pages left of the tractate when I came to the rabbinic injunction to "repent one day before your death" (153a). The rabbis question how anyone can know when he will die, and conclude that he should repent every day as if it were his last. The day of death and the day of birth are similarly unpredictable, I mused. And it was during that very musing, while lying in bed with my Talmud open, that my water broke.

Daniel and I agreed that the most sensible thing to do would be to get a good night's sleep before the contractions became more painful. He turned over, closed his eyes, and promptly drifted off. As soon as I heard his breathing slow, I stealthily turned on my bedside lamp and opened tractate Shabbat, which I was sure I could finish. On the penultimate page (156a), which I reached in that last hour before dawn just as the contractions grew more intense, the rabbis discuss a series of astrological predictions based on the relationship between the day a child is born and the shaping of that child's character: "One who is born on Sunday will be strong; one who is born on Monday will be quarrelsome; one who is born on Tuesday will be rich and fornicating. . . ." Rabbi Yehoshua ben Levi associates each of these destinies with the creation story. For instance, just as the waters were divided on the second day of creation, a baby born on this day will participate in divisive exchanges. On the other hand, if the twins were born on the Thursday that was then dawning outside my bedroom window, they would be committed to loving-kindness, because this was the day the fish were created. Rashi explains that fish do not work to find their own food but rely on the loving-kindness of God, who supplies them with all they need. It sounded sufficiently auspicious to me.

In the morning Daniel and I dropped Matan off at gan and then walked home slowly. "How are you feeling?" a neighbor asked as we passed by her on the sidewalk. At that point I was stopping every ten minutes to breathe my way through the contractions with my hands on my knees and my head hanging down between my legs. Luckily she caught me just after the worst had subsided. "I'm fine," I assured her, forcing a smile, because those early stages of birth seemed too intimate to share. I was not in a rush to enter the medicalized environment of the hospital with its needles, monitors, and harsh fluorescent lighting, and I told Daniel that I preferred to proceed by candlelight at home. Daniel humored me for just a few more minutes, until it became clear that it was time to go.

As I both feared and anticipated, as soon as I got to the hospital an anesthesiologist came in to ply me with the promise of relief that an epidural would afford. I was adamant in my refusal; I had not taken any medicine when Matan was born, nor did I wish to do so now. I wanted to feel the labor in all its intensity, not to be deprived of any aspect of the experience. And so I turned down the anesthesiologist, an older man with a long gray beard and a black kippah. "You don't understand," he told me. "I give women epidurals as a way of helping out the Shechinah. The divine presence is in pain whenever a woman is in pain. I relieve the woman's pain so as to relieve the Shechinah." Oh dear, I rolled my eyes. So now the doctor was trying to win me over with religious precepts.

Not to be outdone, I thought back to a passage from tractate Shabbat (88a) in which the Talmud, amidst a long excursus on the giving of the Ten Commandments, quotes a biblical verse about the children of Israel's preparations for this event: "And they took their places at the foot of the mountain" (Exodus 19:17). The rabbis explain, "This teaches that the Holy One Blessed Be He forced the mountain over their heads like a bucket, and said to them: If you accept the Torah, well and good. And if not, this mountain shall be your grave." I quoted this passage to the anesthesiologist, insisting that he was holding the epidural over my head like a bucket, threatening to drop it upon me. If I refused to accept, this would be my grave, I told him, punning on the Talmud's use of the same word for "grave" and "womb." Suffice it to say that he left me alone after that.

By the time I was ready to push the two babies out, the room resembled a cocktail party, with two midwives, two pediatricians, one obstetrician, and the defeated anesthesiologist milling around. I howled and screamed and shrieked and closed my eyes, too scared to look. A girl! She was a beautiful blonde with big blue eyes, and Daniel joined my parents, who had been waiting behind a curtain, to greet her as the pediatrician took her Apgar. But I was still kneeling over the bed, struggling to birth her sister. I tried to block out their voices as they fawned over the baby's long fingers and her nails the size of sesame seeds. "Now, now, push!" yelled the doctor above the din. I felt the second baby's head as it tore at my flesh like a searing hot iron, and then they were both in my arms, the blonde who had come out first and a delicate brunette, also a girl, also with bright blue eyes. Sisters! After God holds the mountain over the head of the children of Israel, the Talmud recounts that He made a condition with all of creation: if Israel accepts Torah, creation will exist; if not, the world will be restored to a formless void (88a). I sat propped up in my hospital bed gazing from one girl to another, awed by creation.

෨ඏ

In the days following the twins' birth, Daniel and I devoted many conversations to the question of what to name our daughters. This was surprising given how much of my childhood I spent dreaming up names for my future children—though I'd come a long way from Azalea Rendezvous and Regatta Serenade. The only thing I knew for certain was that they would have to be names that we could pronounce. Daniel and I speak Hebrew with American accents, and our R's—which sound nothing like the Hebrew letter *reish*—are most jarring. I didn't want a situation in which I would yell at my teenager to go to her room, and she would respond insolently with, "You can't even pronounce my name right." We also wanted names that all our American relatives would be able to say without twisting their tongues, which meant I'd probably have to give up on the multisyllabic Hebrew names I liked—Chavatzelet, Shlomtzion, Achinoam.

As we leafed through the name dictionary, I thought of a midrash about Jacob's struggle with the angel in the book of Genesis. Jacob asks the angel to identify himself, and the angel challenges, "Why do you ask my name?" (Genesis 32:30). The midrash on the book of Genesis (Genesis Rabbah 78:4) connects this verse to another encounter between a human and angel that appears in the book of Judges: Samson's father Manoach asks the angel his wife has encountered for the angel's name, and the angel responds, "Why do you ask my name? For it is a secret" (Judges 13:18). The midrash explains that angels' names remain a secret because they change based on the particular mission the angel is sent to accomplish. I imagined that in choosing names for our children, Daniel and I were also in some sense charging them with unique missions in the world. I pictured thousands of winged angels hovering over us, each representing a different name and each beating its wings in hopeful anticipation that perhaps that angel might be the one whose mission would match the name we chose. With this midrash in mind, we invoked very real angelic presences. We'd named Matan—whose full name is Matan Aharon—for each of our maternal grandfathers, Mordecai and Aharon. Matan is also the Hebrew word for "gift," an expression of our overwhelming sense of gratitude to God for the miracle of birth. The twins, too, had beloved namesakes. We named Liav for Daniel's father, since she was the first grandchild born after his death; the Hebrew word *av*, which is at the root of her name, means "father." Tagel, meaning "she will rejoice," comes from the same root word as Gilla, the name of my maternal grandmother. I hope that we succeed in instilling in them the values of their ancestors, and that they grow to love their names. If not, I will tell them they should be grateful that they are not Azalea and Regatta, and hope that they agree.

Even before we settled on names for our girls, I resumed daf yomi by cracking open tractate Eruvin, which deals with the boundaries within which a person may walk and transport objects on Shabbat. As I lay there nursing, I pretended that the hospital was a study house and I was not a postpartum mother but a disciple of the sages absorbed in the Talmud's discussion of the four domains that relate to the laws of Shabbat: public (a thoroughfare where more than six hundred thousand people pass), private (an area four handbreadths by four handbreadths, marked off from the surrounding space by walls), a *carmelit* (a space neither public nor private), and a *makom petur* (a place exempt from the laws of carrying). The rabbis teach that it is forbidden to carry anything from one domain to another, and it is also forbidden to carry anything more than a minimal distance within the public domain.

I thought about the distinctions between these domains during the three days I spent in the maternity ward following the births. I was in a small room that I shared with two other women. Unlike me, they were ultra-Orthodox, each with at least five other kids at home. We were separated from one another by colorful curtains that hung from tracks on the ceiling. The tracks surrounded the perimeters of each of our beds, with room for just the bed, a small bassinet (or two), and a nightstand. When all the curtains were opened, as they were when the cleaner came to wash the floor on Friday morning, the illusion of three separate "private domains" was shattered, and it became clear just how near we all were to one another. Even with the curtains drawn, I could hear everything they said to their visitors, and they could hear me read aloud from the Talmud's pages to my newborn daughters.

In those early pages of Eruvin, I was struck by the Talmud's discussion of *dyumdin*, the double pillars that were placed around public wells in order to cordon them off into private domains in which it would be permissible to draw and carry water on Shabbat. At the beginning of the second chapter (18a), the Talmud records a discussion in which the rabbis try to determine the etymology of this word, which they posit comes from the conjoining of the Greek prefix *dyu*, meaning "two," with the Hebrew word *amud*, meaning "pillar." They then consider concepts that relate to the prefix dyu, including the two faces (*dyu partsufin*) of Adam. According to the midrash, Adam was created with one face in front and one face in back and was then split down the middle to become male and female. Each of our twin daughters lay in her own plastic hospital bassinet on wheels, with pink tags marked "Kurshan A" and "Kurshan B." Depending on which way the girls were facing as they slept, I'd rearrange the bassinets periodically so that I could see the fronts of their heads. They were my double pillars, supporting my world.

For the first few weeks after I returned from the hospital, it was impossible to leave the house. I had nursed Matan for his first year of life, but nursing twins was something else entirely. The girls needed to eat every two hours, and each feeding lasted over an hour; so there was almost no time when we could be apart. Although my mother urged me to try to feed both girls at once, plying me with a fluffy twin nursing pillow, I refused. My excuse was that I wanted time alone with each of my daughters, but in truth, I wanted a free hand to hold a book. It was while breastfeeding that I encountered a midrash in tractate Eruvin (54b) on the verse, "A loving doe, a graceful mountain goat. Let her breasts satisfy you at all times; be infatuated with love of her always" (Proverbs 5:19). As they often do when confronted with the Bible's erotic imagery, the rabbis interpret this verse as referring to Torah. Just as a doe has a narrow womb and is beloved unto its mate each time anew, so too are words of Torah equally special the first time they are studied and on every subsequent encounter.

Moreover, the rabbis go on to explain, just as a breast is available with plentiful milk every time the baby wants to suckle, so too is Torah always available for those who want to savor its rich insights. I took comfort in the fact that my daughters not only learned Torah with their mother's milk, but the milk they imbibed was in fact Torah.

Learning daf yomi while nursing served as a way to retain some semblance of my former pre-twin life in spite of all that had changed. I was on maternity leave from work, which meant that my professional life was on hold. I also couldn't run or swim yet, since my body was still healing from the birth. And it was difficult to see friends, because I was nursing too frequently to leave the house. I felt like I was on leave not just from work but from so much of my life. And so I was fortunate to have daf yomi as a link back to the person I had been before my whole life contracted to the couch and bed.

Holed up at home, I thought of the story in tractate Shabbat about Shimon bar Yohai and his son, who retreat into a cave for twelve years to escape Roman persecution (Shabbat 33b). A miracle occurs, and a carob tree and a spring of water are created for them so that all their needs are provided for, and they do not have to worry about sustenance. They need only each other so that they can study Torah together, in much the same way as my daughters needed only to nurse and I needed only to feed them. It seemed miraculous to me that my body could satisfy all their nutritional needs; I was the carob tree and the spring and the study partner, all in one.

I did not bother to get dressed in those early weeks, just as Bar Yohai and his son shed their clothes and sat covered in sand up to their necks, like talking heads. On those rare occasions when I left the house to take a walk with my double stroller, I felt blinded by the harsh light of day and bewildered that everyone else was rushing to and from work, going about their daily business. So too, when Bar Yohai and his son leave the cave after twelve years, they are taken aback by the sight of people planting and sowing and working the earth. "They are forsaking the eternal world of Torah for this transient world," they mutter in disdain, their eyes burning up the world around them. A heavenly voice rebukes them for being so dismissive of the rest of humanity: "Have you come to destroy My world?" I confess that I muttered this same question quite a few times when one or another of the girls woke Daniel and me yet again in the middle of the night, preventing us from ever sleeping for more than a two-hour stretch: Dear babies, have you come to destroy our world?

But of course they could not destroy our world because they constituted it, which is a lesson that Bar Yohai learned as well. He and his son are commanded by the heavenly voice to return to their cave, and when they come out again twelve months later and survey the landscape, they conclude, "The world is enough with just me and you." Sitting there on the couch with one baby on the breast and one leaning against me, I looked at them both in weary elation and reached the same conclusion: the world is enough with me and you.

⁊

By the time the girls were a few weeks old we were up to the end of Exodus in the Torah reading cycle, with its elaborate descriptions of the *mishkan*, the portable sanctuary that traveled with the Israelites through the desert. In the midst of the Torah's detailed description of the building of the mishkan, Moses reiterates the commandment to keep Shabbat. This has led generations of commentators to speculate on the relationship between the mishkan and Shabbat. As we learn from tractate Shabbat (74a), the list of the thirty-nine labors that are prohibited on Shabbat is derived from the various forms of work that were undertaken to build the mishkan. In some sense, then, Shabbat is the opposite of the mishkan. The mishkan is about human labor, construction, and creativity, or "thoughtful work," as the Torah describes it at the end of Exodus. Shabbat, in contrast, is about resting and desisting from creative labor. In other words, the mishkan represents the modality of building, whereas Shabbat represents the modality of being.

Following the birth of the twins, I spent much more time "being" than "building." Most days I did not turn on the computer, or cook, or attempt to do much of anything but nurse, change diapers, and nurse some more—and yet somehow, by the end of the day I was always exhausted. I yearned to return to the mishkan modality of dressing for work, leaving the house, and feeling like a productive member of society. This was not a new feeling. I remembered it from Matan's early weeks of life, and I suppose it is familiar to all working women who become mothers—life suddenly stops, or veers off course, and it is hard not to feel completely derailed.

After a few months, though, our family got back on track. The Talmud speaks of the shofar blasts that were sounded to announce the start of Shabbat (Shabbat 35b). The contemporary equivalent is the Shabbat siren, which is sounded all over Jerusalem when it is time to light candles. Nowadays when the siren goes off on Friday afternoons we carry the twins over to the window to light candles, and Matan trails behind with his drill or his electric mixer or whatever electrical appliance he is obsessed with that week. "Put that away, it's muktzeh," we tell him, and at last he understands what that means. The girls, who go for increasingly longer stretches without nursing, will sit in their high chairs and feed themselves bite-sized pieces of chicken as Daniel and I chant Kabbalat Shabbat at the table. I think about how the mishkan and Shabbat may be opposite modalities, but not always. In our very sitting there together, we are building a family.

PESACHIM

❧

Take Two

PART OF THE EXPERIENCE OF LEARNING DAF YOMI IS THE
dissonance between the subject of the tractate under study and
the period it coincides with in the Jewish calendar. I felt this
most acutely when I began learning tractate Pesachim at the start
of summer and continued all the way through the high holiday
season in September, a long time away from Passover. When summer began I learned about how to search the house for *hametz*,
the unleavened products forbidden on the holiday, and when to
burn any remaining traces. By July I was deep into a discussion
about when and to what extent it is permissible to perform work
on the day before Pesach. And with the start of the Hebrew
month of Elul at the beginning of August, when it is traditional
to begin atoning in advance of Yom Kippur, I was instead immersed in the laws of the Paschal sacrifice: when is it slaughtered,
how is it roasted, who eats it, and with whom.

Much of the second half of tractate Pesachim could just as
easily have been included in Seder Kodshim, the order of the Talmud that deals with sacrificial worship. Pesachim had me splat-

tered with blood and knee-deep in roasted entrails and animal fat that must be consumed immediately and may not be left over until dawn, according to biblical law. I watched by the Temple outskirts as representatives of all of Israel arrive in three shifts to slaughter the Pesach sacrifice on behalf of larger groups, who then eat the meat together. As each shift enters, the doors of the Temple courtyard are closed and the shofar blasts are sounded. The priests stand in rows carrying gold and silver bowls for collecting the sacrificial blood, which they then sprinkle on the altar as the Israelites sing the psalms of Hallel. They then hang the sacrificial meat on iron hooks and flay it to prepare for the roasting. I thought of my early morning runs through the shuk, when I sprinted past the narrow alleyways at 7:00 a.m. just when the meat trucks were arriving and opening their back doors to reveal whole animal carcasses dangling from hooks, the blood dripping onto the ground as strapping young men with impressive muscles removed the fresh meat to deliver to the butcher stalls for salting and chopping.

I spent most of that summer ensconced in the Temple, witnessing each stage of the preparation of the Pesach sacrifice. But then again, this is not unlike how I usually spent the month of Elul. For most of my adult life, I led the Musaf service on Yom Kippur in various egalitarian minyanim on both sides of the ocean. To prepare myself spiritually and liturgically, I listened over and over again to recordings of the service on my headphones while going about my daily business. My favorite part of the high holiday prayers has always been the Avodah, the ritual reenactment of the high priest's activities on Yom Kippur. It is the most vivid, embodied aspect of the Yom Kippur service, in which the synagogue becomes the metaphorical equivalent of the Temple and the prayer leader is analogized to the high priest who designates two goats: one as a scapegoat that is knocked off a cliff, symbolically bearing the people's sins, and one as a sacrificial offering whose blood is sprinkled in the Holy of Holies. The Avodah ends on an exultant note, with the singing of a rousing liturgical poem about the radiance of the high priest's face when he emerges unscathed from the Holy of Holies.

But when I learned tractate Pesachim, I did not lead any high holiday services. The twins were seven months old and Matan was a rambunctious toddler, and it was hard enough for Daniel and me to take turns just showing up to synagogue, let alone trying to inspire a congregation. For the first time in over a decade, I did not spend Elul listening to recordings of the Yom Kippur prayers. Without the cries of "Who shall live and who shall die" accompanying me as I went about my daily chores, I felt bereft of my spiritual preparation for the high holidays. I could sooner imagine searching my house for hametz than searching my heart for misdeeds that needed to be righted.

I was lamenting this sorry state of affairs one morning while emptying the dishwasher. I had risen at 5:00 a.m., eager to steal the only quiet moments of the day before the kids awoke. I stood there putting away the previous day's dishes while listening to my daf yomi podcast. The daf mentioned *trumat hadeshen*, the first ritual activity performed in the Temple every morning, which involved clearing away the ashes from the previous day's sacrifices. Trumat hadeshen is not unlike emptying the dishwasher, a ritual that links the day that has passed to the day that is dawning. While trying not to let the glasses clink against one another, I peered out our kitchen window to watch the sun paint the sky above our view of the Old City where the Temple once stood. I froze the breast milk I had pumped the previous day and arranged Matan's place setting with his map-of-the-world placemat and his monkey sippy cup. These were activities I performed every morning; they are "love's austere and lonely offices," as Robert Hayden put it,[34] and they are, in a sense, my version of the *korban tamid*, the daily sacrifice offered every morning in the Temple. Yom Kippur would soon be upon us, but even before that, the kids were bound to stir. So while the gates of prayer were still open, I offered mine: May the high holidays herald a year that is as sweet as the taste of mother's milk on a baby's tongue, and as full of blessing and promise as every new day that dawns.

☙

The fourth chapter of tractate Pesachim considers the matter of local custom, specifically with regard to the question of working on the day before Passover. In places where it is customary to work on this day, work is permitted. In places where it is not, work is forbidden. But what if a person travels from one place to the other? The rabbis teach that such an individual must adopt the stringencies of the place he has left, and the stringencies of the place where he has arrived. If in either place they do not work on the day before Passover, then he must take the day off (50a).

The Talmud's discussion reflects an awareness that customs vary with geography, and a person who moves to a new place must take the time to get to know the customs of the new community. I experienced this lesson firsthand on Shavuot that year, when we received instructions that Matan, age two, was to come to gan dressed in white, bearing a basket of fruit for the holiday. The gan used the biblical word for basket, *tenne*, per Moses's instructions to the Jewish people to bring a basket of first fruits to God: "You shall take some of every first fruit of the soil, which you harvest from the land that the Lord your God is giving you, put it in a basket [*tenne*], and go to the place where the Lord your God will choose to establish His name" (Deuteronomy 26:2). The only basket we had at home was the large brown straw basket we'd used to carry our newborn Matan during his *bris* (circumcision) ceremony, so we threw in a few peaches and nectarines, dressed Matan in a white T-shirt and beige shorts, and sent him off to gan, relieved that we had remembered to follow the special instructions for that day. Little did we know.

We realized our mistake even before we entered the building. Outside the gates leading into the playground we watched as the other toddlers filed out of their parents' cars decked out in their Shabbat finery: white lacey dresses for the girls, and white sailor suits (or at least crisp button-down shirts) for the boys. It seemed they were all carrying identical white wicker baskets, about a fifth the size of the monstrosity that poor Matan could barely balance in his tiny arms. Their baskets were decorated in flowers and leaves; Matan's was utterly bare. Daniel and I looked at each other and grimaced, cognizant, yet again, of how difficult it is to be new immigrants to the Jewish homeland, whose customs and mores seem both deeply familiar and incomprehensibly foreign.

As I left the gan, my head hung in embarrassment for Matan and for myself, I was reminded of one of my favorite children's picture books, *Molly's Pilgrim*. Molly is a Russian immigrant to the Lower East Side. Just before Thanksgiving, her teacher assigns all the students to make a pilgrim doll and bring it to school. When Molly's mother learns the definition of a pilgrim—a new immigrant who came to America for religious freedom—she creates Molly's pilgrim in her own image, a babushka-clad lady in a long skirt. The other children tease Molly because her pilgrim looks nothing like theirs, but the kind and sympathetic teacher assures Molly that "it takes all kinds of pilgrims to make a Thanksgiving." And indeed, this is essentially what Matan's teacher told me at pickup that afternoon, when I apologized that we had sent Matan in the wrong clothes, bearing the wrong basket.

Shavuot is a pilgrimage festival, one of the three holidays when Jews are required to come to the land of Israel. Like Thanksgiving, which coincided with the American pilgrims' first successful harvest, it too is a harvest festival and a time of thanksgiving, in which we offer our first fruits in gratitude to God. This holiday had particular poignancy for us as immigrants to the State of Israel; we were pilgrims, and Matan was our first fruit. Perhaps it is somewhat appropriate, then, that the basket he paraded across the stage at gan during the Shavuot celebration was the basket we used to carry our firstborn at his bris. Still, I could only hope that by the time our second and third fruits reached his age, we'd be better acquainted with the local customs.

❦

For the most part Matan was fine in gan, so long as we remembered to send him with his beloved stuffed Elephant, which he slept with every night and was inseparable from throughout the day. But then one morning the inevitable happened: we lost Elephant. It was at the beginning of the school year, and Matan could not get through the day without his pachyderm. Initially panicked, we searched our home, the gan, and the bike path that connects the two, but all to no avail. Thankfully we were able to avert disaster, because Daniel managed to track down and purchase another elephant just in time. The new elephant was cleaner and less worn than its predecessor, but Matan seemed to accept our assurance that Elephant had merely taken a bath.

And so all was well again, until the gan located the lost elephant a few days later and handed it to Matan. But Matan was already clutching the new elephant, and he looked at us confused. "Two Elephants, one two?" he asked imploringly. He regarded his Elephant as unique and inimitable, and was bewildered by the sudden multiplicity. Which elephant was Elephant? Could both be equally beloved? And if not, what should we do with the other one? Fortunately, all of these questions were addressed on the page in Pescahim I learned right in the middle of the elephant crisis.

The Mishnah (96b) considers the question of what happens when a Paschal lamb is lost and another lamb is designated for the Paschal sacrifice in its stead. There is in fact an entire tractate in Seder Kodshim dedicated to problems arising from replacement sacrifices. This tractate, Temurah, is based on a single verse in the Bible: "One may not exchange or substitute another for it [a sacrificial animal], either good for bad, or bad for good. If one does substitute one animal for another, the thing vowed and its substitute shall both be holy" (Leviticus 27:10). A person may not sacrifice one animal for another, say, so as to save money by offering an inferior alternative. If someone commits this forbidden act, both animals are subject to the laws of sacrifice. If the original sacrifice is a *nedava*, a voluntary offering, then both animals are brought to the altar. But if the original sacrifice is one that cannot be brought twice, such as a *chatat* (sin offering) or a Paschal lamb, then the replacement animal cannot be sacrificed and it also cannot be treated like a regular, unconsecrated animal. The only option is to let it graze until it develops a blemish, at which point it is unfit for sacrifice. Then it is sold, and the proceeds are used to buy another sacrifice.

In the case of a Pesach sacrifice, as the Talmud teaches, the halachah depends on when the original animal is found. If it is found before the replacement lamb was slaughtered, it is as if that animal was actively "pushed aside" when its replacement was sacrificed, so it cannot be brought as another offering but must be left to graze. If the original was found after the replacement was sacrificed, then the original can be brought as a *shelamim*, a similar and related sacrifice.

So what did all this mean for Elephant and elephant? In our case, the original elephant was found after the second elephant had already been consecrated. That is, Matan had already transferred all his love and affection to the replacement elephant, thereby designating it as Elephant. Thus the original elephant need not be left to graze, and both elephants were valid sacrifices. We decided, therefore, to leave one Elephant at gan and one at home, in the hope of avoiding similar problems in the future.

Fortunately our twins, who started gan at the age of nine months, were not yet attached to stuffed animals. They were, however, very attached to me, which made it hard for us to be apart. Each morning I was beset by doubts about whether I should be entrusting them to another person's care. Could someone else really replace their mother? The answer, I discovered, was yes and no. Someone else could play with them and feed them baby food and put them to sleep, but only I could breastfeed them. Perhaps this was why I never taught the twins to drink from bottles; on some level, I realized that it was only breastfeeding that made me truly irreplaceable.

Throughout that year I ran to the gan twice a day to nurse. Each day I arrived at the gan breathless, my breasts full and bursting, and a Talmudic aphorism running through my head. When Rabbi Shimon bar Yohai begged Rabbi Akiva to teach him Torah in prison, even though the Romans had outlawed Torah study, Rabbi Akiva responded: "More than the calf wants to suckle, the cow wants to nurse" (Pesachim 112a). Still, though my need was more urgent, the girls were just as excited to see me as I was to greet them. The moment I walked in the door they grinned at me from ear to ear and raised their arms above their heads with joyous squeals. Each was my one and only beloved: inimitable, irreplaceable, and unique.

⁓

I loved greeting the girls at the end of the day, but I dreaded having to decide whom to pick up first. Sometimes I would be lucky—I'd arrive at the gan and Tagel would still be sleeping, so I'd pick up Liav and spend a few moments alone with her before bringing her with me to wake her sister in the back room lined with cribs where all the babies slept. But other days I'd show up to find the two of them sitting on the floor, each eagerly crying "Emma, Emma" (they could not yet pronounce long vowels, so they pronounced the Hebrew word for mother, *ima*, like the Jane Austen heroine). If only I could swoop them both up simultaneously, but they were usually on opposite sides of the room. I wished that I could perform a feat worthy of King Solomon—not to divide one child for two mothers, but to divide one mother for two children.

Whenever I found myself forced to choose between the two girls, I thought of the rabbinic principle that "one does not pass over mitzvot." This principle, which appears in Pesachim (64b) and throughout the Talmud, means that if there is a commandment that is right in front of you, you should fulfill it before searching for other commandments. Thus, when the priest walks over to the altar to sprinkle sacrificial blood on its four corners, he should start off with the corner that is closest to him, because "one does not pass over mitzvot." I recited a version of this principle in my head: "One does not pass over twins." Like the priest who may not walk past one corner of the altar to sprinkle blood on the next, I would not pass over one daughter to reach another. Inevitably that meant that her sister would burst into tears, and then I would have to set down one twin to retrieve the other, by which point they would both be crying.

Whenever I described to my friends the challenges of parenting twins, I received expressions of sympathy and incredulity, of the "I-Don't-Know-How-She-Does-It" variety. Even the Talmud seems to be wary of things that come in pairs, as we learn from the tenth and final chapter of tractate Pesachim. Unlike the previous nine chapters, which deal with the Paschal sacrifice, this is the one chapter that covers the ritual of the Passover seder: the four cups of wine, the eating of matzah and bitter herbs, and the recitation of the Hallel psalms. All is explained in a clear and orderly fashion until the middle of the chapter, when the rabbis seem to get drunk on seder wine as they break from the halachic discussion of the seder to engage in several pages about superstition, demonology, legend, and lore.

The rabbinic discussion of the danger of pairs begins with the Mishnah's statement that a person should not have less than four cups of wine at the seder, even if he is so poor that he has to rely on communal funds. "Four cups of wine?" asks the anonymous voice of the Talmud. "How could the sages legislate something that is so dangerous? After all, we are taught that a person should never eat two of anything, or drink two of anything" (109b). The rabbinic discussion reflects a prevalent belief in destructive forces that we with our modern sensibilities would likely dismiss as superstitious. One such belief was the fear that doing things in pairs was hazardous. It was always safer to do something an odd number of times. But if so, how could we possibly be obligated to drink "two times two" cups of wine?

The sages offer various justifications. Rav Nahman suggests that since the Torah describes Pesach as "a night of vigil" (Exodus 12:42), we need not worry, because Pesach is guarded from demons and harmful spirits. Rava says that the third cup, used in the Grace after Meals, is a "cup of blessing" that serves as part of a mitzvah, and could never combine for evil purposes. And Ravina posits that since these cups are a symbol of freedom, they do not combine in pairs with one another, but each stands independently in its own right.

These explanations notwithstanding, the sages remain preoccupied with the danger of doing anything in pairs and go on to relate several stories about the lengths they would go to avoid such behavior. Whenever Abayey would drink a cup of wine, for instance, his mother would immediately hold out two more cups, one in each hand, lest he inadvertently drink just one cup more and become susceptible to demonic forces. If a person inadvertently stops after two cups and finds himself besieged by demons, the Talmud instructs that he should hold his right thumb in his left hand, and hold his left thumb in his right hand, and say: "You, my two thumbs, and I make three!" But even so, there is no guarantee that he will be protected.

The very same day that I learned about the Talmud's fear of pairs, my friend Shira happened to forward me an article written by the parents of twins. The article, entitled "25 Tips about the Horrors of Raising Twins That You Will Never Learn from

Movies and TV," reminded me of the beginning of *Anne of Green Gables*, when orphan Anne is told that she will be sent to take care of Mrs. Blewett's two sets of twins. "Twins seem to be my lot in life," Anne miserably laments. The article warned that with twins, the pregnancy is harrowing, the early months of the babies' lives are more than twice the amount of work, and the first year is so exhausting that the parents don't even remember any of it.

As I wrote back to Shira, I must beg to differ. Yes, parenting twins is exhausting and all-consuming. But the rewards are not double, but exponential. Each night after the girls were born I watched them fall asleep in a single bassinet. I laid them down beside one another, each with her head facing away from her sister and toward one side of the crib. But invariably within the first few minutes of settling into sleep, they would each turn so that they were facing each other, their noses just centimeters apart. I thought about the cherubs in the Temple which would face each other whenever Israel was doing God's will, but turn away from each other when Israel had sinned. My angelic twins wanted all to be well with the world.

And then there was the reward of knowing they had each other. The article Shira sent recounted horror stories about mothers who could not go to the bathroom when they were home alone with their babies or who went days without showering because they had no time alone. This never happened to me. When I needed time to myself, I laid the girls on their stomachs facing each other, with a few toys between them. Tagel amused herself by trying to catch Liav's eye and cracking up any time Liav looked in her direction; Liav mostly ignored Tagel because she was intent on moving all the toys onto her section of the mat. Every so often I had to separate them because Liav did not realize that the "toy" she was yanking on with all her might was actually Tagel's hair. But for the most part, they played together quite nicely, at least for long enough for me to run to the bathroom or jump in the shower.

As they got older, we were able to witness their increased interactions with each other. Tagel learned to crawl several months before Liav, so she scrambled around the house searching for books and toys to deliver to her sister. Once they learned to feed themselves, we sat them down in adjacent high chairs and they passed food to each other. Liav placed her sandwich on Tagel's tray, and Tagel reciprocated with her cucumber slices. Yes, on one of those occasions when I took advantage of their camaraderie to transfer the wash, I returned to find the two of them painting each other's hair with strawberry yogurt. For a moment I began to wonder whether the Talmud was on to something in its association between pairs and demonic forces, but then I could only laugh as I took a wet washcloth and wiped the pink streaks out of their hair.

Throughout those early months Daniel and I were often beside ourselves with exhaustion, with food to cook, kids to bathe, diapers to change, and no time to work or sleep—let alone to enjoy a glass of wine. But the joy of observing our own pair grow and develop and interact with each other has been indescribable, and even if our cup is overflowing, we never doubt for a moment that it is a cup of blessing.

⁊

Tractate Pesachim takes its name from notions of doubling and pairs: there is not one Pesach but rather two Pesachim. The first, known as Pesach Rishon, is the normal Passover celebration that takes place on the anniversary of the exodus from Egypt. The second, known as Pesach Sheni, is the make-up opportunity offered one month later to those who were ritually impure or too far from the Temple on the fourteenth of Nisan to bring the sacrifice then. And so Pesachim symbolizes the opportunity for second chances and a new lease on life. In that sense the holiday has something in common with Yom Kippur, which is also a chance to wipe the slate clean and begin anew.

When I look back on my own life, and on the span of time between the start of my daf yomi study when I lived alone in Jerusalem and its culmination as a mother of three, I think about how I, too, was blessed with a second chance. When I started learning Yoma, I was quite certain that I would never get married again. But there are multiple versions of every story, and ours, too, has a take two. One fall evening at the beginning of my study of Bava Kama I attended a Shabbat dinner where I met a guy named Andrew, who had baked the challah loaves for the meal. His challah was delicious, and I asked him if he baked every week. He told me that he had recently been injured in a bus accident, and he had to quit his job; he was baking and selling challah as a way of earning money. Poor guy, I thought, resolving to purchase his challah weekly. He delivered it to my house every Friday, and I enjoyed fresh home-baked loaves.

Reader, as you know, I did not marry him. But several months later, just a few weeks before Pesach in 2009, I ran into Andrew's roommate. His name was Daniel and I recognized him from the weekly class taught by Avivah Zornberg that we attended together, though we had never spoken. Daniel said he had been meaning to get in touch because Andrew had returned to America for surgery, leaving his unsold merchandise behind. Before his departure, he'd instructed his roommate to distribute the remaining loaves to his most loyal customers. "Pesach is coming and I'm stuck with a freezer full of challah," Daniel told me. "Can you help?"

The first chapter of Pesachim treats the commandment to rid one's house of all leavened products before the start of Pesach. In a sense, then, I was merely helping Daniel perform a mitzvah. But as I'd learned in Yoma, "One cannot compare a person who has bread in his basket to a person who does not have bread in his basket." A few days later Daniel stopped by and filled my freezer with six loaves of challah, which I, living alone, could never possibly finish in time for the holiday. I asked him if he wanted to come over for sandwiches, still unsuspecting that he was my match, my pair, my second chance. We have been breaking bread together ever since.

SHEKALIM

~&

Weaving the Talmudic Tapestry

TRACTATE SHEKALIM DEALS WITH THE FINANCES AND organization of the Temple, and specifically with the half-shekel coin that must be donated each year by Jews the world over. With the conclusion of this tractate, I completed seven and a half years of daf yomi and came full circle, since the end of tractate Shekalim hearkens back to Yoma. The final chapter of Shekalim deals with items of uncertain purity status that are discovered in Jerusalem. What happens if one finds spittle lying on the sidewalk. Do we assume that it belongs to someone who is pure or impure (21a)? This leads to a discussion of what to do when various holy objects in the Temple become impure, including the *parochet* (21b), the woven tapestry that divided the sanctuary from the Holy of Holies.

The rabbis debate the nature of the weave of the parochet, which the Torah describes as "a curtain of blue, purple, and crimson strands, and fine twisted linen" (Exodus 26:31). The Talmud cites a source stating that in fact each strand was made of thirty-two threads, based on a more sophisticated understanding of the

Bible's use of the term *moshzar*, twisted linen. Adding a further twist to the debate, a third sage asserts that each strand was actually made of forty-eight threads—and thus the parochet is woven into an increasingly textured tapestry as the Talmudic text unfurls.

The Talmud, too, has proven increasingly textured the more I learn. If any page ever seems simple and straightforward upon first read, it is generally because I have not studied it carefully enough. Or, as one rabbi rebukes another at various points in Talmud, "If you have read it, you have not reviewed it. If you have reviewed it, you have not gone over it a third time. And if you've gone over it a third time, they've not explained it to you well." Only as I look closer and begin to unravel the various strands of argumentation do I begin to appreciate the rich texture of the material. Where do the rabbis get twenty-four threads? Because had each strand been made of one thread, the Bible would simply have said *chut*, a thread; had it been made of two threads, the Bible would have said *chut kaful*, a double thread; had it been made of three threads, it would have said *shazur*, an entwined braid. But it said *moshzar*, which must be double the shazur, and so there were six threads. Moreover, the Bible lists four different strands—blue, purple, crimson, and linen—and so we must multiply six by four, yielding twenty-four. This is quite a thick weave. Indeed, the Mishnah states that the parochet was so heavy that it took three hundred priests to lift it and carry it to the ritual bath when it needed to be immersed for purification purposes. I, too, received much help with the heavy lifting, not from three hundred priests but from countless rabbis and teachers whose notes and podcasts guided me through my daf yomi study, revealing the text in its true colors.

The Mishnah goes on to relate that the parochet was the product of eighty-two thousand myriads. The Talmud's term for "myriads" is *ribo*, which, according to Rashi, relates either to the cost of the veil's production or to the number of threads from which it was made. But according to some scholars, ribo may also be short for *ribot*, meaning "young maidens," referring to those who wove it. The Torah states explicitly that the parochet was women's handiwork: "And all the women that were wise-hearted spun with their hands, and brought that which they had spun: the blue, the purple, the crimson, and the fine linen. And all the women whose heart raised them up in wisdom spun the goats' hair" (Exodus 35:25–26). And so it was women who wove the textile, just as it is women, increasingly, who are beginning to weave their voices into the Talmudic conversation.

I feel fortunate that I have found my voice in the Talmud's pages. Academic scholars of Talmud use the term *makbilot*, parallels, to refer to textual passages that appear in identical or similar form in various Talmudic contexts. Thus, for instance, the description of the parochet appears not just in Shekalim, but also in Hulin (90b), Tamid (29b), and throughout Yoma. And so I studied this passage not just at the start and end of my daf yomi cycle but also during my maternity leave after Matan was born, when the parochet reminded me of the various hand-woven blankets we'd received as baby gifts, and then again when we found out we were having twins, as we thought about how to partition our second bedroom to make room for an additional baby. Scholars of Talmud consider how the text is informed and often even changed by its contexts; the same is true, perhaps, of the personal contexts in which I have encountered these passages. The text seems to change with each encounter because it resonates in new ways, and I, in turn, am transformed by each encounter.

The Talmud explains that the weave of the parochet was double-sided, with a lion on one side and an eagle on the other, such that the high priest would see one image when he entered the Holy of Holies and another image when he exited. As a double-sided divider, the parochet was both a way in and a way out. I am reminded of the inscription on Dexter Gate, which I used to walk through countless times a day as a college freshman: "Enter here to gain in wisdom," reads the side leading into Harvard Yard; "Depart to serve better thy country and thy kind," reads the side leading into the busy traffic of Massachusetts Avenue. Every point of entry is also a point of exit, and every end is also a beginning. This is why graduation ceremonies are called "commencement," and this is why as soon as one finishes reading the Torah or studying the Talmud, it is traditional to begin immediately again.

When completing a tractate of Talmud, it is customary to recite a prayer known as the *hadran*: *hadran alach v'hadrach alan*. Hadran comes from the word for return, though in modern Hebrew it is used to refer to an encore. This is one way the rabbis use the term, suggesting that the text continues to go on even after we have finished it, since there is always more to learn. According to this understanding, the prayer means "may we return to you, and may you return to us": May we have the opportunity to study this tractate again (because inevitably we'll forget some of what we learn), and may it come back to us (because we hope that some of what we learn will stay with us). The prayer gives voice to my fervent belief in the power of learning to make the world endlessly interesting—there is always more to learn, which means that there is always a reason to keep living. But in classic Talmudic wordplay, hadran, from the word *hadar*, also means "beauty" and "glory." So the prayer can also mean, "Our beauty is from you, and your beauty is from us," which conveys the notion that we, with our own individual life experiences and our own unique perspectives, can beautify the study of Talmud; and Talmud can beautify us.

At the end of tractate Shekalim (21b) the rabbis teach that after the parochet was woven by eighty-two thousand maidens and then immersed by three hundred priests, it was spread out to dry on the tallest place on the Temple Mount for the entire nation to admire the beauty of its craftsmanship. I have tried to do the same. These are the texts that I will come back to and the texts that have come back to me, woven together and spread out before you with trembling hands.

YOMA

⁓

Encore

IN KEEPING WITH THE TRADITION OF RETURNING TO
the text, I write these words as I am well into my second cycle
of daf yomi, on the eve of the twins' first birthday. Last week I
completed Yoma for the second time. I would say that relearning
Yoma was a positive experience were it not for the fact that I
broke another bone. Seven and a half years ago, when I first learned
Yoma, I broke my foot while jogging in the early morning. And
then two months ago, during an uncharacteristically severe Jerusalem snowstorm that made international headlines, I broke my
arm when I slipped on the ice on my way to dispose of a bag of
dirty diapers.

Unlike seven and a half years ago, this time my injury wasn't
just inconvenient, but nearly impossible. Daniel and I joked
that we had a one-working-arm-to-child ratio. I learned to carry
the twins in the crook of my arm, to cut vegetables with one
hand, and to fold laundry with my elbow. All the while I was
following the high priest through the chambers and courtyards
of the Temple, observing as he gathered up the incense to take

into the Holy of Holies. He took a pan in his right hand and a ladle in his left, a task that I could not have completed without two working arms. Nor could I have performed *kemitza*, which involves scooping up the incense underneath the middle three fingers of the hand while extending the thumb and pinky (47a). The rabbis describe kemitza as the most difficult part of Temple ritual—even without a cast extending from elbow to knuckles.

In order to heal, bones have to set, and so I think about what has set in my life in the time between my two encounters with tractate Yoma. The word Yoma is Aramaic for "the day," and refers, of course, to Yom Kippur, the holiest day on the Jewish calendar. But in Hebrew the word for "the day," *hayom*, is also the word for "today," which points to a significant difference between my study of Yoma then and now. Seven and a half years ago, when I learned Yoma for the first time, I never had any doubts about how I was spending "today." Each morning I learned Talmud with a study partner and then headed to my job at the literary agency. In the evenings I attended various classes throughout the city—a lecture on the weekly Torah portion one night, a discussion on Jewish philosophy the next. When I came home late in the evening, I leaned daf yomi and collapsed in bed so that I could wake up early to jog the next morning. Each day had its own schedule, mapped out like the order of the priest's activities on Yom Kippur. And each day was full of activities I enjoyed—learning Torah, working with books, exercising, attending classes, spending time with friends.

Even so, I could not have told you where my life was heading, and it wasn't just because I had one broken foot. I did not know if I would ever advance in my job, or fall in love again, or become a mother, or stay in Israel. All the big questions were still unanswered. Indeed, part of the reason I began learning daf yomi in the first place was as an attempt to shore up against a terrifying future in which nothing seemed certain except that I was getting older. By the time I finished the cycle, I'd be thirty-five. This seemed terribly old to my twenty-seven-year-old self. If I hadn't had children by then, I thought, then surely I never would. And if I hadn't reached a satisfying place in my career, I thought, then surely it was all over for me professionally. All future Yom Kippur observances would be full of regret at missed opportunities, and I would never be able to forgive myself.

Returning to Yoma for the second time, after seven Yom Kippur holidays have elapsed in the interim, I see it all in a very different light. The night before Yom Kippur the young priests were responsible for ensuring that the high priest did not fall asleep, lest he have a seminal emission and become impure. If he started to drift off, they would beat with their middle fingers and tell him to stand up and then lie himself down on the cold floor so as to jolt himself awake (19b). These priests were also charged with determining exactly when the sun rose on Yom Kippur morning by looking out at the sky in the direction of Hebron, at which point they would announce "Barkai"—the sun is up (28a)!

This is not unlike how Matan spends his early mornings. Daniel taught him that he is not allowed to wake up until the sun rises, and we leave his shade open a crack at night so that he can make this determination for himself. Then he bounds into our room in his furry one-piece pajamas and announces, "Sun is up! Time to play! Get up, Ima!" Before I can listen for the morning traffic on Hebron Road or even open my eyes, he is beating his fingers on a puzzle box, encouraging me to come help him. No sooner have I gotten out of bed than I hear the girls clamoring for attention in their cribs, eager for me to come in and take them out. The rest of the morning unfolds in a tired blur of diaper changing, nursing, dressing the girls in their pink (Liav) and purple (Tagel) outfits, and reheating the French toast that I fried in a pan the night before, first dipping leftover challah in egg and milk and then scooping in some cinnamon with my middle three fingers.

These days I have significant doubts and insecurities about how I spend each "today." I wish I could say that when I drop off the kids at gan, I forget about them until pickup. But in fact I continue to think about them as I edit and translate books in my office across the street. My work is stimulating and challenging, but I would not say that I have discovered my true calling in life or that I am engaged in divine service. From the moment the high priest immerses himself in the ritual bath for the first time on Yom Kippur morning until the people of Israel accompany him to his home at the end of the day, the Talmud details every single step he takes. As such, tractate Yoma is a model for what it means for all our steps to be directed toward the service of heaven. In this sense I have a long way to go.

On the other hand (and I do not take my two hands for granted), while I can't say I'm satisfied with how I spend each and every "today," many of the larger questions of "someday" seem to have resolved themselves. The Talmud speaks in Yoma of the lotteries conducted to assign the various priestly duties, and there is no doubt in my mind that when I married Daniel, I won big time. I could not imagine a kinder, wiser, more loving life partner, even if I rarely have time to tell him that anymore. Our children are beautiful and beaming, though not a day passes when I don't worry about the one who refuses to feed himself or the one who still hasn't learned to walk. From the back window of our home in Jerusalem we can see the Temple Mount where the high priests once performed the Yom Kippur service. If given the opportunity to enter the Holy of Holies and offer only a short prayer, as the high priest was instructed on Yom Kippur (52b), I would use those precious moments to thank God for my many blessings.

It took two cycles of daf yomi, but I feel that I have finally learned the lesson of this tractate, namely that Yoma is about the convergence of both meanings of hayom. It is about that day when "today" is "the day," the most important day on the Jewish calendar. But it is also about realizing that this convergence happens every day. Our lives at this moment are not merely prelude to a future someday, but this is it, Barkai, the sun is up, Ima! No sooner does this realization dawn on me than I get out of bed, extend my arms to embrace my son, and step forward into the rest of my life.

ACKNOWLEDGMENTS

The Talmud (Berachot 54b) teaches that there are four types of people who are obligated to bring a Korban Todah, an offering of thanksgiving—one who walks through the desert, one who is healed from sickness, one who is released from prison, and one who goes down to the sea. The Babylonian Talmud is often compared to a sea because of its vastness and depth, and so after over a decade of daily Talmud study, I count myself among the seafarers duty-bound to offer thanks.

For putting the wind in my sails, I am indebted to my beloved agent, Deborah Harris, my devoted editor, Elisabeth Dyssegaard, and to Laura Apperson and Alan Bradshaw at St. Martin's Press.

For staying my course and offering feedback on early drafts of this manuscript, I thank Rebecca Bardach, Ilana Blumberg, George Eltman, Misha Feigenson, Rachel Furst, Rabbi David Golinkin, Miriam Goldstein, Debbie Greniman, Debra Kaplan, Ayelet Libson, Peggy Samuels, Shuly Rubin Schwartz, Paola Tartakoff,

Ron Wolfson, and especially Tammy Hepps and Jason Rogoff. Thanks, too, for the longstanding support of Susan Weidman Schneider and Naomi Danis at *Lilith* magazine, always a favorite port of call.

For helping me navigate the journey, I am deeply grateful to my parents, Neil and Alisa Rubin Kurshan, my siblings, Naamit, Ariella, and Eytan, and their spouses and children.

To my co-captain, Daniel Feldman, and to our children, Matan, Liav, Tagel and Shalvi—may we merit to immerse ourselves in words of Torah for many years to come.

NOTES

1. Biblical translations are my own, but heavily influenced by the *JPS Hebrew-English Tanakh* (Philadelphia: Jewish Publication Society, 2003).

2. Yehudah Marks, "It's Question Time at Daf Yomi Kollel: Jews from around the world can get instant answers—in English—to their questions on Gemara, halachah, and many other areas of Jewish interest," *Hamodia* 24 (May 2012), pp. A30-31.

3. Sándor Ferenczi, *Further Contributions to the Theory and Technique of Psychoanalysis*, translated by Jane Isabel Suttie and others (New York: Boni & Liveright, 1927), pp. 174–77. Quoted in Judith Shulevitz, *The Sabbath World* (New York: Random House, 2010), p. 10.

4. Pinchas H. Peli, *On Repentance: The Thought and Oral Discourses of Rabbi Joseph Dov Soloveitchik* (New Jersey: Jason Aronson, 2000), pp. 97-98.

5. Martin Buber, *Tales of the Hasidim* (New York, Schocken Books, 1991), p. 219.

6. Jane Austen, *Northanger Abbey* (New York: Penguin Classics, 2003), p. 71.

7. Edna St. Vincent Millay, "Time does not bring relief; you all have lied" in *Collected Poems* (New York: Harper Perennial, 2011), p. 562.

8. D.H. Lawrence, *Lady Chatterley's Lover* (New York: Bantam, 1983), p. 30.

9. Ibid., p. 68.

10. Virginia Woolf, *A Room of One's Own* (Boston: Mariner Books, 1989), pp. 27–28.

11. Ibid., 44.

12. Ibid., 43.

13. Ibid.

14. Amos Oz, *A Tale of Love and Darkness*, translated by Nicholas de Lange (Boston: Mariner Books, 2005), pp. 24–25.

15. Woolf, *A Room of One's Own*, p. 8.

16. Billy Collins, "Taking Off Emily Dickenson's Clothes," in *Picnic, Lightning* (Pittsburgh: University of Pittsburgh Press, 1998), p. 74.

17. Madeleine L'Engle, *A Circle of Quiet* (New York: HarperOne, 1984), p. 211.

18. Colleen McCullough, *The Thorn Birds* (New York: Avon, 1979), front matter.

19. Kenneth Koch, "To You" in *The Collected Poems of Kenneth Koch* (New York: Knopf, 2006), p. 80.

20. Robert Graves, "Love without Hope" in *The Complete Poems* (New York: Penguin, 2003), p. 227.

21. Jack Gilbert, "Waiting and Finding" in *The Dance Most of All* (New York: Knopf, 2003), p. 15.

22. Edward Hirsch, "Dates" in *The Living Fire: New and Selected Poems* (New York: Alfred A. Knopf, 2011), p. 185.

23. Walt Whitman, "A Noiseless Patient Spider" in *The Complete Works of Walt Whitman* (Wordsworth Editions, 1998), p. 333.

24. Eliza Griswold, "Tigers" in *Wideawake Field* (New York: Farrar, Straus and Giroux, 2007), p. 39.

25. William Matthews, "Misgivings" in *Search Party: Collected Poems* (Boston: Mariner Books, 2005), p. 306.

26. Edwin Arlington Robinson, "Eros Turannos" in *Selected Poems* (New York: Penguin, 1997), pp. 91-92.

27. Samuel Taylor Coleridge, "Frost at Midnight" in *The Complete Poems* (New York: Penguin, 1997), pp. 231–233.

28. Mary Oliver, "The Summer Day," in *New and Selected Poems, vol. 1* (Boston: Beacon Press, 2004), p. 94.

29. Leah Goldberg, "Teach Me, O God" in *Poems*, vol. 2 (Tel Aviv: Sifriyat Poalim, 1986), p. 154. See also "Poems of the Journey's End" in *Selected Poetry and Drama*, trans. Rachel Tzvia Black (New Milford, CT: Toby Press, 2005), p. 97.

30. Wallace Stevens, "Sunday Morning" in *The Collected Poems* (New York: Vintage, 2015), p. 71.

31. Alexander McCall Smith, *The Careful Use of Compliments* (New York: Anchor, 2008), p. 116.

32. Stevens, "Sunday Morning," p. 73.

33. Alfred Lord Tennyson, "Ulysses" in *The Works of Lord Alfred Tennyson* (New York: Wordsworth Editions, 1998), p. 162.

34. Robert Hayden, *Collected Poems*, ed. Frederick Glaysher (New York: W.W. Norton, 1985), p. 41.